D1158224

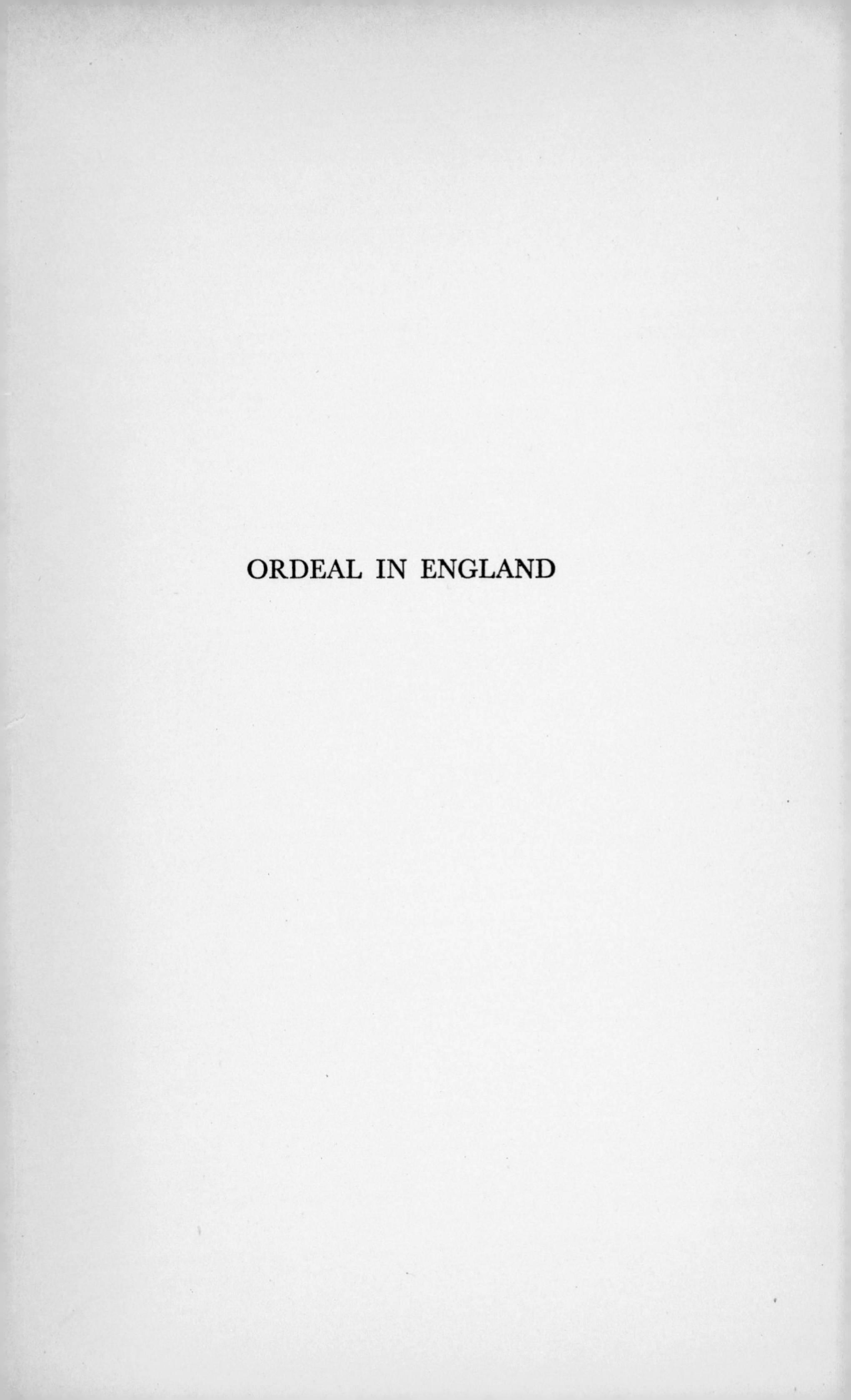

ORDEAL IN ENGLAND

Books By

PHILIP GIBBS

ORDEAL IN ENGLAND
CITIES OF REFUGE
ENGLAND SPEAKS
BLOOD RELATIONS
EUROPEAN JOURNEY
THE CROSS OF PEACE
THE ANXIOUS DAYS
THE GOLDEN YEARS
THE WINDING LANE
THE WINGS OF ADVENTURE
and other novels
THE HIDDEN CITY
DARKENED ROOMS
THE AGE OF REASON
THE DAY AFTER TO-MORROW
OUT OF THE RUINS
YOUNG ANARCHY
UNCHANGING QUEST
THE RECKLESS LADY
TEN YEARS AFTER
HEIRS APPARENT
THE MIDDLE OF THE ROAD
LITTLE NOVELS OF NOWADAYS
THE SPIRIT OF REVOLT
THE STREET OF ADVENTURE
WOUNDED SOULS
PEOPLE OF DESTINY
THE SOUL OF THE WAR
THE BATTLES OF THE SOMME
THE STRUGGLE IN FLANDERS
THE WAY TO VICTORY
2 volumes
MORE THAT MUST BE TOLD
NOW IT CAN BE TOLD

THE BOGEY OF EUROPE

ORDEAL IN ENGLAND

By PHILIP GIBBS

ILLUSTRATED BY EDGAR LANDER

DOUBLEDAY, DORAN & COMPANY, INC.
Garden City 1937 New York

PRINTED AT THE *Country Life Press*, GARDEN CITY, N. Y., U. S. A.

FIRST EDITION

Contents

ILLUSTRATIONS

ILLUSTRATIONS

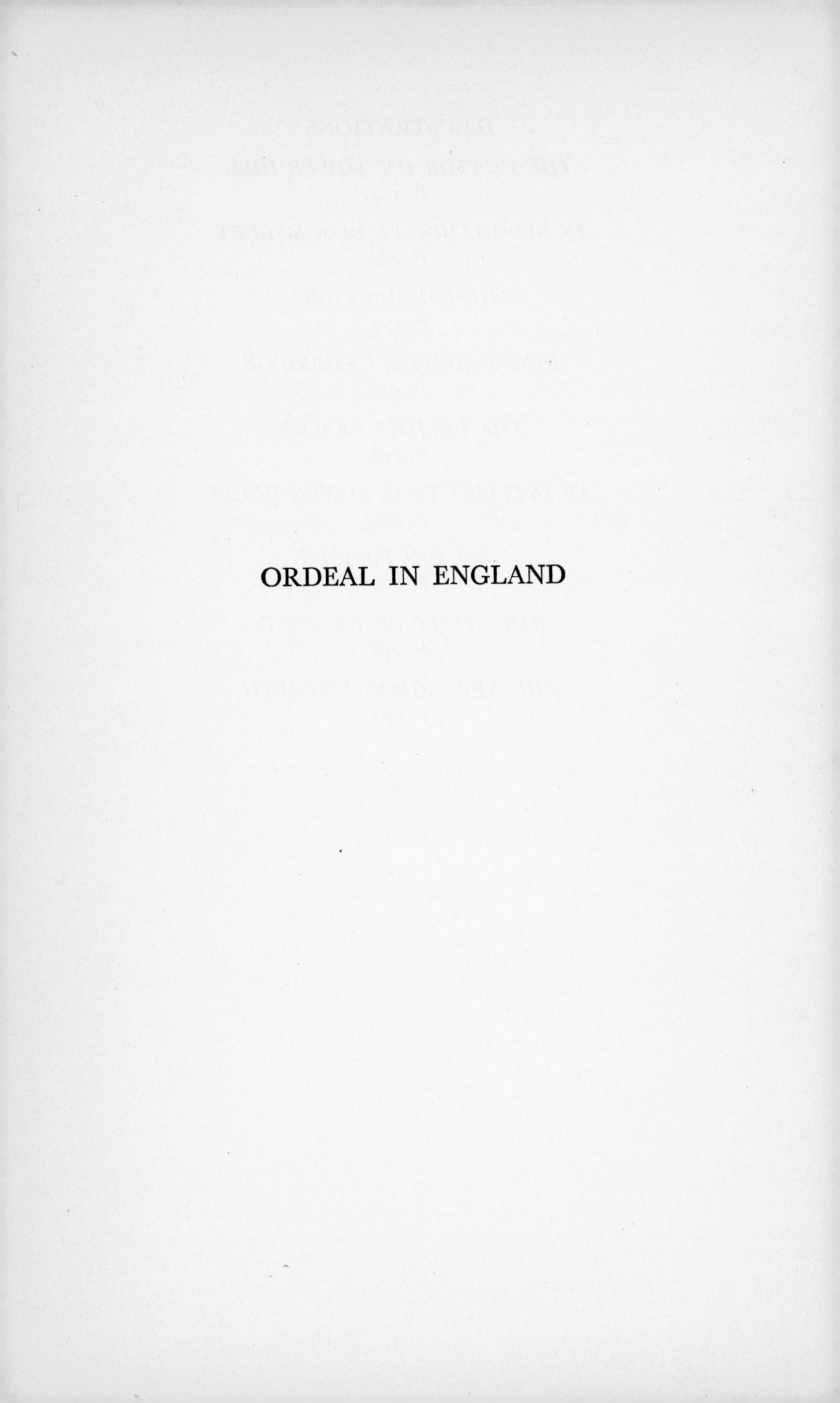

ORDEAL IN ENGLAND

I

The End of a Reign

1 The Dying King

ON THE EVENING of January 20, 1936, there was a small crowd outside Buckingham Palace. Lately there have been crowds very often outside the gates of that palace—a new habit, it seems, of Londoners and visitors to London who won't leave it alone and stand there, staring at the sentries and through the railings, impelled by some sense of drama or romance, excited perhaps by the picture papers and the daily bulletins about royalty which reach them over the wireless.

On this day what special reason had brought this crowd of silent people to the gates? They were waiting for a bulletin. The King—who was George V—was ill at Sandringham. He was dying, perhaps. It was only a few weeks after he had spoken through the microphone his Christmas message to the nation, when millions of people had listened to his rich throaty voice in which there was great kindliness, a really fatherly benevolence, and, once or twice, an emotion which enriched the words he spoke and that last "God bless you all."

It was only half a year since his Jubilee celebrations, when he had been surprised by the tremendous warmth of popular enthusiasm and affection which greeted him on his way through the streets and from every part of the country. Vast crowds had surged up then to Buckingham Palace on those wonderful May nights so warm and fragrant and strange for an English spring. They had chanted, "We want the King! . . . We want the King!" until he had come onto the balcony to receive their cheers and listen to their singing of the national anthem.

He had been surprised and touched by this, as we heard afterwards from those close to him. He had had no idea that he had made such a place for himself in the hearts of the people. He had thought that it was his son, the Prince of Wales, who had captured the imagination and idolatry of the crowds.

He had been physically strengthened even by this new awareness of popular devotion. To the astonishment and relief of his doctors and friends he went through the fatigues of these celebrations and street processions without signs of exhaustion. They had been anxious. They knew that he had no reserves of vitality. That lung was not functioning. It was almost a miracle which had saved him during his desperate illness after taking a chill at the Cenotaph. But during the Jubilee he had shown astonishing endurance and had even asked for more than he need have done by making unexpected drives with the Queen through the poorest districts of London, as though eager and happy to hear the shrill cheers of millions of young children who rushed out at the news of his coming, and to warm himself at the fire of this popular homage which, he could see and feel, was personal and affectionate. He had tried to serve them by doing his job. He had been through the war with them. They understood. This was his reward.

Now he was dying. What did the crowd expect to see, staring through the railings at those blank walls and unlighted windows?

They were speaking to each other in low voices.

"I hope he'll pull through."

"We can't afford to lose him."

"No, that's right. He's been a good King, and all of us know it."

"The world's in a troubled state, isn't it? If King George goes . . ."

2 *Another Vigil*

As I passed the palace and stood for a moment in the crowd a strange memory came back to me. I was here, inside those gates, beyond the railings, on the night when George V became King. It was the night of May 6, 1910. Then King Edward VII was on his deathbed here in Buckingham Palace.

The last official bulletin had been hopeful. As a writer on the old *Daily Chronicle* I had been received with other newspapermen by Lord Knollys, who had assured us that the King was quite comfortable and that there was no reason for immediate anxiety. I had reported this to the office and prepared to go home to a little house in Kensington, but the news editor—a ruthless fellow in times of crisis!—desired me to spend the night outside the palace "in case anything happened." It seemed to me an abominable idea and quite unnecessary, but with a colleague named Eddy—now a famous K.C.—I obeyed orders.

It was Eddy's idea that we should charter a four-wheeled cab and make ourselves as comfortable as possible during the night of waiting. It was an admirable plan, and after dining in a Fleet Street restaurant we hired the "growler"—that extinct vehicle—and, by the magic password of the Press, drove through the gates and "parked", as we should say now, in the great courtyard.

It was about half-past eleven at night. Outside the railings there was a crowd made up of all classes and types of London life in those days, which now seems incredibly remote because of all that has changed since then. There were many society men and women; young bloods of the town in top hats which have now gone into forgotten dustbins; and soldierly men who had not yet lost all the bronze of the South African war days; and actresses, and coster girls, and the old doss-house types; and people who had just come out of the theatres, in evening cloaks and coats. We could see their faces in the white glare of the lamps by the fountain.

Eddy took off his boots and proposed to sleep. Being a nicotine addict, I had a craving for a last cigarette and stood smoking it in the empty courtyard. Presently—I forget how long it was—a carriage and pair came quietly through the archway and passed me as I stood by one of the standard lamps. Their gleam passed across the carriage window. Inside were two people with white faces and glistening eyes. I had known them by sight as the Prince and Princess of Wales.

I went to the cab and spoke in an agitated voice.

"Eddy, I believe something has happened. I believe the King is dead."

Eddy put on his boots. We went hurriedly into the equerries' entrance, which was open. Before a fireplace a gentleman of the household was standing.

"How is the King?" I asked.

He was standing there as though a little dazed.

He looked up at a clock over the fireplace and answered me.

"His Majesty died a few minutes ago."

Those who had passed in the courtyard were the King and Queen. George V had begun his reign.

Now, nearly twenty-six years afterwards, he was dying at Sandringham.

3 *The Reign of George V*

That night I sat in a little old farmhouse under low beams. There was a log fire burning on the hearth, and it was very quiet outside in fields going down to a wood. But a voice was speaking in the room which was heard by hundreds of millions of people, in many countries, listening for the latest news about King George, by the miracle of the radio, which is dramatising life and death and all the human puppet show. The announcer had put on his mourning voice, infinitely sad.

"The King's life is moving peacefully towards its close."

It was the last bulletin from the King's doctors, and the announcer read out their names.

Every quarter of an hour for hour after hour the same words were spoken by that mournful voice.

"The King's life is moving peacefully towards its close."

It became unbearable at last, that constant repetition, but all over England, and all other countries where British subjects were within reach of this wireless transmission, the people listened and could not bring themselves to switch off until they had heard the announcement of the end.

George V was dead, and something had gone with his passing. It seems so often that something goes, some change happens, in the spirit of our nation at the end of a reign, as though the personality of the sovereign stamps itself upon the character of the time. History is not cut off into slices like that. One era merges imperceptibly into another. But the Victorian era itself with its manners and moralities seemed to go when the old Queen departed. The Edwardian period, that short reign of Edward VII, seems, falsely perhaps, to stand for a definite transition from Victorianism to "modern" ways of thought, less rigid, less formal, and less reticent. What did George V mean in our history book? What difference would his passing make?

His reign had begun with some political trouble, as I remembered on that night of his death. There had been that struggle —was it the last fight?—between the Lords and the Commons. Asquith had threatened to swamp the House of Lords with

Liberal peers if they would not pass a budget which, they asserted, went beyond a financial measure. A number of "Die-hard" peers—the name was newly coined—had threatened to resist to the last ditch in defence of their privileges. But Asquith had the King's agreement to create the new peers if the House of Lords refused to yield their power of obstruction. They had not been pleased with His Majesty for that. When he came to open Parliament there were murmurings among the peers and peeresses in the long painted gallery where I happened to stand among them as an onlooker.

"This is the end of all things," said a lady by my side. "After us the deluge. Oh, that man Asquith!"

The King was very nervous but read his speech in a steady guttural voice. It was noticed that he wore no gloves, contrary to all tradition. Something had happened in the royal coach to spoil them. The Queen's face was extremely pale, and in that white face her eyes seemed to burn—almost as though cut out of the Cullinan diamond at her breast, which quivered with light as though little white flames were leaping from it.

After that there was the Irish trouble, when the officers at the Curragh decided to disobey orders if they were to be moved against Ulster, arming under Carson. Then came Churchill's angry cry: "Then it will be the Army versus the People!" There were always the Suffragettes. . . . Certain newspapers raised a scare about the navy and a secret increase of the German fleet. Churchill demanded more cruisers. "We want eight and we won't wait."

How difficult it is to recall all that now! And how little it seems to matter! The reign of George V will be remembered always for one chapter of history which lasted for four and a half years—the most terrific ordeal ever endured by our nation and race; the cause of the most tremendous upheaval in the minds, manners and moralities of our people; smashing caste, breaking down the last stronghold of feudalism, changing everything, except something unchangeable, it seems, in our character and tradition. George V was King during those years of war and played his part with a courage, a lack of dismay even in the darkest days—which were very dark—and a kindly sympathy for all the suffering of the younger men which somehow reached out to them, though he was never emotional and never dramatic.

He came out to France and Flanders during the war and insisted upon going up to the front when it wasn't at all "healthy", as we used to say. His generals were very nervous about him. The enemy's shellfire was no respecter of persons. It came very close to him when he stood on the Messines Ridge looking over the enemy lines, and it followed him when he stood by one of the enormous craters blown up by our mines.

I listened to his conversation with the young officers in trenches and dugouts. He had a cheery naval voice and manner, though he looked odd in khaki and steel hat because of his beard. He laughed now and then in the fields of Armageddon. With him at these times was a young officer who was Prince of Wales, rather bored with the litter of battlefields which interested his father. It was all very familiar to him.

I was within a yard or two of the King when he sat on a restive horse reviewing a battalion of Air Force men near Béthune. They cheered him, and the horse, frightened by this queer noise, reared up three times and then fell over sideways in the mud with the King beneath its body. He was seriously hurt when "brass hats" dismounted hurriedly, rushed to him, and carried him to a car. Next day an ambulance passed through Lillers, where thousands of ambulances went their way in those war years with loads of wounded men whose muddy boots stuck up beyond the stretchers. Only a few of us knew that in this ambulance was the King, suffering horrible pain. It might have been another Tommy on his way to a casualty clearing station. The young Prince was scared about it and saw the shadow of the crown creeping closer to him.

Crowns were falling into the mud. Dynasties were crashing. Revolutions were breaking out towards the end of a struggle among the human tribes which had called for more than human endurance and had become a warfare of machines, a mechanical routine of slaughter, an endless maiming and killing of the world's manhood. When at last it ended, one king, almost alone—except for the King of the Belgians—received the homage of the men who had gone through those fires. It was King George.

On Armistice night enormous crowds mostly in uniform—or hospital blue—went towards Buckingham Palace and called for him. It was the first time they had ever demonstrated like that outside the palace, though now, as I have said, it seems to be a habit. They cheered themselves hoarse and sang "God Save the King" with tireless enthusiasm.

Up there on the balcony was a bearded man with kind eyes puckered by little wrinkles. He was not one of the war lords. He had never dressed up in shining armour. He had never played the part of a great general moving masses of men about—to the wrong places, perhaps. He had done his job as head of the state without any limelight or any greed for power.

"I'm a very ordinary fellow," he said of himself. Perhaps because of that, because he was supremely the ordinary English fellow, quiet, and good natured, and keen on his duty, and unfussed by disaster, and above all the intrigues and dissensions and despairs which had happened behind the scenes, the men of the Services paid their call on him and said "Good old George!"

They liked him. And he was their King and therefore stood as the symbol of "the whole show", as they called it, meaning the frightful and heroic adventure of those war years, the spirit of a people—their pals, themselves—who hadn't done badly, damn it; who had died or gone forward to the fires with something in their souls and blood which went back to Agincourt and Crécy; who had endured the muck and mud for something more than the oaths of a sergeant major; who now had fought the way to peace, with something saved out of the ruin and the wreckage. England was saved. The Empire was saved. Good old George!

They were sorry he had pegged out.

4 *The Ordeal of Grief*

"This is getting a bit too much," said a friend of mine, drawing a deep breath. "What with the newspapers and the B.B.C., I'm beginning to think that the death of the King is the greatest event in human history since the Crucifixion. And that isn't true, you know, in spite of due respect."

There were other people—many of them—who felt like that.

"We can't go on wallowing in grief to such an extent," said a lady of practical mind, averse, like many English women of the old stock, to exaggerated sentiment and emotional expression. "The B.B.C. are making an orgy of it."

The B.B.C. were overdoing it, though with reverence, a sense of drama, and all their resources of solemn music, tolling bells, reciting of poetry, hymns and prayers. Their news service was devoted almost entirely to the Lying in State and funeral procession, with an account of all the grief and sympathy of the world expressed by rulers and peoples to the British nation for their great loss. But it lasted too long. There was too much of it. The voices of the announcers were lowered to a minor key for too many hours of the day and night. It is one of the dangers of this present period of history. The wireless, the Press and the cinema are competing in the overemotionalisation, the overdramatisation, of contemporary events. The microphone especially is dangerous because it can so easily produce mass excitement and mass hysteria. Towards the end of the funeral ceremonies I noticed a tendency to cynicism among intelligent people who wish to keep a mental balance and proportion.

"I'm almost becoming antimonarchical," said a friend of mine who is no Communist.

A group of elders, very wise and distinguished, sat in their usual places, beyond the draughts, in a corner of a club smoking room. The eldest and the wisest of them was saying something about all this fervour of grief for the dead King.

"It's because people are giving up belief in God," he said. "They must have something to worship. So they are indulging in King-worship and raising the state, or the leader, to the position of Godhead. It happened in Rome in the time of the Caesars."

That was an inevitable reaction against the exaggeration of printed and spoken words. But it didn't touch the great mass of the nation. They did not think it was overdone. They delivered themselves over to its emotion and were utterly sincere in their regret for the passing of King George. He had spoken to them. They had heard his voice. He belonged to every little household in the country and in the Empire. They had actually come to regard him, I think, as the father of the family of nations which make up the Commonwealth. There was a personal warmth in their affection for him beyond their traditional loyalty to the King—in which, as the Americans can hardly understand, or, if they understand, condemn—there is something mystical, whatever the character of the King, and something which has its roots far back in their history and soul.

OUTSIDE BUCKINGHAM PALACE

5 *The Cross on the Crown*

I was in the crowd not far from the Marble Arch when the coffin of the dead King was brought on a gun carriage—after the train journey from Sandringham—to Westminster Abbey. An officer of the guards with drawn sword walked immediately behind the coffin and then came the new King, Edward VIII, whom all of us had known as Prince of Wales, so that it was very difficult to speak of him as the King. His brothers walked with him that long way. He looked tired, I thought, and others thought so too.

"I'm sorry for him," said a voice over my shoulder. "He looks hot and bothered. No wonder!"

His feet dragged a little towards the end. Several times he wiped the sweat off his forehead as he walked bareheaded in ordinary clothes with a dark overcoat.

On the gun carriage above the flag which covered it was the Imperial Crown, jogging as it went.

I remembered something about that crown having once read its history. It is St Edward's crown. In the gold framework of this diadem are three thousand diamonds and the sapphire of the Confessor's ring, and above all, in the cross, that "fair ruby, great as a rocket-ball", given to the Black Prince, and worn by King Harry in his helm, upon St Crispin's Day.

Something had happened to the top of the crown where the cross stands. The jogging of the gun carriage had shaken it loose and presently shook it off. It fell first on to the ledge of the gun carriage and then into the mud.

King Edward noticed it and gave a startled exclamation. The officer with the drawn sword stooped down and picked up the fallen piece and put it in his pocket, where it stayed until he reached the Abbey, where it was screwed on again.

"*Absit omen!*" said a voice in the crowd quite close to me, and I turned and looked into the eyes of the man who had spoken those words. He was a tall, lean youngish man with a little dark moustache. I happened to know him slightly, having met him in one of the small rooms of St James's Palace.

6 The Lying in State

King George's Lying in State in Westminster Hall was the most impressive evidence of the personal respect which he had gained among the people who passed into that old hall, which is one of the shrines of our history and very full of ghosts.

It was a slow and long ordeal on winter days and evenings, with wet pavements and a cold wind blowing, and no shelter for women and children. But all day long, day after day, there were queues stretching far and waiting patiently for this moment's glimpse of a coffin and a crown and four sentries of his Life Guards standing like statues with bowed heads at each corner of the catafalque. For half an hour they were the new King and his brothers.

The crowds moved at a snail's pace with many halts after each few yards of progress. I passed along their lines and watched their faces. They were of all classes and types, though mostly belonging, I should say, to the outer suburbs, where they live in little houses in long streets where there is not much margin of money for those who have a wireless set in the sitting room, paid for on the instalment system. They had come up by buses and tubes after office hours if that was their only free time. They looked very grave, as though they had lost their best friend or even their own father. They spoke hardly at all to each other and then in whispers. The children with them were stricken dumb by its solemnity. There was no commotion, no attempt to steal a place, no back chat. This long line of damp and shabby people in raincoats seemed never to end. It never ended until nearly a million had passed that way.

One of them—a lady—spoke to me on her way out of Westminster Hall. It was one I knew, and the last I expected to see. She is a humorous lady with a caustic wit, despising sentiment; and she is delicate, and fragile in physique.

"You here!" I exclaimed.

"Of course," she answered. "Why not? I had to say good-bye to a man who gave me my medals. I couldn't shirk that. A soldier's daughter!"

It had taken her two hours, and she looked dead tired with a very white face. She had served in the war in hospital wards, going down on her knees to cut off the muddy rags of wounded soldiers. She was not wearing her medals, but somehow I saw them on her breast.

Among those hundreds of thousands who lined up in queue to pass for a moment past the coffin of King George—that very ordinary fellow, as he called himself, as in many ways he was—there were great numbers of men who had gone, I am sure, in the spirit of that nurse, "For King and Country." Hadn't they gone out when that call came? They had been "fed up" all right. They had cursed the war. They had had a poor deal afterwards, perhaps. But somehow, for some reason which they would have shirked putting into words—they don't talk about patriotism or loyalty—they came to give a last salute to the King, and it was not for a peep show.

7 *The King's Funeral*

I was in the crowd again to see the funeral procession pass up Park Lane on its way to Paddington, where it would entrain for

Windsor. There was a vast multitude in the Park and along Piccadilly and down St James's Street. Its pressure became dangerous, especially around the Marble Arch, where it checked the progress of the procession and spoilt the timetable. There was a window in Grosvenor House to which I had been invited, but I stared up at it across many lines of people and knew that I should never get there. I thought also that I should not get even a glimpse of the funeral pageant as I stood in a hollow with rising ground in front of me, densely packed. Those people in front were more selfish than was quite justified. They stood on park chairs, utterly obliterating any view to be had by a hundred thousand eyes behind them. But those people without a view were wonderfully patient and good humoured about it. I talked with some of them.

"Not a hope!" said a man next to me with his wife and little girl. "But after all, we haven't come for a show, exactly. It's to show respect. Some of these folk are a lot too cheerful! I don't feel like laughing myself because a few boys are behaving like monkeys up them trees. I've come to see the last journey of King George, or, anyhow, to take my hat off when he passes."

He was severe on the demeanour of the crowd, which I found very orderly and quiet. Only now and again before the first sound of funeral music a few trivial incidents aroused a murmur of laughter—a man falling off one of the chairs, a young fellow hanging on to a branch, a dog hurrying along the empty roadway, scared by the multitude on each side.

A girl near me defended herself for a moment's levity.

"Oh well, the King wouldn't mind a smile or two while we're waiting for him. It's only natural. I suppose we're all choking down our secret feelings."

She spoke of the King as though she had known him well—as though he might have taken tea with her quite often—so that she knew he wouldn't mind a smile or two while these folk were waiting for him. She belonged to that type and class which sits down to a light meal of tea and sandwiches after a funeral and says, "It's just how he would have liked it, poor dear!"

"I must say it's a nice day for it," said the father of the little girl. He kept making friendly remarks to me but I couldn't place him exactly. He was perhaps a French polisher. I find quite a number of men I talk to by chance are French polishers. He had hoisted the plump little daughter on to his shoulder and hoped she could see something.

Heavy clouds were scudding across the sky, and a soft wind was blowing, and sunlight flickered between the bare trees of the park.

"I'm thinking a lot of the new King," he told me. "Great responsibility for a young man, of course! Well, he'll be equal to it, no doubt of that. He has the people behind him, and all the young folk. They'll follow him anywhere if he lifts a little finger. It's his pluck they like. No end of spirit, eh? And he gets on with the working classes. He knows how to talk to them. He showed up the state of the distressed areas when the politicians wanted to forget them. A young king will be good for the country in my judgment. Not that he could do better than the man who's gone. Everybody says so. He was all right."

There was a determined attempt to force a line through the chairs. Women who had been firmly planted on them since the early hours of the morning refused to budge but could not resist enormous pressure from behind. Some cunning fellow moved a chair or two in the sudden scrimmage—enough to let in a raiding party. By sheer luck and blind force I was one of those pushed forward onto higher ground from which I could see the roadway through the railings.

A few moments later I heard the beat of drums and the sound of Chopin's funeral march—that lovely, pitiful and triumphant tune of the spirit's victory over death. Very slowly came the long procession of mounted and marching men, preceding the King's coffin and the royal mourners, and the representatives of many countries. It was a long walk for them, and the pace was set to a slow beat. Some of them were elderly men and looked exhausted before they had gone as far as Marble Arch. I caught a glimpse of faces I knew by sight—generals and admirals and princes. The richest colour in this moving picture was made by the flame-red capes of coachmen, which spread over the boxes of the old-fashioned coaches in which royal ladies were driven, as though they had come from the Court of Queen Anne. King Edward VIII looked very pale and strained in his naval uniform as he strode alone behind his father's coffin, which was drawn by long lines of naval men holding white ropes attached to the gun carriage.

There was utter silence among those hundreds of thousands of people, standing with bared heads along the short line of route which I could see. There is something always uncanny in such a sudden and continued silence in London. One seems to hear the beating of one's own heart in that multitude of humanity. The birds were frightened by it and rose circling above the trees and roofs. Then the silence was shocked by the firing of guns. So King George passed on his last journey, which would end at Windsor.

"Very impressive, don't you think?" said a man who had stood next to me by the railings and had made way a little so that I could see something.

"Vastly," I agreed.

"Now it's the reign of Edward VIII. I suppose we'll get used to it, but I still think of him as the Prince of Wales. How's he going to shape out, do you think?"

"He has fine qualities."

My friendly acquaintance—he was a well-dressed man of

middle age who looked like a family doctor or lawyer—waited with me until the crowd had thinned out a little.

"A pity he isn't married," he said. "A bachelor king will feel a bit lonely, don't you think? But he has a great chance. I should say he's the most popular man in the world. It's his spirit. There's something very youthful about him."

We were separated in the crowd. I walked down a passage into Knightsbridge, which was dangerous because of the enormous pressure of people jammed into this narrow way. Two girls—shopgirls probably—walked in front of me.

"I didn't see a thing!" said one of them. "Nothing but people's backs. Still, I must say I enjoyed myself."

"King George was all right," said a man's voice over my shoulder. "He was all right, that's what I say."

"I want something to eat," said a woman. "I always feel hungry after a funeral. Queer, ain't it? Still, it's natural, I daresay."

"I waited three hours to see the Lying in State," said one of the girls. "I wouldn't have missed it."

London had seen a King go to his grave, and as I listened to the sullen shocks of gunfire and the sound of tolling bells swept by the moist wind, and the murmur of vast crowds, I had a sense of all the history that has passed in this old monstrous city, and of many crowds gathered under the clash of bells from many churches for crownings and burials, and tragedies and triumphs, and pageants and processions, through the centuries. This consciousness of the past, this sense of historical drama, this awareness of ghosts, is, I believe, very real in the minds of London crowds when they go out to see their kings and princes, dead or alive. They are sensitive to old vibrations. The most ignorant get some thrill of romance out of their heritage of history. They learn a bit of Shakespeare in the schools; and it's in their blood.

II

King Edward VIII

THIS YOUNG KING who followed his father had with him the heart of England—and of almost all the world—when he began his reign.

He had made a place for himself in the imagination of many peoples beyond his realm. They had seen his face and figure so often on the screen, and in picture papers, and on postcards in a million shopwindows, that he belonged to the portrait gallery of their minds and they liked the look of him. There was one of his photographs in naval uniform, laughing, which was pinned over many mantelpieces and many desks. It made one feel good to look at it, it was so youthful, so gay, so "English", as we like to think.

As Prince of Wales he had been truly the Prince of Youth. The Germans called him "the Prince" as if he belonged to them. The Americans called him "Wales" and had a hero-worship for him since that time he went to visit them, and fingered his tie with extraordinary shyness, and laughed at the pretty girls, and, unfortunately, fell into the wrong set on Long Island.

"How are you falling, Prince?" asked Will Rogers at a time when the Prince had been unlucky as a rider.

"All over the place," said the Prince of Wales, and Will

THE LYING-IN-STATE OF KING GEORGE V

Rogers, who had the ear of America, told his own people that if the United States liked to join the British Empire when this prince should be King it would be all right as far as Will Rogers was concerned.

The world liked his courage, and restlessness, and eager spirit to try anything new. He was often in the air and could handle his own plane. He liked any kind of game and once, as I know, got into trouble in Canada for liking one too much when he ought to have been lunching with his elders.

He spoke well and wittily, and sometimes made up his own speeches, or put bits into those prepared for him.

"Gentlemen," he said to a gathering of Press photographers, "I am the raw material of your industry."

There are not many princes who can make a *bon mot* like that.

He was easy in his ways with the common folk, whom he liked best—"the likes of us"—who live in small houses on small means; and the ex-service men, and craftsmen and mechanics and jockeys. He had a soft spot in his heart for the unemployed and the underdogs; and his speech over the wireless after his first visit to the workless districts in Wales was very moving because of its genuine sympathy and eagerness to get something done about such conditions.

He had a sense of humour uncommon in princes. If there were an orchestra in the room he liked to play the traps or the big drum. He even did rather well on the bagpipes, which might daunt a less fearless man.

I had seen some of his appearances from boyhood onwards. I stood within a yard of him when he heard his father proclaimed King from the walls of St James's Palace, when he looked over the garden wall of Marlborough House.

I saw him that day in Carnarvon when, as a boy, he looked a fairy-tale prince with golden hair as he was presented to the

Welsh people as Prince of Wales with ancient ceremony in castle walls.

I met him on the roads of France and Flanders when he rode a push bike, and the troops, slogging forward through the mud and rain, didn't know who he was and didn't care because they had an ugly job ahead of them.

I stood close to him when, as a young lieutenant, he watched a battle from a hill in Flanders. There were lots of generals about and he saluted them respectfully, and they took no notice of him.

I saw him with his brother officers of the guards, laughing at their jokes and going into dirty places which were not "health resorts", as we used to say.

"Crowns are cheap today, gentlemen," he remarked one morning in his mess when dynasties were crashing.

There was something of Prince Hal in him. He would have exchanged wisecracks with old Falstaff. He preferred the company of Poins and Bardolph to that of lord mayors and aldermen. I had often seen him looking very bored—painfully and elaborately bored—when he had to sit through long dull speeches at long dull tables. He was always restless at such times, moving about in his chair, touching things, shifting his position continually. "That lad is suffering," I thought. Anybody who would make him laugh could get that laugh. He loved to be amused. He loved to laugh. It was rather dangerous for a Prince who one day would be King and have to keep his dignity and put away his jesters.

But he had a serious, even spiritual, side to his nature. In another book I have told how he went one night to the crypt below St Martin's Church in Trafalgar Square where homeless men sleep. It is not a pleasant place. The atmosphere there is not sweet. The men have damp clothes from which there comes a sour stench. But he stayed there for two hours, talking to each man as he came down the steps to get his pillow for a hard bench. He was in evening clothes with his overcoat collar turned up. Not a man knew who he was. There were no newspapermen lurking about. No word of this visit was published. It wasn't a publicity stunt but something he did for his own interest.

He was keen on Toc H, that society of earnest and religious young men who hand on the torch of faith to the younger crowd. He entered into the spirit of it when they lit the lamps of Remembrance, and he often used to go to one of their houses to sit down on bare boards and join in a singsong, with "Tubby" Clayton leading the chorus.

He would get into a small car and drive himself to workingmen's districts, like Hoxton, and spend an evening in workingmen's clubs. He might have been having a good time with his own friends in more comfortable surroundings. There was no public kudos in it. It wasn't advertised.

He knew the Empire and its peoples. He had gone through the cities of India when their shutters were closed because of Ghandi's boycott. He had talked with Indian princes and received their homage. He had a ranch in Canada where he lived a free life. He had broken down the solemnity of South African chiefs and native tribes. He had donned the headdress of Red Indians. Everywhere he went he put off pomposity and had the human touch, frank, kindly, very winning. He made friends too easily perhaps with those who made him laugh. He was impatient with friends who didn't make him laugh but criticised or advised him.

Now he was King. It was time to put behind him the carelessness of youth and boon companions of Alsatia. He was King Emperor. What a power, and what a chance to give the world a new leadership! The people believed in him. He stood for something very special in their imagination and in their fairy tale of life. They knew none of his faults, his obstinacies, his tempers, if he had them. They knew only that he was a young King with a will of his own and a democratic mind. They believed he would lead them forward to a new age, with youth in the saddle behind him.

III

Arms and the Man

1 A Royal Commission

ON A WINTER DAY two years ago—when I began an adventure which dragged on until September of last year—certain village post offices were disturbed by telegrams which they could not deliver, summoning me to see the prime minister.

Telephone messages asked for me in vain. I was completely lost until—alas!—I was found at the tick of time to appear before the prime minister in his private room at the House of Commons at the hour appointed. It was Mr Ramsay MacDonald, who was so kindly and friendly when I came that I did not suspect the mantrap into which I walked. Before I left his room I had agreed to serve on a royal commission to enquire into the alleged abuses in the private manufacture of arms and the trading in weapons of war, and to decide whether it was possible, or desirable, to substitute a state monopoly in this industry.

Here, I thought in my simple soul, is a chance of doing something for world peace. How can I refuse, having seen the massacre of the world's young manhood in the greatest war in history?

In due course I received a document from His Majesty King George V, who was good enough to call me his "Trusty and Well-beloved."

"Now know ye," said His Majesty, "that We, reposing great trust and confidence in your knowledge and ability, have authorised and appointed, and do by these Presents authorise you and appoint you," as one of the members of the Royal Commission.

It sounded important and awe inspiring, but I was aware that there are many pigeonholes in Whitehall stuffed with the reports of royal commissions which have laboured long and then have been forgotten. Nevertheless, I hoped to do a good job.

The chairman of the commission was Sir John Eldon Bankes, a veteran of the High Court of Justice; and the other members were Dame Rachel Crowdy, Sir Thomas Allen, Sir Kenneth Lee, Professor Gutteridge, K.C., and J. A. Spender, the famous journalist and historian.

I knew none of them but Spender when we first met, but before our report was issued we came to know each other's minds and mannerisms and instinctive leaning to this side or the other of that complicated case we had to examine. Gradually I came to be looked upon by Sir John Eldon Bankes, I fear, as the Bad Boy of the Family, and I see now that I caused him at times grave anxiety and, but for his great good nature and unfailing courtesy, considerable annoyance. Dame Rachel Crowdy was, in his mind, I think, the Girl Who Took the Wrong Turning.

For Sir John himself I shall never cease to have the most profound respect and admiration. He was over eighty when the Royal Commission first sat but he looked twenty years younger, with a straight back and the complexion of a new-born babe, and the blue eyes of a Saxon thane. His mind was alert and clear, and he could handle a mass of evidence presented to him with the mastery of a judge—as he was—who finds a contradiction between a paragraph on page fourteen and another paragraph on page seventy-four and would like to know the reason why.

He had one little mannerism of which he was unaware. Whenever a witness was making statements with which he profoundly disagreed—as often he did—or whenever one of us asked questions which seemed to him objectionable, he tapped a pencil on which there was a little ring, and it tinkled until the witness had allowed himself to be interrupted or switched off by another question. That little bell often rang when I was examining the witnesses and asking questions of which the chairman disapproved. I knew by its tinkle that I was on dangerous ground, and it needed moral courage of a high quality to ignore this fairy tintinnabulation and pursue my enquiry to its bitter end.

Dame Rachel Crowdy, who had done fine work at Geneva to check the opium traffic, is a humorous lady with an amount of moral courage which I found stupendous.

Nothing daunted her—not even the blue eyes of Sir John Eldon Bankes—not even the long array of representatives of Vickers Limited and Imperial Chemicals. In the most charming voice she would ask the most deadly questions. With an agreeable smile she would dig a grave for a reluctant witness or, by some quotation from a document before her, bring a blush to the cheek of an arms' manufacturer who had been indiscreet in his correspondence.

Sir Thomas Allen, an old leader of the Co-operative movement, was one of the Wise Men of the West. He said very little, but when he spoke it was with words of power, though Sir John Eldon Bankes, who was a little hard of hearing now and then, seldom heard them.

Sir Kenneth Lee, one of the great industrialists of this country, was our dark horse until the end, when he became a shining light.

Professor Gutteridge, K.C., was learned in the law and especially in international law, and, though in his heart he is the most genial of men, he used to alarm some of his witnesses by an abruptness of questioning in the voice of a sea captain, which made them imagine that he had a grudge against them.

J. A. Spender, as most of us know, has a mind as finely balanced as the most delicate instrument of the clockmaker, and a spirit steeped in the old Liberal tradition which once was the glory and strength of this country.

Our secretary had the noble and significant name of Twentyman—Edward of that ilk—and was a picturesque figure with golden hair and beard, like the German idea of John the Baptist, purely Nordic. He was an impressive specimen of the Treasury Official, perfectly efficient, but with an acute sense of humour which he kept for private use untouched by red tape and sealing wax. A romantic man, yet cynical now and then, but sometimes very surprising in his sudden blaze of idealism which came up from some smouldering fire within his soul.

He had as an assistant a young civil servant named Haigh—who, I suspected at times, was wiser than any of us but too considerate to let us know.

We were those who were lagged for this job.

2 *England in the Witness Box*

For many long and weary months we were burdened by this task, which was unpaid—and some of us had to earn our daily bread—and unpleasant, to me particularly, because I am a man who hates to hurt anybody's feelings, or to be harshly hostile to other people's points of view, or to act as a moral judge of other people's actions; and yet I felt that it was my duty sometimes to be like that for the sake of getting at the truth, which was the job with which we were charged.

Postmen in town and country must have cursed this Royal

ARMS AND THE MAN

Commission, for it added considerably to their burdens. Sitting in my room, I could hear a desperate struggle to get a bulky document through an average-sized letter box. It dropped to the floor with an awful thud, and from a yard away I could see the letters "On His Majesty's Service" and knew that I should have to read more pages of close print or faintly copied typewriting.

These documents poured in. No letter box would take many of them. They filled a large despatch box before we had had many sittings. Before the end had come they were as thick as leaves in Vallombrosa. They nearly blinded me, those figures, graphs, charts, appendices, notes in the smallest possible type on the worst possible paper. All of them had to be read and studied and, if possible, remembered. It was like the labour of Sisyphus, that most unfortunate wretch.

But this experience was valuable and not without human drama.

It brought us into close quarters with opposing schools of thought on a subject which arouses passion in millions of minds who hated war and therefore—not with strict logic—hated the makers and traders of the instruments of war.

Into the court rooms, where we sat for public sittings, came, as witnesses to be examined by us, many interesting figures—some of them famous in our chronicles—and many odd characters, whom Charles Dickens would have put into his notebooks as good stuff for his picture gallery of English life—old admirals with the quarter-deck manner and mind; generals who had been responsible for the supplies of war when this nation was hard pressed; scientists, inventors, chemists, pacifists, Communists; old boys of the bulldog breed, young advocates of the Marxian faith; old-fashioned industrialists, and builders of ships, and forgers of steel; the heads of enormous combines—like Sir Harry McGowan of the Imperial Chemicals, and the representatives of the Vickers group; a trafficker in secondhand arms and any old weapons for any new war; government officials with minds like card indexes; the pioneers of aviation; and other figures in the passing pageant of English life.

This Royal Commission summoned to its witness stand many remarkable minds and men, in the public arena of political life or behind the scenes in workshops and laboratories and quiet rooms where thought—sometimes very dangerous—is active.

Our first witnesses presented the case for the prosecution, as one might say, against the private manufacturers and traders in war material.

Our chairman decided to give them the widest possible latitude in presenting their case and to ignore any restraint to the full expression of their views, even if they were not strictly supported by evidence. Both they and we ourselves, however, were limited in this enquiry to the consideration of abuses alleged against our own arms industry in this country, whereas many of the gravest charges and suspicions and acknowledged facts of evil significance were of foreign and international character. That was a severe limitation, as the corruption of the Press, the bribery of officials, pressure upon governments by arms manufacturers, and many notorious scandals in foreign countries could not be dealt with as evidence before us.

Then again, we did not adopt the methods of the Nye Committee in the United States, which had enquired on this subject and had employed large numbers of investigators who seized private correspondence of manufacturers and traders to search for any scandalous affair which they might fish out of muddy waters.

Nevertheless, the case for the attack on the private manufacturers and traders did not lack force when presented by men like Lord Cecil on behalf of the League of Nations Union, Sir

William Jowett on behalf of the Union of Democratic Control, Mr Arnold-Forster for some twenty-six peace societies, and Mr Philip Noel Baker for himself and the Labour party.

Their main contentions were based upon the list of alleged evils set out in a report of a commission to the League of Nations Assembly in 1921:

That armament firms have been active in fomenting war scares and in persuading their own countries to adopt warlike policies and to increase their armaments;

That armament firms have attempted to bribe government officials both at home and abroad;

That they have disseminated false reports concerning the military and naval programmes of various countries in order to stimulate armament expenditure;

That they have sought to influence public opinion by the control of newspapers in their own and foreign countries;

That they have organised international armament rings by which the armament race has been accentuated by playing off one country against another;

That they have organised international armament trusts which have increased the price of armaments to governments.

In addition to those abuses charged against manufacturers the opponents of that private industry urged that wars may be prolonged by supplying arms to opposing nations, and that arms may be supplied freely to a potential enemy.

They also argued that private trading in arms leads to the disturbance of good international relations, the touting for orders among foreign powers leading to an increase in explosive forces and the disclosure of secret information to possible enemies.

Finally, they advocated a system of state monopoly, or nationalisation, in order, as they thought, to check the abuses and establish a more efficient method of national defence—

private firms being unable, in their opinion, to create the necessary expansion in time of war.

That is a very brief outline of the main body of attack upon the system of private manufacture and it was sustained by allusions to alleged scandals at home and abroad, by quotations from speeches made by directors of armament firms at company meetings, and by letters from representatives of those firms produced in the American commission, which suggested a sinister connivance for trade purposes between international armament rings, and hostility to efforts on behalf of international peace.

There were frequent allusions to an affair called the Mulliner case, in which a gentleman of that name was accused of organising a scare campaign against Germany in the British Press before the World War and among members of the Government and the Opposition, in order to obtain Admiralty orders for his own firm. There were many suggestions and charges of bribery, influence exerted upon foreign governments by private traders, and other abuses based upon circumstantial evidence, inferences, and suspicion rather than upon exact facts which would satisfy a court of law and produce a verdict of "Guilty."

I confess that instinctively, emotionally and intellectually I leaned to the side of that case against the private manufacturers in their international dealings. I had heard many dark stories about the Comité des Forges and its black hand in the political corruption of France. I couldn't disbelieve information given to me by men deeply familiar with armament scandals in Central Europe. I was not at all shocked by the sensational titles given to certain pamphlets published by peace societies extreme in their hostility to the trade in arms, such as one called *Merchants of Death.* Those titles did not, and do not, seem to me too strong for armament firms who, with the utmost cynicism and by many means of bribery and corruption in foreign countries, provide all the machinery of scientific slaughter to any nation, or collection of savages, able to pay for them; who will stimulate the trade by playing one enemy against another; and who will supply the material and weapons of war even to those who are most likely to attack their own people. There was, I thought, a strong prima-facie case that these things do happen in many countries and that our own virtue is not like that of the angels—we have the greatest export trade of war material among all the other nations—though we may be—and I think are—less corrupt in our methods, less brazen in bribery, than some of our competitors.

But we were a court of enquiry, a kind of judicial body, who could only deal with evidence produced and proved, and who were bound in honour to try this case—enormously complicated in its details and ramifications—without prejudice or passion. I found that difficult, and I lapsed now and then, but there is the report to prove that we subordinated prejudice to pure reason, cold logic, and a judgment of which Solomon himself might approve.

3 *One of the Cecils*

Lord Cecil appeared before us, and there was a stir in court when he rose with his long stooping figure and falconlike face—one of the Cecils whose family ruled England in more than one era.

His high-toned voice, suave and conciliatory, reminded me of days when I had seen him in the Council of the League of Nations, holding that body together, in times of international crisis, by some ingenious formula which smoothed over conflicting interests and pouring diplomatic oil upon the troubled waters of national passions. But for him the League would have died in its early years. If he had been there in recent crises it might not be so sick.

He made a masterly exposition of the case against the private arms manufacture and trading. With his legal training and fine judicial mind, he never stepped beyond the mark of what might be fairly considered legitimate inference of available evidence. Who could dispute his description of what happened in the recent savage war between Bolivia and Paraguay according to the findings of the commission appointed by the League of Nations?

"The armies engaged are using up-to-date material: aeroplanes, armoured cars, flame projectors, quick-firing guns, machine guns and automatic rifles. The arms and material of every kind are not manufactured locally, but are supplied to the belligerents by American and European countries."

The Merchants of Death—Sir John Eldon Bankes did not approve of that title—were making good profits out of this traffic in a murderous war which was no concern of theirs. They have done so recently in Spain.

Lord Cecil did not minimise the importance of the emotional hostility to this form of trade and quoted with approval a passage from a speech by Lord Halifax which afterwards we placed prominently in our report:

"This is one of the questions that arouse a very sincere and very profound feeling in the minds of our people. . . . Rightly or wrongly, the great majority of them conceive this question of the private manufacture of, and trade in, arms to be directly connected with the great issues of peace and war, on which they feel more deeply and more vehemently than upon anything else: and therefore, regarding war, as they do, as the greatest evil to which the nation could be exposed, and regarding it indeed as only justifiable in cases of ultimate and extreme national necessity, they are disposed to regard the preparation of the implements of war as too high and too grave a thing to be entrusted to any hands less responsible than those of the State itself, fearing intrusion into so dangerous a field of any interests less imperative than those of national security or national honour."

Not stressing too much the emotional side of the argument, Lord Cecil based his views upon points of principle and upon such evidence of admitted evil—scanty, as one must admit—such as he could find.

I watched him curiously as he gave his evidence, and when afterwards I was privileged to question him; and I thought how strange and significant it was that this man of aristocratic tradition, rather cold and aloof in temperament, intellectually Conservative, with a mind stored with knowledge reaching far back into history, should, by some concealed flame in his spirit, stand like this in public support of extreme views against a system defended, as it was bound to be, and as afterwards it was, by the Conservative government, by all the Services, by all, or nearly all, the people of his own party and class. He was in alliance on this subject with Communists, Socialists, all the Reds, and all the Pinks, and all the pacifists. He had been responsible for that Peace Ballot in which eleven million people had voted for the principles of the League of Nations, including the policy of sanctions against an aggressor nation, which for a time had considerably impressed Mr Stanley Baldwin and his colleagues who had objected to it.

4 *A Passionate Advocate*

A youngish man of dramatic personality appeared before us later and made another prolonged indictment of the private manufacturers. I watched him with some amusement, remembering a day—I was a boy then, in a top hat—when his father asked me to see him safely to a railway station. He was William Arnold-Forster, and his father—a most remarkable man, with the bluest eyes and the most passionate industry of any man I have known—was H. O. Arnold-Forster, once secretary of state for war, secretary for the admiralty, and my first chief in a publishing office off Ludgate Hill.

"You may sit down if you prefer to give your evidence that way," said Sir John Eldon Bankes benevolently.

"I prefer to stand, sir," said Mr Arnold-Forster.

He stood and gave his evidence with great dramatic intensity, and as I watched him I saw him, not in the courtroom of the Westminster Guildhall, but in Paris as a Jacobin in the days of the French Revolution, proclaiming the Rights of Man.

Though he had prepared a formidable indictment in which he crammed all the facts he could find or suggest—we had a lot of suggestion!—in his introduction he was disposed to minimise their importance and relied upon general inevitabilities—human nature being what it is, and businessmen being what they are, in his opinion.

"The firms," he said, "which make and sell armaments for private profit MUST desire conditions in which there is an effective demand for their products; and this motive-force, operating under present conditions, MUST have the effect of promoting an expansion of sales of armaments, and of impeding agreement upon that all-round reduction of armaments which the world urgently needs."

I shall not forget the gesture with which he flung out his arm at that mighty and indisputable MUST which rang through the court and raised a slight smile on the lips of Sir John Eldon Bankes.

In a brilliant passage of pure imagination he anticipated the objections of these unfortunate manufacturers whom by that MUST he had handed over to predestination.

"Do the firms in this country, whose business is largely concerned with armament production, desire conditions in which there is a demand for their products? Of course they do, just like the producers of beer and soap. They do not find it prudent to advertise the fact on the hoardings; they do not invite us with picture postcards 'to say it with tanks' . . . 'it's nicer with mustard gas.' But of course they desire the business.

"I dare say," he went on, "that spokesmen of some of the firms in question will presently assure the Commission that they do not desire war. Let us accept their assurance at once, without reserve (though we should be realistic enough to take note of the colossal profits made by certain firms manufacturing armaments, especially during the war period). . . . But that is not the real point at all. I dare say that all the directors and managers of these firms, when reading their morning newspapers at breakfast, want to see the nations settling down nicely together. . . . But can it be doubted that these same individuals, when they go to the office after breakfast in their capacity as managers of great businesses, have to switch over their attention to the job of expanding that business so as to produce dividends for their shareholders and employment for their staffs and plants?"

This was pretty good stuff and I enjoyed it. But my judicial mind—sitting on the right hand of Sir John Eldon Bankes I remembered that I had to be judicial—waited for the conclusion of that rhetoric which, in fairness to the arms manufacturers, demanded some show of proof that when they wished to expand their business in tanks, high explosives or machine guns they were able to impose their will upon the government or so to stir up international trouble that their goods would be in greater demand. I remembered that their success in this direction had not been very notable during our long period of economy in armaments. On these points Mr Arnold-Forster's evidence was not convincing, as far as our own manufacturers are concerned, though he brought out some very unpleasant allegations, a few incriminating facts, and some very plausible inferences, not quite good enough as evidence. He was an advocate of first-class quality.

5 *The Listeners*

There was always an audience at our public sittings, and I used to watch them from my place aloft and wonder who they were and why they should come to listen to evidence which was sometimes very technical.

I began to recognise the faces of certain regular attendants. Below me on the right was a pale-faced lady who never failed to come and who made detailed notes. Now and again I caught her eyes upon me—once, I fear, with a rebuke in them. It was when I laughed at the evidence of a certain witness who was a complete moral bandit and rejoiced in doing good business in the traffic of arms wherever he could find his customers. He faced us—and we were a severe-looking lot—with cheerful effrontery and undisguised cynicism. There was something comical in his outrageous defiance of any moral attitude and in his swashbuckling account of his own career. It was like having a pirate before us, waving the skull and cross-bones under the very nose of Sir John Eldon Bankes. I find it impossible to account for my laughter, but certainly I laughed, as did others of us, and the pale-faced lady looked at me with astonished and painful disapproval.

There was another lady who seldom failed to be in court. She was young, "easy on the eye," as the Americans say, not at all alarming in appearance or manner. But I became rather nervous of her. At first she sent up little notes to the judge, asking him to put certain questions to the witnesses who defended the private manufacture of arms, which sometimes he did. Then she turned her attention to me, evidently thinking that I was a sympathetic soul on her side of the argument, which was the extreme Left. Her questions which she wanted me to put were very penetrating and proved that she had studied the case, even in its technical aspects, with great industry and intelligence. But I did not wish to be coached by a young woman who was acting on behalf of Communists, and, anyhow, I had studied my own brief—those masses of documents which were piled on my shelves—and had my own line of examination. I fear I must have pained her by returning her sheafs of notes.

On the benches below us were groups of middle-aged men who looked very bored sometimes but did their best to keep awake after lunch. They were representatives of the Services and the arms manufacturers. They became alert on days when the directors of Vickers and Imperial Chemicals were giving evidence and when the examination of these gentlemen led to some drama and heat.

It was impossible for me to take this case with any kind of levity, though we had some cause of laughter now and then, especially when we gathered together in our retiring room. Dame Rachel Crowdy had a merry wit; and our secretary, Mr Twentyman, with his blond beard and blue eyes—we ran to blue eyes—had an ironical mind; and Professor Gutteridge told some very good stories. Sometimes we had to readjust our facial muscles before standing very solemnly in court for the arrival of the chairman who had been Lord Justice of Appeal.

But I was always conscious that we were to be judges in a case which to some extent might involve the lives of those now approaching manhood and might have some influence upon the peace of the world. Because this traffic in arms—to me the most important aspect of the case—might be a cause of explosion somewhere which would hurl us all into the furnace of another war. Its prevention by international control—if we could ever get that—might do something to remove evils and dangers and immoralities, not the direct cause of war perhaps, but an indirect cause, maybe, of fear and hatred and competition in lethal weapons.

In that Royal Commission I was marked out by some of the peace lovers as one who would defend their cause and would not let them down. I knew that because I had letters from them urging me to put up a good fight against "Mars, his Idiot", against vested interests in the instruments and material of war, against armament rings whom they believed to be agents of iniquity. I was to go out against this Moloch.

So when I sat in my seat, like a white mouse, I felt, below the judge's chair, I had a grave sense of responsibility to a public bigger than that in court—to millions of men and women desperately anxious for peace in our time, and for the safety of their children, and for the security of what civilisation there is or may be.

I felt extremely nervous because of that task. I had had no training in cross-examination or the mastering of a complicated brief with innumerable and difficult facts and figures; and it was no easy thing to face an array of arms manufacturers, or official experts, and ask the right questions, and follow a line of examination with self-assurance, and ask offensive questions —necessarily offensive—without flinching, because they displeased those to whom they were put and that very charming and courteous old man sitting up aloft who didn't think it helped at all.

There were times when I was preposterously nervous, so that my voice became harsher than I intended, and my manner more repulsive than I had ever thought possible of myself, and my temper less under control than it ought to have been. It was all due to nerves and a sense of strain. I am astonished now at the ferocity with which I tackled some of those witnesses, but they can afford to forgive me. They are making handsome profits again. Are they not making munitions of war as fast as they can—and not fast enough—for the government rearmament plan?

6 *Times of Crisis*

During the course of the commission there were two episodes in history which bore down upon our enquiry and seemed to make it foolish and futile.

The first was Mr Mussolini's adventure in Abyssinia, after he had flouted all his pledges to the League of Nations, mocked at that assembly's condemnation of an aggressive war against one of the member states, and gone straight ahead with his attacks and reinforcements, despite the sanctions imposed upon him by many nations. When he sent a large body of troops to Libya and tried to stir up trouble in Egypt, things began to look serious between this country and Italy. When the proposed settlement by Sir Samuel Hoare was passionately repudiated by public opinion in this country and our fleet concentrated in the Mediterranean, things looked more serious. Italian propaganda was furious against us. Mussolini uttered threats of war. M. Laval, prime minister of France, had sold the pass by a secret agreement with Il Duce and was a reluctant ally of ours in any use of force—a possibility repugnant to French opinion. If there were any war with Italy it would be our war, though we were acting in the name of Collective Security.

"I find it difficult to face any more public sittings during this crisis," said Sir John Eldon Bankes one morning, and we agreed with him, because, after all, it was difficult, if not absurd, to discuss the alleged abuses of private manufacture of arms when the Admiralty was sending rush orders for naval shells, and when the private firms were put under sudden and immediate pressure to make good the deficiencies of supply which had fallen too low—alarmingly and dangerously low—should the horrid spectre of war beckon us to follow him. No condemnation of ours, no recommendations, no plan of a new system, would be of the least avail if Italian aircraft flew over our battleships with loads of bombs, or if Mussolini, suffocating with rage, touched the button of a bell in the Palazzo di Venezia and ordered his submarine commanders to sink some British battleships, whatever hell might follow. That nearly happened. . . .

This crisis passed, but its shock and its warning did not leave things as they had been. Mussolini's repudiation of the League revealed, as though by a flash of lightning, the impotency of that body to establish law and order, or to prevent a war if one of the big powers decided to risk it.

The Pact of Paris, by which many nations had renounced war in support of their national policy, was now a dead letter.

Other pledges and pacts were being broken. Germany was breaking them, and Germany was rearming with an intensity which alarmed her neighbours and former enemies. Mr Winston Churchill called the attention of the House of Commons to the rapid and costly programme of German rearmament, especially in the air, and his lurid words, based upon evidence which is not now challenged, seriously disturbed the British government, who had hoped for a general measure of disarmament—although their political opponents could not congratulate them on the work of their representatives in Geneva, who had always raised pettifogging obstructions and had "missed the boat" more than once when the tide was flowing in the direction of that ideal and possibility.

The British government issued a white paper on the subject of national defence and rearmament while the Royal Commission was sitting. Neither the prime minister nor any of his colleagues thought it well to send us a word on the subject, though we were supposed to be—and were—charged with the duty of considering many of the aspects of that problem and had in our possession all the available facts.

They based all their reliance upon the old system of private manufacture, with its profit making and its limited possibilities of expansion, and its lack of co-ordination and control. Here we were—this Royal Commission—sidetracked and ignored. It was not a pleasant position, nor very encouraging to our labours. One or two members suggested resignation. The others begged the chairman to go straight ahead, as though the white paper had never been issued, and as though we had to deal—as indeed we had—with general principles unaffected by passing events. The chairman agreed, after an adjournment.

I can see him sitting there during these crises in our history with a faint look of anxiety and worry on his usually placid face. He sat, during our private sittings, with his back to a wide window overlooking the garden of Buckingham Palace or, in another room we used, looking on the way from Wellington Barracks to St James's Park. Every morning there was the sound of gay music and the beat of drums. The guards were on their way to the King's house. We turned in our seats to watch those young men marching by, their arms and legs swinging in perfect unison, with their machinelike precision. The colours passed.

"A good sight!" said Sir John Eldon Bankes.

7 *The House of Vickers*

As the greatest armament firm in this country, linked up with many subsidiary companies and a network of international interests, Vickers Limited stood in the public imagination, and in actual fact, as the stronghold of that system of private manufacture and trading in arms against which all their critics were passionately hostile. Considerable public interest was aroused when it was known that the directors of this firm were coming to give their evidence and to be examined. The court was crowded on the days when they appeared, and the Press was in full attendance.

The members of the Royal Commission were, I think, all feeling somewhat highly strung as they took their places to face these directors and experts of Messrs Vickers headed by Sir Herbert Lawrence, the chairman of that company, with Sir Charles Craven as its managing director, and Mr Yapp among its important officials.

Our chairman knew that the examination of these witnesses after they had put in their own detailed case would not be of a mild and amiable character. He was apprehensive, I think, that some members of the commission might go too far in their probing of matters of scandalous allegations. He was not sure of our ability in cross-examination or of our being willing to conform to judicial discretion. By this time, I fear, he had mild suspicions of Dame Rachel Crowdy and myself as a couple of hot-heads who might cause trouble.

There was a mass of material before us. Many letters by Sir Charles Craven, not meant for the public eye and addressed to American firms, had been seized by the American arms enquiry; and certain phrases and statements in them suggested some of those very methods in the sale of arms which had been charged against this industry.

I had dimmed my eyes by the study of those documents. I had made enormous numbers of notes which I had to abandon in court. I felt frightfully ill at the time, and when I took my place next to the judge I was as nervous as a cat on hot bricks. But I tried to steel myself to face this duty of examining the most powerful group of arms manufacturers in this country or the world. They would be hard nuts to crack, but I was determined that I would not allow them to gloss over any of the charges brought against them, or let it be said that this Royal Commission had been an eyewash affair, evading the possibilities of revealing scandals and abuse. Outside that court were millions of men and women who had a deep and passionate hope that this Royal Commission would put its searchlight upon this industry, which they believed—without much direct evidence—was very sinister in its power and practices. I steeled myself to an unpleasant task.

Sir Herbert Lawrence was very courteous and bland when my turn came. He knew that I was trying to find holes in his armour and that there was no button on my foil, but I must admit he parried my thrusts without the slightest touch of anger, even when I pressed him rather hard. On a minor point in which I was interested he professed remarkable ignorance. It was about the personality of Sir Basil Zaharoff—who had been closely associated with the firm of Vickers over a long period of years. None of my questions would draw him out on that subject, and, looking at the facts published after the recent death of that extraordinary man, who was the greatest commercial traveller in lethal weapons, I feel that his forgetfulness was remarkable. On all the points raised in criticism of his firm's activities he would admit nothing that might suggest any low or immoral motive. Vickers, he thought, was incapable of anything but the most spiritual ideals. He was shocked that I should suggest otherwise.

All this was by way of preliminary to the evidence of Sir Charles Craven, who had to deal in detail with the suggestions against the actions and methods of his firm. Those letters of his which had been published by the American Arms Committee needed a lot of explaining, and there were many transactions with which he had been associated which called for most penetrating enquiry.

Sir Charles Craven has an apparent air of boyishness, geniality and the breeziness of a naval man. He is a good-looking, fresh-complexioned man who would inspire immediate confidence in Chinese generals or Japanese admirals as a simple, honest Englishman. He faced the commission like a schoolboy who has not learnt all his home lessons but hopes to get away with it.

The chairman, Professor Gutteridge and Dame Rachel Crowdy took him through those indiscreet letters and would not let him get away with them easily. Dame Rachel made him look very uncomfortable by some of her quotations and her inferences from them. She quoted a letter he had written which suggested that he deplored the possibility that the League of Nations or some other "fancy convention" might abolish large-sized submarines, and she put it to him that he would rather have an increased sale of the products of his firm than any form of peaceful settlement.

Sir Charles Craven objected to this interpretation of a phrase in his private correspondence.

Dame Rachel Crowdy: "But you have no great feeling in favour of any attempt at peace by diplomacy?"

There was a wave of laughter in court, greatly to the surprise of Sir Charles Craven, when he made the following reply:

"I think that the League of Nations was the most wonderful ideal that has happened in our time."

I leave out the dingdong examination of all the points raised by the methods of Vickers and its associated companies. It was a severe ordeal for the representatives of that firm, and the chairman and members of the commission dealt fully with every case alleged against them. There was no eyewash here. I had a verbal duel with Sir Charles Craven which became rather heated. It appeared that we did not like each other very much, but I can truly say that there was nothing personal in my endeavour to get at the truth of things, and that it was a kind of duel between one brain and another as might happen between a counsel for the prosecution and a difficult and important witness. Sir Charles resented, it seemed, many of my questions.

"Most unfair," he said. At times he appealed to our chairman, who was not happy but supported me in upholding my right of questioning.

"I think you had better answer that," he said to the witness.

There was a sensation in court when I asked leave of the chairman to call for the private files of correspondence between the head office of Vickers Limited and their agents abroad. It was after Sir Charles Craven and his fellow directors had thwarted all my efforts to obtain more light on the way in which their agents abroad were instructed in their methods of obtaining orders.

The representatives of Vickers looked at each other and had a whispered consultation. The chairman upheld my request but enquired whether such files as I desired to see could be brought in a pantechnicon or a motorcar.

"Would it not be much easier," asked Dame Rachel, "for Sir Philip to go and read them on the spot?"

"Quite," said the chairman.

My heart sank within me. I knew that I had asked for trouble and had got it. I should have to read innumerable files, and my eyes were suffering from severe strain.

I immediately applied for leave to be supported by Dame Rachel Crowdy, and I had a nod from her of very gallant agreement to come to my rescue.

It was decided that we should study the correspondence of Vickers relating to their business in China, Japan and Manchukuo over a certain period of years, and Vickers raised no objection whatever to this examination. After that whispered consultation they played up remarkably well.

By this time, however, Sir Charles Craven had decided, quite definitely, that I was treating him as a hostile witness, and I did not dispel this idea by my subsequent examination.

I fear that there was a certain sultriness, a certain suggestion of forked lightning, in my intensive questioning which may have suggested to him that I was prejudiced against the great firm of which he was managing director. Shall I go to the extreme lengths of candour in saying that I was?

8 Bluebeard's Chamber

But I must pay a tribute to the courtesy of Sir Charles Craven and his colleague Mr Yapp when we met them on private ground, so to speak, after this affair in the public arena.

It was a sensational moment when Dame Rachel Crowdy and I appeared for the first time at the portals of Vickers House, in the neighbourhood of St James's Park Station, in order to examine the files. Word had gone forth in that great building that we were expected. By some mysterious telepathy it was known that we had arrived. Hall porters and office boys saluted impressively. Clerks bobbed their heads out of various doors. Directors and heads of departments had assembled to receive us. They offered us tea with great solicitude. They provided us with cigarettes. They pressed on us their services to show us the system of filing and to answer any questions which might be raised by us. It was all very touching and in the best tradition. All we wanted, however, was to be left alone with the files, and finally we were able to make this clear to them. We were left alone with the files.

It was a Bluebeard's chamber, I thought with a shudder of horror when I first gazed around that room where all the files of correspondence—at least all those of an official character—had been packed and arranged for our examination. They were piled high upon the tables. They flowed over to chairs and sofas. Even to examine them cursorily would take enormous time. A sense of comedy, and a sense of melodrama, took possession of us. We wanted to laugh but were afraid of listening ears. We wanted to exchange sensational remarks about the task ahead of us and to frighten each other by melodramatic suggestions.

"Heaven help us," I murmured, sitting down at a desk barricaded by those files.

"Heaven helps those who help themselves," said Dame Rachel, who is very matter of fact.

She grasped one of the files and then withdrew her hand as if it had bitten her. They had not been dusted for years. After half an hour's work among them my hands were like those of a coal heaver and Dame Rachel declined to shake hands with me after our first afternoon's labour.

Dame Rachel Crowdy has the eye of a hawk. In fifteen minutes she had found strange mysteries in the cross-index system of Vickers Limited regarding supplies of certain articles to Japan. They led to great trouble in Vickers House. But there was no trouble too great for them it seemed. Mr Yapp was so charming, so helpful, so honest—his honesty was almost embarrassing—that we both came to have a soft spot in our hearts for him. We had to goad each other to ask impertinent questions and pursue certain enquiries with relentless zeal and painful results. It positively hurt us to take advantage of his candour and good will in revealing the full history of certain transactions which aroused our inquisitiveness.

Sir Charles Craven, that breezy type of naval manhood, insisted upon putting his car at our disposal after office hours. It was an enormous Rolls-Royce into which Dame Rachel Crowdy sank with a sigh of ease. She was handed out at her dwelling near Hyde Park Corner. I was driven further and alone.

"This is a scandalous affair!" I thought. "If only a *Daily Herald* reporter could see me in this tremendous car, belonging to the managing director of Vickers Limited, the public would have doubts of my integrity."

I hadn't the moral courage to let that car drive up to the little house where I lived. The car was almost larger than the house.

9 *English Characters*

Such incidents provided humorous relief to a task which nearly killed us all. At least we thought it was going to kill the most frail among us, and few of us thought we should survive its long ordeal. Dame Rachel bet me half a crown that I should pop off first and Sir Thomas Allen second. She hasn't yet paid me, now that she has lost. We were all agreed that the only possible survivor would be Sir John Eldon Bankes. There was a time when the entire Royal Commission, with the exception of that hardy veteran, were lying over the countryside in hospitals, nursing homes, or private beds. But we staggered up and on, jeered at in the Press for delays which were not of our making but due mostly to the difficulty in getting our witnesses to prepare their cases.

Those witnesses were as good as a stage play of English life in 1936.

They were, in some cases, types who are passing from us and perhaps will never be bred again in our island's history, because character is changing and tradition is breaking. Will such old sea dogs as Sir Reginald Bacon walk the quarter-decks of future fleets? He thoroughly enjoyed being questioned on his views, and when I hoped that I was not tiring him he looked up with a sunny smile and said cheerfully: "I love it!"

He believed that the peace of the world could only be kept by a strong British navy, and repudiated heartily the idea that competition in armaments might lead to war. He asserted that the war in 1914–18 only happened because we weren't strong enough to stop it, by overwhelming supremacy at sea. Perhaps he was right.

Generals appeared before us. They were men who had organised our machine in the world war. One of them, most responsible for that business, alarmed me by his simplicity of mind which made him reveal the frightful lack of intelligent organisation at that time without being aware that there was anything wrong with his system. But he was the most charming type of old gentleman, *sans peur et sans reproche*, and it was impossible to be rude to him.

Before us came many high officials of the Services, and as they gave their evidence I felt a sense of admiration for their perfect poise, their perfect good form, their ability and their character. These men, I thought, are beyond all suspicion of corruption. In no other country, perhaps—at least in few—would one find such integrity, such reliability, such devotion to duty. But their minds were rigidly fixed into a certain framework of ideas, conventions and traditions. Also, they were speaking to an official brief in favour of the continuance of private manufacture, but I think they were also expressing their own convictions.

So it was with some of those engaged in shipbuilding and steel production. These men of old established firms could hardly be suspected, except by cankered souls, of dark and murderous methods for profit's sake. One could not regard them as "Merchants of Death." They were builders of ships and manufacturers of steel plates, and not stirrers-up of strife for the sake of dividends. Most of them disarmed one's suspicions by their simplicity of character, though there were other witnesses who were not without guile, and not without a hard cynicism which made one distrustful.

One episode caused a sensation in one of the public sittings to everyone present except the man most concerned, who was Sir John Eldon Bankes, totally unaware of what had been said because he was busy with his own notes.

It was when Mr Harry Pollit, representing the Communist party of Great Britain, was giving evidence. He was a Communist, but butter wouldn't melt in his mouth. He stated his case with a moderation and gentleness which reminded me of Bottom in the *Midsummer Night's Dream.* "I will roar you as gently as any sucking dove."

It was towards the end, when our chairman thought he had had quite enough rope and was becoming a little impatient, so that his fairy bell was tinkling. Mr Pollit read out a list of public men who had blocks of shares in armament firms. So and so, so and so—a long list—and Sir John Eldon Bankes, the chairman of the Royal Commission on Arms!

I started back as if I had been shot. Mr Twentyman, the secretary, turned round to look at the chairman with stupefaction and alarm. The audience drew its breath deeply. The reporters began to write hurriedly. It was a sensational moment. But Sir John Eldon Bankes went on writing without turning a hair. It was our duty to tell him afterwards what had happened, and at the beginning of the next public meeting he made a statement that a number of United Alkali Shares, recently converted into Imperial Chemical Shares, had stood in his name as trustee of a relative's estate, but that all the trust had expired, and all the shares had passed out of his name, months before he had been invited to become a member of the commission.

10 *Lloyd George*

Among the historical characters who appeared on our stage was that great old actor and man of action, the Right Honourable David Lloyd George, the Wizard of Wales; and he was at the top of his form.

As minister of munitions he knew all that had happened in the early days of the war when there was a frightful shortage of shells, guns and everything else needed by the armies in France. He had helped to organise the whole industry of the country in this desperate and awful necessity of providing the vast flow of war material which afterwards poured out of the national factories. His dynamic energy had driven the wheels faster, and his magic had solved, by reckless prodigality of payment, the labour troubles which threatened to check the output. Dr Addison, who also gave us valuable evidence, had been his successor as dictator of supplies.

Mr Lloyd George arrived rather early for his examination. He was as fresh as a daisy in spring. His blue eyes twinkled merrily. His shoulders were squared. His hands were restless. All his movements were those of a young man. He didn't seem a day older since a morning in Paris, in 1915, when I met him outside the Hotel Crillon and said: "How are things going, sir?" and he answered brightly: "I can tell you something that's going, my lad, and that is English gold. We are the milch cow of Europe." He didn't look one hour older, though it was twenty years since a morning when I had had breakfast with him in Downing Street after the battle of Loos, of which I had been an eyewitness and of which he knew very little then, though prime minister of Great Britain, because of some holding back of information after that bad show. He didn't look a day older, I thought—perhaps mistakenly, for one forgets the imperceptible touch of time—than on a day when he had come out to France to talk to our generals, who detested the little man until they met him and then fell over each other's spurs to get near him and hear his words of wizardry. He had always been very kind to me until one day he was very unkind and very unfair to me in one of his books.

"I have a bone to pick with you, sir," I said laughingly before we went into court.

"There's hardly a man in England who hasn't," he told me with a smile in his blue eyes—those blue eyes which disarm his worst enemies because of their humour and vivacity. "What's your trouble?"

"You made an unjust attack on me in your last book about the war," I told him without rancour.

"My dear fellow," he said, "it's within my recollection that you attacked me first! I always hit back."

We went into court in a friendly mood. And as a witness he was vastly interesting and expanded provocative argument and sweeping statements which wiped the floor, from his point of view, with private manufacturers and their whole system. He was all for the nationalisation of the arms industry.

That morning he was good enough to invite me to lunch with him at the House of Commons, and it was an amusing interlude. He gave a rapid series of character studies of the members of the Royal Commission in his finest style of caricature, and he didn't spare us.

This little man, I thought, is, after all, the most amazing character we still have among us. He will never be forgotten in history. He has what now we lack so much—dynamic energy, miraculous vitality, the spirit of great adventure, courage, genius, laughter, magnetism of personality. He has been very wicked at times—diabolical!—and will go on being so until he dies, but, all the same, he is a great child of nature, not often placed in the cradles of humanity by fairies and goblins.

He wanted to know a few points about the battle of Passchendaele. A secretary, who must lead a harried life, was called upon at the luncheon table to take down some notes, between roast mutton and sultana roll provided by the House of Commons. Miss Megan listened to her father with an enjoyment which does not stale. Before parting with me he shook hands warmly.

"This is the peace of Passchendaele!" he said, alluding to my little feud with him.

11 Sir Maurice Hankey

Utterly different, in every quality of mind and personality, was another witness who came before us to present the strongest argument against nationalisation possible to make by any human intellect in possession of the fullest knowledge, and after the most intensive study, and with the most passionate, though unemotional, conviction. It was Sir Maurice Hankey, chief of the Committee of Imperial Defence and secretary of the Cabinet.

Sir Maurice Hankey had devoted an enormous amount of time to a study of the case for and against the private manufacturers of arms, extending over many years. During the war he had been secretary of many bodies controlling its operations, such as the War Council and the War Cabinet. After the war he became secretary of the Peace Conference, secretary of the Cabinet, secretary general of imperial conferences and disarmament conferences. Since 1901 he had been closely associated with the business of Imperial Defence in all its aspects.

In spite of all his immense labours this astonishing man—astonishing for his industry, his machinelike efficiency of mind, like a card-index system in which there is an immense store of facts neatly classified—found time to prepare two immensely long memoranda of evidence which he desired to place before the Royal Commission.

They dealt in considerable detail with every aspect of the case before us. They were formidable documents with many notes and appendices. He analysed the problems and history of arms manufacture nearly as far back as the Stone Age and came forward relentlessly to the latest type of bombing aeroplane.

His first memorandum was a general survey, and every statement in it was heavily weighted in favour of the private manufacture of arms.

The second memorandum was a close analysis and destructive criticism of the evidence presented by the opponents of private manufacture. As the chairman pointed out to him, he adopted, in his second memorandum, the position of a counsel tearing to pieces the evidence of opposing witnesses upon which we, and not Sir Maurice himself, had to decide.

Sir Maurice wished to adopt the position of a private individual interested in the question of armaments and coming to give evidence before us because of that interest. We could not accept that point of view as to his standing. He was the official spokesman of the Services.

"I have been in close touch," he told us, "with the Government departments principally concerned—that is to say, the Admiralty, the War Office, the Air Ministry, the Foreign Office, the Board of Trade and the Treasury—to all of whom I am indebted for much of my material and for help at every stage. In the Government service team work is very much the order of the day, both in defence matters and other matters, and my two memoranda that I have sent to you may be taken as representing broadly the views of the officials in those departments. . . . At the same time I should like to state personally, although no one has asked me to do so, that I cannot commit other officials to every word that I say. I cannot consult them as to what I say under cross-examination."

This was a complete acknowledgment that he came before us as an official and not as a private individual.

He was careful to point out, however, that any remark he might make in no way committed the prime minister or any other minister. It was obvious to me, and to my fellow members of the commission, that the evidence of Sir Maurice Hankey, enforced by a formidable array of Service representatives, was the official case in defence of the private manufacture of arms, and that the opponents of that system would find in the evidence and views he presented the strongest challenge to their indictment.

It was an astonishing experience, listening to that distinguished government official. I could not help thinking, as I followed his long statements, that here before us was the most influential brain in England, the mind moving behind the scenes of imperial defence and policy. Prime ministers and Cabinet ministers would turn to him for facts and advice, which he would give instantly, with complete confidence in his own knowledge and intelligence. He would never make a mistake on a fact. He would never falter in an opinion. He would just tell them with a quiet self-assurance which would admit of no argument. He would know. He would be patient with their ignorance. He would explain to them in simple language so that they might understand.

I had another thought from time to time. Why, I thought, does he not wear bifocal glasses, instead of having to take off his spectacles every time he wants to have a look at us, and put them on every time he wants to go on reading?

I listened to him hour after hour, on two successive days, with profound admiration and a sense of stupefaction.

Here was a brain beyond competition as a working machine, with a complete mastery of minute detail, historical facts, technical knowledge, classification and order, marvellously well poised. And here was a brain entirely without passion, and entirely unemotional, but extraordinarily limited in its framework, and almost inhuman in its disregard of the sentiment and moral convictions of ordinary humanity.

He was successful, I think, in showing that the case against the British manufacturers was based upon scanty evidence, upon scandalous charges "non proven", as the Scottish verdict says, and upon public prejudice and propaganda exaggerated and, in many cases, unjustified. But, in my opinion still, he overstated his case for the defence. He ignored utterly the moral repugnance of public opinion throughout the world to a traffic in arms which, in its international transactions, cannot be exonerated—in my opinion again—from all such charges as bribery, deliberate incitement of unrest for the sake of orders, the indiscriminate supply of arms, even against the interests and safety of the traders' own countries, the constant competition in efficiency of slaughter, even though their own peoples may be slaughtered, and the cynical disregard of international efforts for limitation of arms and world peace.

He defended the system of supplying arms to both sides in a conflict and even of supplying the latest types of weapon to nations who afterwards used them against our own soldiers.

He found nothing whatever objectionable in our export trade of arms to any country who might like to buy them, even if they might be our potential enemies. On the contrary, he thought, as all other defenders of private manufacture, that this was necessary in order to enable our arms manufacturers to keep going, train their craftsmen, and be capable of expansion in time of war.

He was not cynical. He was just sure that all this was strictly within the moral law. He was not ruthless, or brutal in his sense of realism, but quietly certain that the private manufacturing system is in the hands of men of the highest moral integrity, conducting their business according to the best traditions, and that we should bless them for their labours in defence of this realm and Empire.

If he had admitted one possibility of abuse, one possible departure from moral law, one tiny blot on their scutcheon, he would have been more convincing. But to Sir Maurice Hankey there was nothing but malice, illusion and falsity in the charges brought by the opponents of the arms firms. Nevertheless, I am bound to admit that he did riddle many of the specific allegations against British firms and put up the strongest case against nationalisation.

12 The Report of the Commission

After having representatives of the navy, army, and Air Force, technical experts, scientists, shipbuilders, steel producers, chemists, masters of ordinance, and other witnesses, the Royal Commission concluded its public sittings and sat down in its own rooms to consider a report.

Sir John Eldon Bankes looked anxious at times. There were days I think when he almost abandoned hope of presenting a report at all. In private and public some of us had appeared to him rather more impassioned than was quite in keeping with our quasi-judicial character. Would it ever be possible to get agreement in this team of strongly opinionated people? So he must have wondered. Sitting on his right hand, I could hear his little sighs when argument crossed and recrossed the table, and when discussion became long and animated on first principles, as well as on facts and details. But he had a wonderful self-control, and a very remarkable gift of patience. Never once did he say a discourteous word, never once did he suggest any compromise of convictions, never once did he lose his temper, his beautiful poise, his anxiety to give each one of us a fair hearing for argument or point of view.

Our golden-haired secretary, who had strong views of his own, a sense of humour, and a kind of concealed fire burning behind his blue eyes, suffered exceedingly. It is generally the experience of secretaries on commissions and committees that before the report stage is reached they have a clear idea of the members' views and convictions. But when Mr Edward Twentyman sat down to draft out the report upon our points of agreement he found that we declined to agree to anything without prolonged discussion of fundamental issues. So it seemed to him and so it seemed to our chairman.

Yet the truth was—and it appeared with surprising clarity after this preliminary disorder—that all of us did have the desire, at least, to be judicial and not partisans or advocates of this side or the other. It gradually dawned upon our chairman that we were reasonable people with a certain judgment upon matters of fact and evidence, and that no member of the commission was out for his or her point of view, regardless of such evidence. We were, indeed, sincerely anxious to be honest in our summing up of all we had heard and to shirk nothing that should be taken into account on one side or the other. It was our duty to draw up recommendations which would, if possible, remove the possibilities of evil in a dangerous trade, and to formulate some plan which would be more efficient in producing the armaments required for national defence.

The drawing up of our report, which proved to be unanimous, was a proof of certain qualities in our racial character which keep us fairly steady and fairly sane through all our crises and all our problems. To me it was a valuable experience as a study of human nature and of reason working without fanaticism. Some of us felt passionately about the things upon which we had to report, but we subordinated passion to the test of evidence and common sense. We were like a jury of twelve ordinary citizens who had listened to a great trial and were now called upon to deliver a verdict. I believe we did so with the honesty and sincerity one finds in the jury box. But we were also judges, not to be swayed by emotion or brilliant advocacy. I am, for myself, only claiming the quality of a juryman and the intellectual morality of—shall I say?—a county court judge. I was no intellectual equal in this sort of job to men like J. A. Spender, or Professor Gutteridge, or Sir Thomas Allen, or Sir Kenneth Lee, to say nothing of our secretary, who was a master at drafting what he hoped to be our final conclusions. As for Sir John Eldon Bankes, I cannot pay him too high a tribute for his leadership, his long-suffering patience, his skill in seeing the implications of a phrase or a comma.

Perhaps I am not claiming too much in saying that this spirit of reason, overruling partisanship, is what carries on the life of our nation in an orderly way which is the envy now and then of other peoples. Anyhow, we signed a report which was heartily disliked by almost everybody and may, therefore, have been good. It was.

That report now lies in the pigeonholes of Whitehall, and many copies of it have gone into many dustbins and no doubt have now returned to pulp for other paper and other words. Nobody will ever read it again unless, later in history, some inquisitive fellow, anxious to study a forgotten episode, takes it out of the British Museum and finds to his astonishment an analysis, a judgment and a plan on the subject of armaments, of quaint historical interest.

The Labour party, the Socialists, the Communists, the peace societies, and, strange as it may seem, Lord Cecil of Chelwood were disappointed and angry because we did not report in favour of a complete state monopoly of the arms industry, but they failed to perceive that our recommendations gave them everything for which they had pleaded, apart from the blessed name of Nationalisation.

One aspect of the case against nationalisation which we had to take into consideration was the clear evidence we had, and afforded by history, that governments are by no means more virtuous than private firms, and that the worst cases of bribery, corruption of the foreign Press, stimulation of fear and hatred, arming of one nation against another, and every kind of evil practice have been done, and are still being done abroad, by government agents, government policies, and government funds in many states. What has happened in the Spanish Civil War is proof enough of that.

We urged upon the government as our first conclusion that the most effective and available means of removing or minimising the objection to the private manufacture of arms and its foreign trade would be the limitation of arms by international agreement.

Although we decided, on the evidence, that the total abolition of private industry in this country was undesirable in present conditions, and that no sufficient case had been made out for taking so drastic a step, we insisted that the government should assume complete responsibility for the production and sale of arms by a rigid form of control and the necessary collaboration with private industry. This responsibility should be exercised by a controlling body presided over by a minister responsible to Parliament, having executive powers in peacetime and wartime over all matters relating to the supply and manufacture of arms and munitions, their costing, and the authorisation of orders from abroad.

We recommended that the government's own arsenals should

be fully equipped for the production of naval, military and air armaments; that they should specialise in scientific research; and that they should be responsible for the training of technical experts, taking the initiative in the production of designs and the improvement of machine tools, and the formulation of mass-production methods, not only for their own manufacturing requirements but for the use and instruction of the private industry of the country.

By this means the government establishments would, in time of emergency, be ready with specifications, gauges and particulars of machine tools, necessary for rapid expansion by private firms. They would provide standards by which costs would be checked. They would develop instruction in mass-production methods and would have a trained personnel available for service as instructors in time of emergency.

It was our opinion, strongly stated, that "there is unquestionably something revolting to the conscience of ordinary men and women in the thought that killing, and the supply of killing power, is profitable to particular groups of people; and the conception that war and the preparation for war ought not to be the occasion of private gain is, we believe, the fundamental conception from which the moral objection to the private industry springs. To this conception is added the fear and anxiety that arise from the recognition of the possibility, undoubtedly inherent in the system of private industry in the supply of arms, that those engaged in it may be stimulated by the profit motive to practices which are socially undesirable in themselves and, in the case of the arms industry, are fraught with danger to the peace of the world."

We therefore recommended measures to restrict the profits of armament firms by a rigid system of control and costing under the responsible body whose function we outlined. The removal of the profit motive, we said, is felt to be the one radical and effective method by which it is possible to prevent abuses. We were confident that public feeling in this matter, which we believed to be widespread, intense, and genuine, ought not to be disregarded.

We made a series of recommendations for the control of the export trade and, as we stated, some of the members of the commission were in favour of its total abolition.

We recommended the complete cessation of the private export trade in surplus and secondhand arms and munitions of war.

We recommended that public officials (whether serving or retired) should not accept appointments with armament firms except with the approval of the minister in charge of the department in which they are serving or have served.

There was some pretty good stuff in this report, largely ignored by the Press and utterly ignored by the government. I quote one passage which stands as a judgment of what happened in history and as a warning of what may happen again.

"There is no question about the part which armaments have played in the development of modern war. They have not merely reflected, they have intensified, the fears, suspicions, and jealousies of nations, and enormously increased the scope and destructiveness of war. Through the enlistment of the highest scientific and engineering ability in the design and making of weapons of destruction, the whole nature of war has been changed. Montesquieu said that kings should so make war as to have done one another the least possible damage when peace was restored; modern governments seek to arm themselves with weapons which inflict the maximum loss and suffering upon their opponents.

"The effect of the competition in armaments which preceded the Great War can be traced in the records which are now available. These show the military staffs of all the principal powers in a state of increasing alarm lest they should either lose the lead which they supposed themselves to have gained, if further time were permitted, or be surprised before their own preparations were complete, if war came sooner than they expected.

"In both the European groups the military staffs were anxiously discussing what would be the 'favourable moment' for the conflict which they assumed to be inevitable, and both fixed it at the point at which they assumed, or hoped, they would be at the height of their power as measured in armaments."

I went to hear the funeral service of the Royal Commission Report. It took place in the House of Commons and was very decently done. Two or three Liberal members urged, in a mild and gentlemanly way, that the report should be adopted. They failed, I thought, to bring out its strength and purpose. Then Sir Thomas Inskip rose and, after a tribute of respect to Sir John Eldon Bankes, professed that he did not understand some part of our recommendations, and that, anyhow, the government had appointed some experts to elucidate them.

Considering the utter simplicity of our plan and prose, it does not say much for the intellectual ability of Cabinet ministers and their advisers.

Sir Thomas Inskip did not like the report, it seemed, and damned it with faint praise and sent it to its grave.

The Labour party had nothing to say for it, having glanced at it with displeasure after seeing that it did not recommend nationalisation.

I knew from a private source that it had angered some members of the Cabinet. It was too radical for them in its recommendations. If they took notice of it, it would upset their rearmament plans, which utterly ignored, and intended to ignore, all our decisions and proposals for limiting profit and checking abuses. It was too radical for the Conservatives and not radical enough for the Opposition.

So it died, and so it was buried, and the members of the Royal

Commission had wasted their time, except for having gained a little more knowledge of human nature, and the benefit of an intellectual exercise as harmless as a crossword puzzle, and, in its public sittings, a close-up view of characters, famous and obscure, with high ideals and low ideals, sinister, brazen faced and cynical, or aflame with fanaticism, or inspired by spiritual purpose. Before us came a procession of those who make the wheels go round, and those who pull the strings of our puppet show, and a few old ghosts of ancient history who walk across our English stage. It was, in its way, a performance of *Cavalcade*. But when the curtain rang down I had had enough of it. It was a tragedy with a few comic interludes—tragic, because it dealt with the very instruments and powers of world tragedy, and the failure of civilisation which defends itself precariously by this competition in armaments and drifts steadily to the explosion point. We few, we band of brothers—and one sister—had done our best to remedy some of these evils and suggest a better way out of their consequences by control and limitation, but we had failed.

I made a bonfire of all the papers which had been thrust through my letter box or handed in at doors opened wide enough to take in their bulk. The flames leapt up as high as the roof of an old cowshed in my backyard. I laughed as they turned those documents to white ash. It was a great relief after much futile labour.

Now the munition factories are working overtime. The government has launched a stupendous programme of rearmament, almost without opposition. Metals are booming on the Stock Exchange. New millionaires are arising out of the profits of an industry which produces the instruments of destruction. The house of Vickers is having a happy time. Everybody seems pleased, so why worry?

IV

The Crisis of the Crown

1 The Bombshell

AT THE BEGINNING of December, in that nightmare year of 1936, England and the British people were shocked by something that seemed to hit them like a bolt out of the blue and was so incredible, so unprecedented in their history, so alarming, that they were stunned. It was the sudden breaking of self-imposed silence in the Press about King Edward's love for an American woman named Mrs Simpson—twice married and not yet fully divorced—and the warning that this affair might lead to a crisis endangering the Throne or leading—it was already hinted—to the abdication of the King.

During the ten days that followed, England was shaken by profound emotion which went deeper than a sense of sensation or scandal in high places. Every man and woman felt personally affected, with a sense of calamity as close as their own household and touching all their loyalties, and all their code of moral values, and any tradition that was in them. They waited under an intolerable strain for the outcome.

Comparatively few people in England had heard of Mrs Simpson until the news broke so suddenly, although for months past the American Press had opened its columns to stories of the King's friendship with this woman and her set. They published descriptions and details of their meetings at Biarritz, Cannes and other places, with snapshots of them on the King's summer cruise in the Mediterranean; and gossip raked up by their Peeping Toms and sent across the cables at great expense. It was the most sensational serial story for the yellow Press of America, and even the presidential election was secondary in interest.

At first they treated it as a royal scandal, and the lowest class of American journal—though never the best—wallowed in it as "debunking" of royalty and unmasking of British hypocrisy.

At first they had no respect for Mrs Simpson. In one chain of newspapers she was called by a disreputable name, and they dug out stories of her early life to show that she was not much, anyhow, in social standing. Her mother had once taken in lodgers at Baltimore, where this girl "Wally", as they called her, had helped in the work of a poverty-stricken household. Then suddenly their tone changed when the idea occurred to them that there might be a royal marriage and an American queen. "Wally" was, after all, a great little lady. The Warfield family—she had been Wally Warfield—was of Norman descent, almost royal, really. She was witty, charming, elegant, and a perfect specimen of American womanhood. Correspondents in touch with Mr and Mrs Rogers, her best friends and friends of King Edward, were able to assure the American public and their own editors that the King was very serious in his intentions.

On October 26, 1936, there was a headline in enormous letters across the front page of a newspaper with one of the biggest circulations in the United States.

KING WILL WED WALLY
MRS SIMPSON WILL BE EDWARD'S CONSORT IN JUNE

Beneath this announcement, on that day in October when not a whisper about Mrs Simpson had reached the mass of people in England beyond London dinner tables and small groups, there was a leading article from which I quote a few sentences:

> Within a few days Mrs Ernest Simpson of Baltimore, Maryland, U.S.A., will obtain her divorce decree in England and some eight months thereafter she will be married to Edward VIII, King of England.
>
> King Edward's most intimate friends state with the utmost positiveness that he is very deeply and sincerely enamoured of Mrs Simpson, that his love is a righteous affection, and that almost immediately after the Coronation he will take her as his Consort.
>
> It is stated definitely that King Edward is convinced that this is both the right thing to do and the wise thing to do.
>
> He believes that it would be an actual mistake for a King of England to marry into any of the Royal Houses of the Continent of Europe, and so involve himself and his Empire in the complications and disasters of those Royal Houses.
>
> He believes that the most important thing for the peace and welfare of the world is an intimate understanding and relationship between England and America, and that his marriage with this very gifted lady may help to bring about that beneficial co-operation between English-speaking nations.
>
> Primarily, however, the King's transcendent reason for marrying Mrs Simpson is that he ardently loves her, and does not see why a king should be denied the privilege of marrying the lady he loves.
>
> So in all human probability, in June 1937, one month after the ceremonies of the Coronation, will follow the festivities of the marriage of King Edward VIII of England to the very charming and intelligent Mrs Ernest Simpson of Baltimore, Maryland, U.S.A.

This extract was sent to me by a friend in New York and I read it with stupefaction. Not a word of this had reached the mass of people in England. Not one hint of it had appeared in the British Press, though here and there American newspapers, or cuttings from them, reached various individuals and all the newspaper offices in Fleet Street and its tributaries. In private circles, at dinner parties in town and country, in clubs and restaurants, people of a certain social class in touch with the court, or with friends who had heard these stories, were talking in low voices about it and getting anxious. It was already raising moral questions, and disturbing loyalties, and causing heated discussions or flippant and frivolous remarks among the light-headed. But the idea of marriage between the King and Mrs Simpson was brushed aside as preposterous nonsense—one of the absurdities of American journalism. It was not as serious as all that, they thought.

2 *The Unknown Lady*

The first time I ever heard of that lady was when a taxi driver was in a conversational mood after I had paid him off one night in Bryanston Square.

"I often drive the Prince of Wales this way," he said with genial good humour. "One of his lady friends! Me and my mates know the address quite well now. Mrs Simpson is the lady's name. An American, they tell me. Well, it's human nature to want female companionship. I have a wife myself and two kids. I couldn't do without them, you know. I often thinks to myself as I'm driving around . . ."

I daresay he thought some very good things, but I've forgotten them. Curiously enough, that name of Mrs Simpson stayed in my memory.

I heard it again a few months later, when the Prince of Wales had become King.

I was lunching with a friend and we were talking about the plans for rearmament and the King's coming trip to the Mediterranean and other matters of interest.

Suddenly he looked me in the eyes and said:

"What about Mrs Simpson?"

"Mrs Simpson?"

The talk of that taxi driver came back to me.

He looked over his shoulder and lowered his voice.

"The King sees a lot of her. It may become dangerous. It may drag him down. The English are still Puritans in the mass. Sometimes we forget that, between Piccadilly and Mayfair."

Presently, at any dinner table, in the corner of any drawing room, one heard that sibilant *s* when people lowered their voices. The *s* of Mrs Simpson's name. The social conscience was not prepared to be hard on the King at that time—the easy conscience of sophisticated people not rigid in their moral code, not by any means Puritanical.

"As long as he keeps her in the background, I don't see that it's anybody's business."

"He has a right to his private life as long as he does his job."

"After all, his grandfather . . ."

I listened to these conversations secretly perturbed. That friend of mine was right when he said that we forget that the English are still, in the mass, Puritans. It would be abominable if our new King, with all his splendid promise, should spoil his chances by some frightful scandal. That American stuff was getting too hot to keep from burning our ears. One day the self-imposed censorship of the British Press would break. Then there might be grave trouble.

"I happen to know the lady," said a man at a London dinner table.

He could not have made a more sensational announcement if he had mentioned casually that he knew Cleopatra or Helen of Troy.

"You know her? What's she like? What sort of a creature?"

"I found her charming," said this man, with a pleasant awareness that he was the centre of interest.

"Good God!" said one of the other men.

"How does she speak, how does she look?"

The women were excited.

"She's quite good looking, especially full face. Not my type exactly, but attractive, I should say. Neat. Rather elegant. Perfectly sure of herself. A fairly pronounced American accent."

"Good God!" said one of the men again.

The man with the information continued.

"She seems to have taste. Her flat is a proof of it. She arranges her own flowers and looks after her own dinners. There's nothing she doesn't know about that kind of thing. I can't say I know her well, but friends of mine who do say that she's very amusing, in the American way. Full of 'wisecracks', as they say!"

"Good God!" said the man who had made use of these words before.

I met a lady who knew Mrs Simpson. It was in a country house where a small crowd had gathered after dinner. The window blinds had not yet been drawn and one could see fields, and a flower garden, and hedges, and rose-tipped feathers in a sky still full of light.

The lady next to whom I sat confirmed the statement that Mrs Simpson was good looking, neat, rather elegant, and amusing. Rather too amusing sometimes, she thought. She called the King fancy names in public. She had no awe or reverence for royal etiquette.

"American women of good social standing don't like her set. They belong to the wrong crowd."

It was an American woman who was speaking to me.

It was another American woman of Virginia who was hardest of all on Mrs Simpson.

"You people ought to bump her off," she said, as though giving out a good idea to solve the problem. "You ought to take her for a ride."

3 *Stupefaction*

A weekly publication of American make-up which had been perfectly obscure until then on English book-stalls began to have an increased circulation, owing to titbits and snapshots of the Mediterranean voyage when Mrs Ernest Simpson was on the yacht Nahlin, as one of the King's guests. But it didn't reach very far. There were still vast numbers of people—the overwhelming majority, including generals, literary men, and the old-fashioned gentry—who had not yet heard the name of Mrs Simpson even as late as the end of November, though it had appeared in the Court Circular and she had been a guest at Balmoral. They had heard nothing of a divorce at Ipswich, though the bare fact of it had been published in English newspapers. But in London anxiety was growing and, in some minds, a dark apprehension of impending tragedy.

I took tea with a lady who knows "everybody"—that is to say, the powers behind the Throne, as they used to be and still seem to be. I happened to speak of the Coronation and she looked at me strangely, I thought.

"Will it happen?" she asked, as though she knew something which she dared not say.

"What do you mean?"

The lamps were dim in her room. We sat in a gloaming which was almost dark, except for the fitful gleam of a little flame in the fireplace.

"I'm afraid something may happen to prevent it," she said. "This affair with Mrs Simpson. It's becoming serious. He talks of marriage—marriage with a woman who is not yet divorced and has two husbands still living. It's impossible. That divorce—what dare one say about it? Who would accept that woman as Queen? It would drag everything down—the Crown itself."

It was by a kind of accident that the storm broke, as it was bound to do sooner or later. The Bishop of Bradford made an allusion in a sermon to the King's way of life with an implied rebuke that he was not so faithful as he ought to be to the teaching of the Church. He afterwards denied that it had any reference to the affair with Mrs Simpson, and that the sermon was written six weeks previous to the crisis. But advantage was taken of it by a Yorkshire paper to break silence about the King's private life, and immediately other newspapers abandoned this self-imposed censorship and flooded their columns with the whole story of Mrs Simpson, as collected from American correspondents, and published portraits of the lady. At the same time the public was informed that the Cabinet was gravely occupied with this subject and that a constitutional crisis of the first magnitude was impending.

To say that this news excited England and the whole British Empire would be untrue. It was not excitement but stupefaction which overwhelmed public opinion. The possibility of abdication seemed beyond imagination and utterly incredible. No such thing had ever happened in our history. No such thing, we thought, could ever happen. Under the stunning blow of the first shock there were few people who believed that it would ever come to that, or be allowed to come to that. King Edward not only had the loyalty of his people in the mass but he had their hero-worship. The younger generation, especially, looked to him as their leader and as their friend who understood their point of view, who had the courage, the individuality, the spirit, which they most admired. Long before this crisis a young manufacturer in the North had spoken to me about the influence of the Prince, as he then was, among "the lads" of northern England, in such cities as Newcastle, Sheffield, Wigan, and the industrial areas.

"They would follow him to the death," he told me, "if he

raised one beckoning finger. They worship him and get a lot of pleasure out of everything he does. They have no envy for his wealth and position. It gives them a kind of self-satisfaction when he goes racing, or flying, or hunting. He is their Prince. They like to know he is doing himself well, having a good time now and then, doing all the things they would like to do. 'He's one of us,' they say. 'He understands us. He knows how to talk to us without pomposity or side. He sympathises with the unemployed chaps and any of us down on our luck. He wants to make those politicians get a move on. That's why he went down to the black areas and spoke on the wireless. He's a real democrat and is on the side of the people. And he's impatient of red tape, and official humbug, and political trickery. He's the only man in England we can trust, and, by God, we trust him.' "

Those words were spoken with knowledge and sincerity, and they did, I believe, tell the truth about the King's hold on popular opinion. No other King after Harry of Agincourt has had such hero-worship in the crowd. Was it then possible to even contemplate the idea of abdication?

4 England Speaks

It is very difficult to set down accurately and completely the psychological experience of the country during these ten days of frightful tension.

It was not without conflict and differences, according to classes and types of mind. Among the professional classes and what might be described as the non-church-going class I could not find at that time any moral indignation because the King had fallen in love with a married woman whom he wished to marry after she had obtained a divorce. The bishops were over-confident afterwards that the entire nation had been shocked by this question of morality. What shocked those who are not rigid in their principles about marriage and divorce was their conviction that Mrs Simpson was not the right woman to be Queen of England. In popular opinion it had nothing to do with her being an American. But the fact that her mother had taken in boarders, and that, according to the newspapers, she belonged to a fast set, made her unacceptable as Queen. They could not see her taking Queen Mary's place. Class consciousness? Yes, and strongest, I found, among the working classes and the small bourgeoisie.

I talked at the time with bricklayers, carpenters, mechanics, and other craftsmen in a country village. I was curious to know what they were saying about this tragic affair. Their views would be an indication, I thought, of what their own class was thinking all over England. It was, I found, unanimous.

"She don't seem to me the right sort for Queen," said a man who was sawing some timber in a yard. He kept his saw quiet for a moment and brushed some dust from his plank. "No class, as you might say. Not like Queen Mary."

I talked with an old soldier who has a soft job as night watchman and was warming his feet at a coal fire.

"It don't matter to me," he said, "if the King marries a flower girl out of the streets. To me it wouldn't make any kind of difference. Not a bob extra! But this Mrs Simpson, who is she? Good looking, yes. I dare say she knows how to behave herself like a lady. May be a lady for all I know! But the Queen? Well—not quite the class of Queen Mary! Not quite up to scratch, as you might say. Are all our duchesses and dames going to bob to her? I can't see them doing it. One wants a bit of blood for the Queen of England. An American, isn't she? Well, there's nothing against that. But America isn't made up of Mrs Simpsons. His Nibs might have chosen somebody more in keeping with his own set."

THE CRISIS OF THE CROWN—WAITING FOR NEWS

These men with whom I talked were craftsmen, mechanics and labourers. It didn't seem to occur to them that they were talking "class stuff" and acknowledging the caste system. They couldn't escape from the old feudal ideas of their forefathers nor from the mystical idea of kingship in the old tradition. Planted in the middle of their minds was the conviction that a Queen of England should belong to the old "Quality." They expected a high standard of selection. . . . I record these things I heard "without prejudice", as the lawyers say. They are worth recording if we want to get at the minds of our own people.

During this time of crisis for England and all other peoples of the British Commonwealth of Nations I was spending a few days in the Lion at Guildford. The news of the King's trouble broke down the reserve between individuals and classes and I was held up in the passages by waiters, chambermaids, porters and the boots, who wished to express their own opinions and to ask mine.

The headwaiter—a venerable man who has been at this hostelry for fifty-eight years—whispered over my shoulder at dinner:

"A very tragic state of things. The royal family must be suffering great anxiety. I'm very sorry for Queen Mary. It's a pity His Majesty's choice has fallen on a lady who doesn't seem to be —well—not highly suitable, if I may say so."

Through the window of the office two young women who look after the accounts were much perturbed.

"We don't want a Queen who has been Mrs Brown or Mrs Smith," said one of them. "There's something wrong somewhere."

"Everything is all wrong," said the other. "We're all going to pot, it seems to me."

A youngish man behind the counter of a small shop in Swan Lane became confidential in his view on the situation.

"I'm not a moralist, as you might say. I dare say the King

needed a lady friend. But why flaunt her? I'm asking you! Now, no one would say a word if he put her into a nice little house and paid her a friendly visit from time to time. He has a right to his own private life, like any gentleman. But private life can't get mixed up with public life. That's where he's made a mistake in my opinion, though I may be wrong. It's a pity, because he's a nice young fellow and we expected a lot from him."

One evening at dinner an old gentleman of a most eccentric type appeared at one of the tables with a friend. He announced to the headwaiter that he liked a good dinner, and pretty ladies, and old wine.

"A bottle of your best old sherry," he demanded. "In this time of national anxiety one has to keep one's spirits up, and old brown sherry is a good beginning to any meal."

He raised a glass of that liquid and proposed a toast to his friend, who was nervous of this old gentleman's resonant voice.

"God save the King—and to hell with the lady!"

The venerable headwaiter looked shocked. The other people in the dining room pretended not to hear. One of the waiters was much amused.

In the smoking room there were changing groups of motoring folk who come for a warm at the big fire and a cup of coffee, or something stronger, before going farther on the road.

They all looked grave, anxious and strained, and did not speak above a whisper to their friends. But that whisper was sibilant. I heard a thousand times the name of the woman who was the cause of all this trouble in the English mind.

5 *Bewilderment*

The lady had left her house in Bryanston Place in the small hours of the morning. Someone said that it had had its windows broken. She had been recognised at Rouen by a French actress. She was on a motorcar journey, being chased through France by French reporters and photographers. A friend of the King—Lord Brownlow—was acting as her escort and trying to put these people off the scent. She reached Cannes and went to the villa of her friends, Mr and Mrs Rogers, who were also among the King's American friends. The French police were guarding the gates from a siege of journalists and sightseers.

The English newspapers were reporting every movement regarding the King's visitors. He remained shut up in Fort Belvedere except for a night journey to Buckingham Palace when he strode through the rooms in search of something and then went back again. There was a constant coming and going between Fort Belvedere and London. The King's brothers were busy on the roads at many hours of the day and night. Officials of the Duchy of Cornwall were in repeated attendance. Members of the King's staff were getting no sleep these nights and travelling to and fro with despatch cases. Mr Baldwin, who had been a sick man, left Downing Street several times for long audiences with the King. What did it all mean? Why this hurrying and scurrying of officials, royal dukes, despatch riders and other messengers? There must be more in it than waiting for a decision by the King whether or not he held to his intention to marry Mrs Simpson.

The newspapers left their readers bewildered. Some maintained that the King could not marry without consent of Parliament. Others asserted definitely that the King was perfectly free to marry any woman he liked without consulting his ministers. Where, then, was the constitutional crisis? Yet the Cabinet remained in almost constant session, and it was announced that the prime minister had consulted the leaders of the Opposition. Mr Baldwin had "sealed lips" again, as once before in recent history—during the Abyssinian crisis. His replies to questions were mainly requests that he should not be questioned. But he admitted that the King had consulted him on November 25 on the possibility of a morganatic marriage with Mrs Simpson, and that, in consultation with the Dominions, this proposal had not been found admissible. No such thing as a morganatic marriage was recognised by the British Constitution or by any precedent in our history.

Mr Churchill rose from his place below the gangway and pleaded that the House should be made aware of the exact situation before any "irrevocable act" had been made. There were some cheers when this request was first made. It still seems to me a right and reasonable request, but when it was made again it was received with angry murmurs in the House and no answer was given by the prime minister.

One evening in the Lion I was rung up by a friendly American voice. The owner of it wanted me to broadcast a short address about all this to the United States.

I refused politely.

"Why not?" asked the friendly American voice. "May I have your reasons?"

"I have an abscess in a tooth," I told him.

It didn't seem an adequate excuse, though it was true.

"Also," I added, "I am in a state of mental conflict about this crisis. I lean heavily in sympathy towards the King but I couldn't bring myself to become enthusiastic about a marriage with Mrs Simpson, and if I take the other view I should offend all my listeners in the United States—or disappoint them. I feel stricken about it. I can't talk about it."

"Now, say," said my unknown American, "that's not so at all. No one speaking from this side is expected to advocate that marriage. On the contrary! It is well recognised in the United States—apart from sentimentality—that it wouldn't be a suitable marriage. You can let yourself go on that."

I didn't want to let myself go on that. I had no fixed convictions at that time. I leant heavily in sympathy towards the King and hoped he would find a way out of his dilemma.

It was, perhaps, the most extraordinary conversation ever held in the Lion at Guildford, whose rafters have heard many strange things.

6 *The Anguish of Doubt*

I went out into the old High Street of Guildford late at night, torn by a conflict of thought about this tragic problem of the King, and I suppose that on this night hundreds of millions of people were suffering the same anguish of doubt between their loyalty and their moral judgment.

It was up to each one of us to decide that issue in his own conscience, for this young man, who was the King Emperor, had gained the personal loyalty and good will of most of us by some quality of courage, and sense of humour, and democratic sympathy. He had taken risks to help the men and women of the distressed areas. *The Times* had grumbled about his recent visit to the black areas of South Wales and hinted that he had gone beyond his constitutional office in bringing personal pressure upon the government to amend their programme and policy. *The Times* might think so, but not the people. They looked to him for this leadership and for something more than the conventional correctness of royal automatism.

Was that hope to be flung away by this love affair with a married woman? Was a man who might be a great leader of a democratic people in an era of enormous danger—needing heroic leadership and new methods—to be hamstrung by a cabinet of mediocrities and a few bishops because he wished to marry a woman who seemed to suit him? Divorce, after all, was accepted by English law and by the Church of England, which is supposed to be obedient to that law. Why should Edward VIII not be given the privilege of the law allowed to his subjects? Why should not Mrs Simpson obtain a divorce from a husband who might be unfaithful to her—what did we know about that?—and be free to marry, without perhaps assuming the dignity of Queen, a man who seemed desperately to need her for his peace of mind and happiness? She might be a second Mrs Fitzherbert who was truly married to George IV but never sat beside him on the Throne.

These ideas, I confess, chased through my mind and troubled me exceedingly, as, I have no doubt, they troubled many other minds that night.

I passed under old gables upon which many moons had shone on nights in Tudor England. Into the yard of an old hostelry, where a lantern threw a glimmering light on the cobble stones, there had been a clatter of hoofs when messengers had come with news of the Armada. I walked past a brick building, through which one sees a quiet quadrangle and old men resting, which was there when James I put his arm round the shoulder of "Dogge Steenie", that handsome fellow, George Villiers, Duke of Buckingham, before young Charles had dreamed of civil war or seen the shadow of a headsman's axe. I looked up at the windows of a house from which the little ladies of Stuart England showed their beauty to the passers-by when the church bells rang for the home-coming of the second Charles who had been in exile. He had come riding this way now and then. There was gossip in the Angel, and tittle-tattle behind those casement windows about Nell Gwyn, and the beautiful Lady Castlemaine, and that French woman Mme "Carwell", as they called her, and other lovely ladies of the court. Charles had many mistresses, but somehow, in this tolerant age, many respectable people have a soft place in their hearts for him. Reginald Blunt, the historian of Chelsea and a man of high ideals, loving all loveliness, has confessed in print that among his English heroines is Nell Gwyn, that lighthearted lady who was mistress of the King. Her name is given to a monstrous block of flats inhabited by many virtuous spinsters who go to church on Sundays. Why then this national crisis shaking the Throne because Edward VIII had set his heart on Mrs Simpson and wished to marry her?

These questions—and these memories of history—crowded my mind as I walked up and down the High Street where a few people were talking together under old archways and in the doorways of shuttered shops.

A voice spoke in the darkness.

"She 'as two 'usbands already. A bit thick for a woman like that to be Queen of England!"

Another voice answered.

"I'm all for 'im. Let 'im marry the woman 'e wants is what I say. Same as any of us."

So English voices had spoken under these archways, this way and that, when the first Charles was being tried for his life in Westminster Hall.

I stood for a moment or two outside an old building with whitewashed walls. It was one of Edward VI's foundation schools, and its stone floors were worn by the clodhopping boots of young English boys who conned their hornbooks even before another boy at Stratford on Avon had written his first line of verse. These walls had been weathered in Tudor England. The clock of the old church at the bottom of the hill, now striking twelve in the reign of Edward VIII, had told the time through many centuries of English history with its triumphs, and tragedies, and wretchedness, and conflict, when Kings and Queens wore their crowns unsafely. But never one of them had renounced the Crown willingly, never one of them had surrendered it for the sake of a woman—saint or slut. I did not believe that the eighth Edward would do this thing.

I went back to the Lion again and could not sleep. England did not sleep easily that night. Its people were conscious that something was shaking beneath their beds—the foundation of the old system of kingship upon which their loyalties are based, which keeps the Empire together and is deeply rooted, in spite of all modern ideas and changes of thought, in their sense of order and tradition. Would there be civil war again in England? Would there be a King's party, and uprisings in Wales, or trouble in the fleet? Such dark foolish thoughts came in the small hours of the night.

Some of the newspapers were trying to organise a King's party against the government. They urged the possibility of a morganatic marriage even when it had been rejected by the government, not only of this country but of the Dominions. It was those papers which announced one morning that the crisis was at an end. Mrs Simpson, over there in Cannes, had issued a statement delivered by Lord Brownlow, the King's friend and hers, that her position had become unhappy and untenable, and that if it would help to solve the problem she was willing to withdraw forthwith.

Many simple souls believed this journalistic optimism that all had ended in the best possible way. Mrs Simpson would eliminate herself. The King would bow to the inevitable and go on with his job. God Save the King!

7 *They Went on Talking*

I went up to town on the day when Mr Baldwin had promised to make an announcement in the House of Commons.

In the railway carriage was an elderly man who became talkative, though not encouraged much by his fellow travellers, who sat rather glum. He looked to me like Uncle Dick in *David Copperfield*.

HIGH STREET, GUILDFORD

"Well, that woman has done the right thing," he announced. "I'm sorry for the King, of course—who wouldn't be?—but, after all, he shouldn't have fallen in love with a married woman. Shocking! In any case, we ask no more of him in giving her up than is asked of many a city clerk or shop assistant who has to give up his girl because he can't afford to marry her, or because he has to keep his mother, or because she happens to be somebody else's wife. See what I mean?"

For some time he elaborated his meaning. In his opinion Mrs Simpson was out of the question as Queen. Equally out of the question as a morganatic wife. "There's no such thing in English law," he asserted, quoting *The Times*. The Americans, he thought, might imagine that the English people had a downer on her because she was an American. That was all nonsense. It was because she was of no standing at all. "One might as well have a mannequin as Queen of England, or some little creature out of Hollywood. The King is old enough to know better. A bit lonely, of course. Likes to be amused. He's touched with the spirit of jazz which undermined the postwar youth. Well, one has to make allowances. But this is a bit too much."

"I'm sorry for him," said a middle-aged man in the corner.

"Of course we're all sorry for him!" said the talkative man. "We're sorry for ourselves sometimes."

"If it came to war we would be expected to give up our lives," said a young redheaded fellow who had been reading his paper in a corner of the carriage.

"Exactly!" said the talkative man. "You'd be expected to give up your life for duty's sake and sing 'God Save the King' before you died. We don't ask the King as much as that. Thank God he has made the right decision."

"How do you know?" asked the young redheaded man, staring him in the eyes.

"Haven't you seen the papers this morning? It's in the *Daily Express*. 'End of the Crisis.' "

"I hope it's true," said the redheaded young man. "I don't see it myself. It's still up to the King."

I went into a club in Pall Mall where as a rule all the morning papers are spread out on a big table. There were very few papers left. They were all being read by silent men, as though one paper might have more news than another, and reveal more light in the darkness of this mystery behind the scenes and the meanings of all the rushings to and from Fort Belvedere. Queen Mary had had a secret meeting with her son. The royal dukes were with him again. Mr Baldwin had had a five hours audience and stayed for a meal. Perhaps the King had made his decision to give up the lady.

This club is not, as a rule, a place in which one hears high secrets of state. One hears more frequently the state of the motor market or the Stock Exchange or the detailed narrative of a game of golf. But I happened to meet a man who told me astounding news as casually as though he were talking about the weather. He was a distinguished soldier in the World War, twenty years back. He had just met a man who was in touch with the situation.

"The King has made up his mind to abdicate. The Duke of York refuses to accept the Crown. There's talk of a regency with the little princess as Queen. Another Queen Elizabeth!"

"Is that so?" I asked, as though this kind of thing was a commonplace. One talks like that to men like that, as when young officers said: "Fine morning!" in the fields of Armageddon.

My soldier friend talked over the situation a little.

"It may be for the best. The life at Fort Belvedere was not a shining example to the nation. No dignity. Jogging about to jazz tunes. Very strange people! Very odd behaviour! I hope the Duke of York will withdraw his opposition. He may have done by this time. Of course it's awkward for him. His own brother! Well, good morning. Glad to have seen you."

Astonishing man! He didn't seem to turn a hair at all this. He had very bright smiling eyes under shaggy brows. He was like any of those brigadiers who had commanded during the war, square faced, with little grey moustaches, and steady eyes, and nerves like steel; the real type of regular soldier of the old school. I was staggered by the words he had spoken so calmly, in such a matter-of-fact way, as though a change of kings had no more importance than a change of uniform.

Could the English people change their allegiance like that? I wondered. Could they let Edward go without violent protest? He was popular in the navy, especially on the lower deck. He was head of the Air Force, and the young pilots had a sense of loyalty to him. He was air minded. He understood their game. He had earned his wings. Wales? The devastated areas? The mean streets through which he had walked; the overcrowded tenements into which he had gone bareheaded with sympathy and kindliness for unemployed and working women and under-nourished families? Would they accept his abdication without a murmur? I could hardly think so. The situation seemed to me full of danger. Underneath this calm in England there might be let loose passionate forces—a sudden outburst of rage. Young Fascists were going about with placards: "We want Edward VIII." Was Mosley going to get his chance as King's champion and leader of the plus-four boys? Who could tell what the next twenty-four hours would bring?

8 The King's Message

On the afternoon of December 10 I stood in the crowd outside the Houses of Parliament shortly before three o'clock. In another half an hour or so Mr Baldwin would be telling the nation, and the Empire, and the world, how it stood with the King. The papers that morning had all been pessimistic. Someone perhaps had given them a tip. "Abdication Feared." Those newspapers which had announced the end of the crisis had changed their headlines and their tone.

I looked into the faces of these people who had gathered in Parliament Square. They were all very grave, but there was no excitement, no demonstration, no look of passion. They were waiting tensely for the announcement of the King's decision, as men might wait outside the law courts for a jury's verdict in a great trial. They were just the type, I thought, which might make up a grand jury: middle-aged businessmen, printers, clerks. Here and there stood a few of the unemployed with scarves instead of collars. There were very few women where I stood; and I noticed an extra number of police and stalwart men who looked like policemen in plain clothes. The crowds moved about a little but obeyed the quiet words of the police and kept clear of the gates through which ministers and members of the House would pass. No one spoke a word in my neighbourhood. I had never seen an English crowd so silent, so grave, except when a coffin passed.

I moved away and had an idea of getting into the House, but I changed my mind and crossed St James's Park in the direction of the Duke of York's steps. I should hear the news quickest in the hall of a club where there would be a tape machine.

Presently I stood by that machine. There was an unusual crowd of members at that hour, when generally the club is deserted. They spoke to each other in quiet voices.

"England," said one of them, "still has a moral conscience. It is still Puritan at heart."

Now and then I heard a laugh, and it seemed to me the wrong time for laughter.

The tape machine was inactive. It seemed a long time before there was a little whir of wheels and a slight movement of the paper.

"It's beginning to work!" said a voice which had a slight Scotch accent. "Now we shan't be long!"

It was this Scotsman who took charge of the tape machine and read out the words when they came, surrounded by this group of men among whom I knew many faces. They were writing men, economists, politicians of past campaigns, lawyers, civil servants.

"Read out!" said several voices.

In a hard clear voice, without emotion, the Scotsman read out words which, I confess, smote my mind as the sentences of a tragic drama.

They had been introduced by Mr Baldwin who had risen from the Treasury Bench and walked to the Bar of the House: "A message from His Majesty the King, signed by His Majesty's own hand."

The tape machine was spelling out the message with jerks and halts.

"*After long and anxious consideration I have determined to renounce the Throne to which I succeeded on the death of My father, and I am now communicating this, My final and irrevocable decision.*"

The tape machine stopped for several seconds.

"He throws up his job!" said the Scotsman. "By God, he's a quitter!"

There was a murmur among the other men.

"It's the best thing that could have happened," said the voice of the man who rejoiced that England still had a moral conscience—that England was still Puritan.

"It's a moral abdication," said another man.

"He went along the wrong road."

"It's the only thing that could save the Throne."

"It was inevitable. He wasn't equal to his high place. His friends—the jazz mind——"

"It's beginning again," said the Scotsman.

"*Realising as I do the gravity of this step, I can only hope that I shall have the understanding of My peoples in the decision I have taken and the reasons which have led Me to take it.*"

"No!" said a harsh voice.

"Quiet there! . . . Get on with it!"

"*I will not enter now into My private feelings but I would beg that it should be remembered that the burden which constantly rests upon the shoulders of a Sovereign is so heavy that it can only be borne in circumstances different from those in which I now find Myself. I conceive that I am not overlooking the duty which rests on Me, to place in the forefront the public interest, when I declare that I am conscious that I can no longer discharge the heavy task with efficiency or with satisfaction to Myself.*

"*I have accordingly this morning executed an Instrument of Abdication in the terms following:*

"*I, Edward VIII, of Great Britain, Ireland, and the British Dominions beyond the Seas, King Emperor of India, do hereby declare My irrevocable determination to renounce the Throne for Myself and My descendants, and my desire that effect should be given to this Instrument of Abdication immediately.*

"*In token whereof I have hereunto set My hand this tenth day of December, nineteen hundred and thirty-six, in the presence of the witnesses whose signatures are subscribed.*

"(*signed*) *Edward R.I.*

"*My execution of this Instrument has been witnessed by My three brothers, Their Royal Highnesses the Duke of York, the Duke of Gloucester and the Duke of Kent.*

"*I deeply appreciate the spirit which has actuated the appeals which have been made to Me to take a different decision, and I have, before reaching My final determination, most fully pondered over them. But My mind is made up. Moreover, further delay cannot but be most injurious to the peoples whom I have tried to serve as Prince of Wales and as King and whose future happiness and prosperity are the constant wish of My heart. I take My leave of them in the confident hope that the course which I have thought it right to follow is that which is best for the stability of the Throne and Empire and the happiness of My peoples. I am deeply sensible of the consideration which they have always extended to Me both before and after My accession to the Throne and which I know they will extend in full measure to My successor.*

"*I am most anxious that there should be no delay of any kind in giving effect to the Instrument which I have executed and that all necessary steps should be taken immediately to secure that My lawful successor, My brother, His Royal Highness the Duke of York, should ascend the Throne.*"

"Well, that's that," said one of those who had listened.

He went off with a friend to order tea and buttered toast. Other men straggled away into the dimly lit hall. They did not seem anxious, perturbed or dismayed by this astounding episode in history. They did not seem to be moved to any emotion of pity by words which were surely tragic, to the heights of Shakespearean tragedy, if one has any sense of drama, of history, or of tragedy. Even now I am surprised by the harsh dismissal of a man who, with all his faults, had a touch of the heroic stuff. Their verdict was one of Guilty without Extenuating Circumstances.

"You look unwell," said a friend of mine as I sat down in one of the club chairs.

"I feel stricken," I said. "I hate to think of Edward VIII going out into the darkness like this."

He was astonished.

"But surely it's the best possible thing? You wouldn't have had him marry Mrs Simpson?"

No, I wouldn't have had him marry Mrs Simpson. She would

never have been accepted by the English people, high or low. At least, public opinion at that time, as far as I could test it, was not in favour of the lady, about whom, after all, they knew next to nothing. But that was not the thought in my mind. What nagged at me was the loss of the man himself and his renunciation of his Crown, and all that it means in service, in splendour, and in opportunities of leadership, for any woman whatever. What made me feel stricken was that Edward VIII, who might have been the leader of a new age with all the nation's spirit behind him, and who, as Prince of Wales, had captured the people's imagination by the touch of youth, by a sense of humour, by gallantry in sport, by his adventures in the air, by something akin to that Prince Hal who quaffed and laughed with Falstaff and his rogues, should not have won the place of Harry the King, of Agincourt, but should walk away from his destiny to follow the call of a siren. Somehow, I felt, it could have been prevented. What shocked me more than a little was the lack of any regret, of any doubt, in the minds of these men that he should go like that when, perhaps, if the affair had been better handled by his friends and by his ministers, he might have been saved.

His ministers might have advised him earlier. His friends might have stood round him closer. That divorce at Ipswich might have been prevented. Pressure might have been brought to bear on Mrs Simpson to leave the country early in his reign.

That night when I travelled by train back to the country I sat in a third-class carriage with six other men. They were all reading the evening papers intently, with glum faces. Presently one man put his paper down and gave a little sigh and shut his eyes. Surely, I thought, these fellows—city men—will begin to give tongue. Here is one of the most extraordinary events in history, never before known in the long roll call of English kings, and surely they will express some kind of view about it. I waited for someone to begin an excited conversation. Not a word was uttered on that journey of fifty minutes. I was tempted to break silence and to ask these fellow travellers what in God's name they thought about it all. And then I realised that this silence was in itself an eloquence. These men were gravely troubled. It was beyond words. They were deeply perplexed by all that had happened.

9 *The Prime Minister Tells His Tale*

We read Mr Baldwin's speech in the House of Commons. It was, in its way—in Mr Baldwin's way—a masterpiece, unprepared and spoken with notes which got all mixed up and were of no use to him. He spoke with emotion, with apparent candour, with an effective simplicity, which moved the crowded House and the country afterwards. But he left a lot of the tale untold, and it has not been told yet. There were some very odd things in his speech which will raise doubts in the minds of future historians about constitutional rights and the prerogatives of the Crown.

Disturbed by a flood of correspondence reaching him from all British subjects in all parts of the world expressing uneasiness at the tales in the American Press, Mr Baldwin had decided—he told the House—that it was a duty which could only fall on the prime minister to warn the King as a counsellor and friend. Accordingly, therefore, on October 18, without consulting any colleagues (an omission for which, he said, they had forgiven him) he asked for an interview—the first and only time that the initiative had come from him.

On October 29 Mr Baldwin told the King of the growing scandal and reminded him that the importance of preserving the integrity of the Crown was greater than ever before, and that its prestige might swiftly be destroyed. He pointed out the danger of the impending divorce case of Mrs Simpson and, after leaving the King to consider his words, reported them to four of his senior colleagues.

On November 16—his narrative continued—he had another conversation with the King at Buckingham Palace and spoke to him for twenty minutes on the subject of marriage. In the interval a decree nisi had been granted to Mrs Simpson. He told the King that marriage with her could not meet with public approval, that the King's wife must be Queen, and that therefore in his choice the voice of the people must be heard. The King said: "I am going to marry Mrs Simpson and I am prepared to go." That, said Mr Baldwin, was grievous news and he must reserve comment.

On November 25 he informed the King of his answer to a suggestion that there should be a morganatic marriage with Mrs Simpson. In his view, he said, Parliament would never pass the necessary bill. The King asked this to be put to the test, though it meant consulting the full Cabinet and the Dominion prime ministers. This was done, and the refusal of special legislation was reported to the King on December 2. The King did not seem surprised, said Mr Baldwin, and, like a great gentleman, never referred to it again. Then Mr Baldwin told him plainly that the alternative seemed to be either to abandon his intention to marry Mrs Simpson or to abandon his Throne. After that it was a week of persuasion, of exhortation, of waiting for the King's own decision between those different ways of choice.

One fact emerges from this plain narrative of events. Mr Baldwin, as prime minister and King's friend, took upon himself to deal with this situation, which involved the Crown and the very foundation of the Throne and Constitution, by personal negotiations between himself and the King, with the one exception of the proposal for a morganatic marriage. The Cabinet left it to him. The Lords and Commons were not consulted at all stages. In the choice of the King's wife, he said, the voice of the people must be heard. But it was not heard. The nation was kept in ignorance of the facts and the alternative choice which the King had to decide. Mr Churchill's reiterated plea for information before any irrevocable act was taken remained unanswered. It was only when the King's Instrument of Abdication was read in Parliament that the nation knew they had lost Edward VIII and could do nothing about it. That method of procedure avoided a King's party and a natural conflict of opinion which would have been very dangerous.

For that reason, no doubt, it was accepted by all parties in the House without a murmur of dissent, except from five members of the extreme Left who uttered harsh and cynical words against what they described as cant and humbug. "If," said one member, "the King is one tenth as good as you say, why are you not keeping him? You want to get rid of him and you are taking the step today."

One may be permitted to wonder whether the way in which King Edward's abdication was arranged and accepted can be quite reconciled with constitutional tradition and the rights of the people. Is not a prime minister taking upon himself too much responsibility and too much power if he plays a lone hand in such a case, even though his actions are ratified, in retrospect, by a Parliament faced with an accomplished act? Is it within a prime minister's power to face a King with an alternative involving abdication, without consulting the people until that act has happened? If so, then the Crown has no safeguard and no support by the people. If so, then a prime minister is more powerful than the King.

The Times ended its summary of that day's proceedings, which recorded for the first time the abdication of a King, with the following words suitable to the discussion of a parish pump.

"With a murmur of relief for a testing day well passed, the House adjourned."

In another column one of its correspondents, describing the silent crowds, wrote: "The people, who made no kind of demonstration, seemed for the most part bewildered by the day's events."

It was not reported that outside Buckingham Palace, according to reliable witnesses, a crowd of from ten to fifteen thousand people made a demonstration in favour of King Edward VIII, with shouts of: "We want King Edward."

Fifteen thousand people are nothing in a nation. Apparently England and the Empire accepted the abdication of Edward VIII and the accession of George VI with astonishing calmness and lack of passion.

Apart from that shouting crowd outside Buckingham Palace, no murmur of passion for the passing of a popular King came from England, or Scotland, or Wales, or any part of the Empire. None, at least, was reported in the Press, and I have heard of none. There was no protest from the Royal Navy, from the army or Air Force, of which Edward VIII had been in supreme command. No single body of men marched out of the distressed areas to demonstrate their loyalty to a man who had been their friend and champion. Did it show a lack of vitality? Does it suggest that our people are incapable of any passion for any cause whatever? The nation stood silent with a passive acceptance of this act of abdication and shifted their allegiance to George VI, who had been Duke of York, with general acquiescence. They cheered the new King outside his private house in Piccadilly. The newspapers were filled with photographs of him and of his beautiful Queen and the little princesses, and everybody found comfort, it seemed, in these pictures of family life—a sense of security. That was the kind of picture they wanted for their royal family.

No doubt it was well that it happened like this. It was supremely good fortune for England and the Empire that there was no King's party, no insurrection, no romantic adventure on his behalf. The Throne remained unshaken, did not totter even for an hour, even for a moment. The people's allegiance to George VI, proclaimed by his heralds so soon after the proclamation of the former King, expresses a loyalty to the Crown above loyalty to any individual who might wear it. With it went a personal sympathy and good will to the person of the new King himself, because he had accepted the office which his brother had renounced—not without anguish, as he acknowledged simply before his council.

10 The Verdict of the People

The world—outside the British Empire—was astounded with admiration for the steadiness of the British people in this crisis. French writers, like most others, searched for words to express their profound respect for the dignity, the nobility, the wisdom, with which the British peoples behaved in a time of trouble which, in most other countries, would have led to rioting, bloodshed, and perhaps civil war. Our own bishops and clergy saw in all this a sign that Christian morality had prevailed over modern looseness, and that the people's sense of virtue had been shocked. Were we as noble as all that? Was it wisdom, or bewilderment, or stupefaction, which caused this change of kings to be made so easily? Was it an outraged sense of virtue which had condemned Edward VIII? One would like to lay this flattering unction to our souls. One would like to bask in a sense of our own morality and spiritual perfection. But is it true?

I tried to find the truth of it as it might be revealed in the minds of the common folk, and of what in the old days of snobdom used to be called the "Quality." It seemed to me enormously interesting to get down to the real workings of their minds over this historical episode. Many, I am certain, were utterly perplexed. They felt that they were not in possession of the full facts. It had all happened so quickly. The King had abdicated before they knew what it was all about. They knew nothing beyond rumour about the divorce at Ipswich. Many people thought the King had been cited as corespondent. They knew nothing beyond gossip about Mrs Simpson. They knew nothing of the argument put before the King until Mr Baldwin spoke in the House of Commons after the Instrument of Abdication had been presented.

But after the abdication something else happened in the English mind. It was anger. It was not anger because the King had got into trouble with a married woman, nor anger because the King's friends seemed to be a poor lot—according to the archbishop—nor anger because he wished to marry "beneath him", as some of them said, but anger because he had "chucked his job."

There was a scene in a mess of the Royal Air Force on the afternoon of abdication. The young pilots of bombing machines had been crowding round the wireless which gave them the news. Suddenly they all started shouting, and arguing, and cursing.

"He has let us down," they shouted. "He has thrown up the sponge. He preferred that damn woman to England and the whole blinking Empire. He ought to have held on to his job, even if it meant chucking that wench. Aren't we asked to risk our lives every day for him? 'For King and Country,' by God! In time of war we should be asked to give up our wives and women for the country's sake; to do our duty and die like little gentlemen. But that fellow wouldn't give a woman the go by—or keep her in her proper place—for the sake of the whole crowd of us; or the pluck to marry her if he wanted and tell Baldwin to go to hell. But he ought to have kept his job. A fellow doesn't chuck his job like that if he's King Emperor—or a clerk in a city office."

So they shouted and swore, greatly excited and very angry. They weren't concerned, these young pilots of bombing aeroplanes, with the moral aspect of the case. They didn't care a curse, they said, for the moral aspect of the case. They weren't Puritans, it seemed.

"It's better to have a leader with guts and no morals," said one of them, "than a fellow with morals and no guts."

It was one of those air pilots who described this scene to me afterwards.

"He has let us down—every one of us," said a man for whom I have a great respect. He is a man of high character and great charm and tender sympathy for humanity, even when he is inflicting horrible tortures upon a quivering human being, as he did that day to me, when he extracted a tooth with a long fang from my jaw, without gas, owing to an abscess at the root of it. He spoke with intense anger, which is rare in him, I am certain.

"We believed in him—and he's let us down. We gave him our loyalty and he's let us down."

I heard that phrase a score of times within forty-eight hours of the abdication.

It was the verdict of the people, as far as I could get into touch with them. They could not forgive him for his abdication. That—and not his love affair with Mrs Simpson—was the cause of their indignation. Kings of England, they seemed to think, do not fling off their crowns for any woman whatever. England and the English stand first, they thought.

I dined next to a man who had been a famous general in the World War. He knew the ex-King well and had a great admiration for his brilliant qualities and charm. He told me many stories of the King's interest in ex-service men and unemployed. He had done things beyond anything he need have done—driving to slum places in his own car without a chauffeur to see how a scheme of slum settlement was getting on, and to keep his friends busy at a work of social service which he had initiated among them.

"The truth is that he had a wrong picture in his mind," said my friend. "He thought that if he fulfilled his public duty and made friends with the people, to whom he was really devoted, they would let him do as he liked in his private life. He forgot that a King has no private life."

There was a proposal to send him a letter of thanks on behalf of ex-service men in many organisations all over the country for all that he had done for them as Prince of Wales and afterwards as King. Many of the delegates were hostile to this idea. They were angry. They turned thumbs down. Those from Wales were the most resolute in refusal.

"He has let us down," they said.

I do not wish to deny—it would be utterly untrue to deny—that the sense of morality of many people in England was shocked by King Edward's love affair with a married woman and by his wish to marry her after a quick divorce. There is still a Puritan strain in England, very strong in thousands of little homes, especially in country towns and villages. There is still a respect for marriage among the great mass of decent living folk. There is still a deep religious spirit centred round the village churches and cathedrals and chapels of this land. That is true, although journalists are always writing of empty churches, and the roads are crowded at week ends with motorists on their way to seaside towns, without any prayer in their hearts or any mercy for pedestrians.

That moral sense of religious-minded people—millions of

them—was disturbed and distressed by the King's departure from the tradition of the royal family since early Victorian days, and by his desire to marry a woman whom they believed was not a pattern of Christian virtue. All that surged up in England during the ten days which led to the abdication.

But this moral attitude was not rigid, I found, in certain minds, not essentially irreligious.

"No one would have objected," said a lady for whom I have a profound respect as a woman of high principle and domestic virtue, "if the King had kept some woman quietly and decently. It's disgusting, but men are like that."

"But, my dear lady," I said, astonished at this point of view from her, "the King wanted to marry a lawfully divorced woman. Surely, that was less immoral? I always thought you stood for the strictly moral code!"

"I do," said this lady with self-assurance. "That's why I am telling you what I think. It's far less vicious and destructive of morality for a King to keep a mistress privately than to take somebody else's wife and degrade the institution of marriage in the face of the whole nation."

"But divorce is accepted in English law," I argued. "The Church has to recognise it, and does."

She hesitated for a moment and then looked up from a crossword puzzle which I had interrupted.

"In any case, the King tried to foist a woman on the nation as Queen who was quite unsuitable. Supposing he had wanted to marry Mae West? She may be very charming and highly virtuous, but she wouldn't make a good Queen of England, I imagine. Let's leave it at that. Unsuitability. The King ought to have known that. In fact, he did when he asked for a morganatic marriage."

She added words which I had heard before.

"He has let us all down."

11 The Tragic Broadcast

Heaven alone knows—or perhaps heaven and Sir John Reith—how many millions of men and women listened to the broadcast speech by the ex-King on the night of Friday, December 11. That morning the Declaration of Abdication Bill had passed through both Houses of Parliament and the reign of King Edward VIII had come to an end at 1.52 P.M. At the same time, his brother, the Duke of York, had succeeded to the Throne. Certain newspapers, utterly misinformed and quite ridiculous, seeing that the ex-King was still the son of George V, had referred to him as Mr Edward Windsor.

"The fellow has the pluck of ten thousand gladiators," said a friend of mine who had been very harsh in his condemnation. "How he can face that microphone after what has happened, and with all the world listening, beats me. I almost feel that I shan't bear to listen to him. It will churn me up most frightfully."

There were many who felt they could hardly bear to listen to that voice over the wireless. It would be too emotional and too tragic. Even those who had turned thumbs down could hardly bring themselves to hear that *apologia*, and that farewell, from a man so recently the emblem of their loyalty.

People, I am told, sat sideways to the radio when, at ten o'clock that night, the King was expected to speak. They were listening all over the Empire and in the United States, where one group, I know, as afterwards one of them told me—they were all "Britishers"—assembled in a club room off Fifth Avenue. They sat, with their faces hidden by their hands, sideways to that microphone from which would come the voice of a man for whom they had sprung to their feet many a time, standing stiffly to attention at the first note of "God Save the King." Now he was down and out, by his own choice and will, it was said.

I was alone with my wife in a country house. We sat at a wood fire. Outside, it was very quiet, with nothing stirring. We didn't look at each other when a deep voice spoke from Windsor Castle and said "His Royal Highness, Prince Edward."

All over the world there was surely a tenseness of silence. Less than a year before this man who was going to speak had spoken on his accession to the Throne of Great Britain, and Ireland, and the Dominions beyond the Seas, and Emperor of India. In a young man's voice, very thin and fresh, he had said: "Most of you have known me as Prince of Wales. I am the same man, though I now speak to you as King Emperor." Now he was about to speak again, after laying down the Crown for a woman's sake. It was not a fresh voice this time. It was a little husky and deeper—extraordinarily like his father's, I thought—except, now and then, when it rang out more sharply or became richer at one phrase.

"At long last," he began, "I am able to say a few words of my own. I have never wanted to withhold anything, but until now it has not been constitutionally possible for me to speak.

"A few hours ago I discharged my last duty as King and Emperor, and now that I have been succeeded by my brother, the Duke of York, my first words must be to declare my allegiance to him. This I do with all my heart.

"You all know the reasons which have impelled me to renounce the Throne. But I want you to understand that in making up my mind I did not forget the country or the Empire which as Prince of Wales, and lately as King, I have for twenty-five years tried to serve. But you must believe me when I tell you that I have found it impossible to carry the heavy burden of responsibility and to discharge my duties as King, as I would wish to do, without the help and support of the woman I love."

It was when he spoke those words "the woman I love" that his voice became richer and deeper.

There was a slight pause and then the voice continued:

"And I want you to know that the decision I have made has been mine and mine alone. This was a thing I had to judge entirely for myself. The other person most nearly concerned has tried up to the last to persuade me to take a different course. I have made this, the most serious decision of my life, only upon the single thought of what would in the end be best for all.

"This decision has been made less difficult to me by the sure knowledge that my brother, with his long training in the public affairs of this country and with his fine qualities, will be able to take my place forthwith, without interruption or injury to the life and progress of the Empire. And he has one matchless blessing, enjoyed by so many of you and not bestowed on me—a happy home with his wife and children.

"During these hard days I have been comforted by Her Majesty my mother and by my family. The ministers of the Crown, and in particular Mr Baldwin, the prime minister, have always treated me with full consideration. There has never been any constitutional difference between me and them and between me and Parliament. Bred in the constitutional tradition by my father, I should never have allowed any such issue to arise.

"Ever since I was Prince of Wales, and later on when I occupied the Throne, I have been treated with the greatest kindness by all classes of the people, wherever I have lived or journeyed throughout the Empire. For that I am very grateful.

"I now quit altogether public affairs, and I lay down my burden. It may be some time before I return to my native land, but I shall always follow the fortunes of the British race and Empire with profound interest, and if at any time in the future I can be found of service to His Majesty in a private station I shall not fail.

"And now we all have a new King. I wish him and you, his people, happiness and prosperity with all my heart. God bless you all. God Save the King."

It was finely spoken, with perfect timing and emphasis on such words as "the other person" and that phrase "he has one matchless blessing enjoyed by so many of you and not bestowed on me"—and that promise "I shall not fail." Only when he spoke the last words, "God Save the King!" were they harsh and strident and overdramatic.

Great numbers of people, I am told, were weeping when this speech ended, and no one will blame them for sentimentality, because, if we have any emotion left for the sense of tragedy, this was a high tragedy which Shakespeare himself would have found in his style. If we have any sense of history, and any touch with old ghosts who were our Kings, and any awareness of dramatic values in life, this farewell of Edward VIII to his people had the quality of greatness and of tragic emotion. It will be remembered with pity and understanding in history, but with the reminder perhaps—for history is cruel—that the matchless blessing Edward coveted might have been his years before if he had chosen luckily, and that the woman he loved was another man's wife.

That night the ex-King drove down to Portsmouth and was challenged at the gates by a sentry who failed to know him in the darkness. Lonely in the night, he left the shores of England for exile abroad, created Duke of Windsor next day as the first act of the new King. He went out of English life but not out of all English hearts, whatever his faults, his weakness, his impatience, his unwisdom, for as Prince of Wales he was our Prince

Hal, with whose spirit he had walked on the field of Agincourt and many fields in France and Flanders during the World War, when he was one of our lieutenants. Shakespeare would have loved him. England loved him for a time. We have lost something.

V

George the Sixth

What manner of man is this who by an act of destiny—the strangest in our history—has been crowned King of Great Britain and Ireland, the Dominions beyond the Seas, and Emperor of India? What character lies behind the grave reserve of his outward expression? What is he like "off parade", as it were, in ordinary social life?

I have seen him many times on public occasions and have heard him make many speeches during which I tried to read the riddle of his personality or to get a glimpse of his individuality—not so expressive, not so dramatic in appeal, as that of his eldest brother, who was King Edward VIII. One thing was easy to tell. He was shy, and, owing to a slight inhibition when he was speaking publicly, so that now and again he paused a perceptible time to get self-control, it was obvious that he was doing something which needed will power and courage. He had all my sympathy, as I hate public speaking and suffer incredibly beforehand.

But I had the good fortune to spend a whole day with him once, and in a day one may size up any kind of man, unless he is in hiding from his fellow beings. The Duke of York as he then was was not at all in hiding, and I was astonished by his easy way of conversation and by his openheartedness. It shows how one can go wrong, I thought. I had no notion that he was like that—so unstiff, so humorous, and, on that day at least, so boyish.

I went with him to his boys' camp at Southwold. This is his particular pet hobby and a little scheme of his own in the way of social service, and he has run it for many years at his own expense. The idea is to get a number of public schoolboys, from Eton and Harrow and the rest, to spend a camping holiday each year with boys from industrial classes and districts, getting them all mixed up in games and all the activities and amusements of camp life.

"You will be surprised," he told me, "how well it works. There is absolutely no class consciousness. And they learn a lot from each other. Anyhow, they have a jolly good time."

I could hardly believe that, I confess. It didn't seem to me possible that Eton could mix with the Mile End Road or Harrow with Bermondsey. Needless to say, I did not express any doubt to the duke himself. One doesn't try to spoil a man's dream.

He was good enough to ask me into his own car and during the journey he chatted on all sorts of subjects. He was very much interested in Australia, I remember. He was also keen on industrial problems and wanted to get more done for young boys just over school age. Then he began talking with obvious admiration about his elder brother, the Prince of Wales at that time.

"My brother," he told me, "is going to make a speech tomorrow lasting something like an hour. I can't think how he does it. To me it would be a tremendous ordeal. But he has a gift that way, don't you think?"

His shyness was revealed to me again. I noticed that whenever the car halted and there was a chance of his being recognised,

KING GEORGE VI, GENTLEMAN UNAFRAID

he drew back in his seat and once pulled down a blind slightly.

"I never get used to it," he told me, but I am sure that by this time he has overcome that particular nervousness, if habit makes any difference.

When we arrived at the camp he was received by rousing cheers from all the boys and I accompanied him on a tour of inspection. But it wasn't at all formal, and he stopped frequently to talk to some of the boys, who were perfectly at their ease, I noticed. What is more surprising perhaps is that he was equally at ease with them, for many men I know find it difficult to take up the right attitude with boys between fifteen and seventeen. But the Duke of York was quite wonderful with them all through that long day he spent there. He went down to bathe with a crowd of them, and without any awe or reverence they played all manner of tricks with him in the water, splashing him with great zest and afterwards rubbing him down with their towels. It was quite clear to me that he was enjoying himself vastly and not allowing all this from a sense of duty or "good form." There was a surprise waiting for him at the corner of one of the little streets of huts in which the boys were housed. A stuffed figure was hanging by the neck from a lantern.

"Someone hanged?" asked the duke. "Not a fellow I'm fond of, I hope."

It was the effigy of an imaginary figure who had failed to live up to the code of the camp. "A Warning to All Dirty Dogs." The Duke of York laughed heartily.

"I shall have to be careful," he said. "If I break any of the rules . . ."

The rules were severe. One of them related to speeches made by the duke's visitors at lunch. They were allowed, I think, three minutes for their oratory, and it had to be amusing. Any pomposity, any trespassing by any fellow, however distinguished, over the allotted time, was quickly brought down. One of the Harrow masters who goes by the genial name of Boss-eye (his real name is Boissier) was entrusted with a pistol and at a given signal off it went with a most alarming report. Down went the speaker as though he had been shot in the heart. I was put up to tell a story. They gave me the three minutes. Then down I went. The duke himself made a very amusing speech, full of the gossip of the camp, which pleased the boys mightily. And at dinner, instead of taking his place at the high table, he slipped away from his seat and dined with a group of boys at one of the lower tables. Among them were a Harrow boy and an Eton boy and some young fellows from the East End of London. They all got on famously. A young humorist with a rich Cockney accent made them all laugh continually. The duke had a great time, it seemed.

I had to withdraw my scepticism about the mixing of classes. All these boys had established perfect comradeship. The team spirit prevailed, the boys being divided into groups who competed against each other in all forms of sports, and an Eton boy, or any other, became terribly keen for his group to do well and coached on the others with excited zeal for honour and glory. What did it matter about class? Young Bill from Bermondsey was the hero if he could run faster or pull harder than his fellows.

"Don't you think it's good?" asked the duke when we started for the journey back to London after a singsong.

"Magnificent," I said with utter sincerity.

His eyes brightened.

"I'm frightfully keen on this," he said, "though it's a very expensive hobby for the limits of my own purse, which has many other calls. I should hate to close it down."

It's not closed down yet.

We went back by train to London and the duke collected a small group of us round him in his saloon car and asked many questions and took his part in a general discussion on the financial state of the country and other subjects. He was very well informed, very anxious to get at facts, and had a shrewd quiet judgment of his own. I was sincerely impressed by his intelligence and still more impressed by his charm of manner, his good humour, his simplicity.

VI

The Dark Shadow

1 The Sense of Doom

IT IS IN THE MINDS of the English people—this dark shadow. It creeps into English gardens where there is beauty and should be, if anywhere, a sense of peace. It sits like a spectre at dinner tables where there is good company, and if one listens, as I do, one is conscious, very soon, of this ghost which haunts the minds of men and women who have been talking amusingly and lightheartedly until, inevitably—at least in the company I keep—the talk drifts, or lurches suddenly, into an argument which begins with fear and ends sometimes with a laugh in which despair is lurking.

I do not exaggerate or overdramatise. This dark shadow is caused by the dreadful apprehension that by some inescapable doom we are all marching, against our will, towards another war more frightful than the last—not the war to end war this time but the war to end civilisation. That shadow lies brooding over our English scene and darkening all our hopes.

What is the use of this "prosperity" proclaimed triumphantly by the government and by the Press (ignoring the distressed areas and other less pleasant aspects of English life) if it is going to be ended, rather soon perhaps (if one can believe the same newspapers), by hostile air raids from some enemy unnamed, unless Germany is named, smashing up our densely populated centres and spreading panic and death by poison gas and incendiary bombs? What is the good of this great scheme of physical training—the outcome of King George's Jubilee Fund—if youth is only to be made fit for the next shambles? What is the good of that Ten Years' Plan for Childhood, advocated by Lady Astor and her friends, if in one year, or two, or three—1940 is generally named as the fatal year by the prophets of woe—these children will be vomiting in gas masks and huddling in cellars which are by no means bombproof?

"I want to frighten people," said Mr Duff-Cooper, secretary for war, anxious to speed up recruiting.

Well, he has been doing his best, but it was hardly necessary. Mr Winston Churchill had done rather well in that direction by speeches and articles revealing the rapid and vast rearming of Germany, especially in the air. The government had not exactly proclaimed a cheery confidence in peace when they launched a tremendous plan for the expansion of our own armaments, by land, sea and air, and in February of this year announced their decision to raise a loan of £400,000,000 to cover expenses estimated at £1,500,000,000 for armaments during the next five years.

Up in Sheffield—I was told—the workers in munition factories were convinced in January last that war was not far off. Otherwise, they asked, why all this hurry?

"Why are we working on day and night shifts? Somebody seems to know something. It don't look good, apart from work and wages."

2 *Ways of Escape*

One Sunday afternoon in the spring of this year I went into two old country houses where pleasant people live, typical, perhaps, of English life at its best. One belonged to a young doctor who had been hard driven by the influenza epidemic and does not get much rest, anyhow, in a practice which extends to many villages. He looked tired, I thought, but was amusing in his conversation as he stood six inches below the old black beams which go across his ceiling. But presently, when we drifted into a talk about psychology, he asked me a curious question.

"Do you think young people ought to escape from this lunatic asylum called Europe if they have a chance of getting out in time before war comes along?"

"Where would they go to find a sanctuary?" I answered by another question.

"What about Rio? That might be a good spot, fairly aloof from trouble?"

He was worrying about that "next war", perhaps on account of his young wife, perhaps as a theoretical question nagging at him as he made his rounds, helping new life into the world, attending to children and young people who might be caught by the fire of Moloch.

It was strange that in the second house I went to that afternoon there were two women who started talking to me about this fear in their minds. One of them was the hostess of a tea party to which a group of young, or youngish, people had come. We talked at the end of the room for a few minutes and presently she asked me a question very seriously.

"Do you think that it might be wise for anyone to get out of this country while the going is good—that is, before another war comes? I've almost given up hope of peace. I'm sorry for the young people—this little crowd, for instance."

It was the same question that the young doctor had put to me. Behind it was the same sense of impending conflict. They were both looking for a way of escape while there might still be time. It was rather startling. It was tragic as evidence of a state of mind creeping into English thought as a deepening shadow. All over Europe, and into millions of minds looking out on life, that shadow lay behind sunlight and the hope of youth.

Another lady in the same room spoke to me in a quiet voice. She had a little scheme in which, she thought, I might be interested. Her idea was that a village like the one in which she lived, and many others not enormously far from London, might adopt a number of school children in the great city and bring them down to a holiday camp once a year. They would be given a good time, but the purpose of it would be to organise a plan of evacuation from London in case of aerial bombardment.

That fear again! That dreadful apprehension of a coming war.

I spoke quietly, as she had done, so that no one could hear in a room where there was a cheerful murmur of general conversation and occasional laughter. It was a good old house which for many generations had belonged to farming folk but now was filled with a company who skim the latest books, and listen to the wireless, and are in touch with London sophistication.

"I refuse to believe that war is coming," I said sturdily. "It seems to me a kind of acceptance of its certainty if one arranges plans for air raids and gas masks for children. That is a surrender of all hope. It's putting emphasis onto preparation and not onto prevention. War mustn't happen."

She was the mother of young children, though young looking herself and beautiful. Reynolds and Romney painted women like her. She looked, I thought, very eighteenth century in a long low room with old-fashioned furniture.

"Besides," I said, "there are nine million people in London. Imagine what would happen in an aerial bombardment frightful enough to create panic. The railways would be used for troops and transport. The roads would be choked. Its horror is unimaginable."

"It might be worth while saving some of the children," she answered.

Somehow, I thought, we must kill this fear lurking in so many minds. How tragic, how farcical, how damnable, that with all our massed intelligence, all our science, all our victories of civilisation, the minds of women should be haunted by this spectre of approaching horror for the children they have brought into the world! Gas masks for babies? The very devil wouldn't think of such abomination.

3 *The Failure of the League*

It was the breakdown of the League of Nations over Abyssinia and the abandonment of the Disarmament Conference which disconcerted the peace lovers and left them rather hopeless, and turned some of them into militarists.

They had pinned their faith to the principles of Collective Security. When Mussolini broke all his pledges to the League, refused arbitration, and massed his troops for attack against the Ethiopians, it looked, for a little while, as though the League would exert its authority and put into combined action its clauses of restraint against a nation judged to be guilty of flagrant aggression against any member nation of the League. By Article 16 of the Covenant sanctions were to be imposed on Italy. Fifty-eight nations agreed to impose them by cutting off Italy from all economic aid, with the screw gradually tightening until the stranglehold would be complete.

Mr Anthony Eden, that elegant young man representing the British government, rapped on the table of the League Council. He took a strong line, supported by his government at home. When Mussolini sent troops to Libya and money to stir up trouble in Egypt and Palestine, the British Lion suddenly sat up and roared. The British fleet steamed into the Mediterranean. It was a great surprise to the world. Many nations had regarded the British Lion as a mangy old beast who had turned pacifist. When it roared and banged its tail angrily it made the world jump. It made Mussolini angry. It seemed to him a very unfriendly act.

There was one day when I felt forked lightning in the air—an oppressive atmosphere. Other people were aware of it.

It was a day when we were within an hour or two of war with Italy, our old friend and ally. Soothing words sent to him by Sir Samuel Hoare prevented that tragedy. In any case, Mussolini held a trump card which made war unnecessary so long as the Suez Canal was open to him. This Collective Security urged by Anthony Eden on behalf of the League had broken down before it was tried out. The prime minister of France, M. Laval—that smiling man—had established a very close understanding with Italy. He had made a secret agreement with Mr Mussolini to turn a blind eye on any adventure in Abyssinia. To please Great Britain he was willing, and obliged, to support the sanctions up to a point, but not as far as oil, not as far as moving a ship or a gun against the Italian expedition.

Collective Security had a wide-open gap. Only military and naval force—that is, war—could stop the Italian army on its voyage to Abyssinia. No nation was willing to go as far as that, not even as far as stopping oil supplies while France under Laval was resolute against it. Any armed action would have to be done by the British navy. That would not be Collective Security. It would be a straight fight between Great Britain and Italy. By a strange paradox only the pacifists were in favour of that kind of war. They believed that if Mussolini cut the throat of Abyssinia the League would be mortally hurt and international law would no longer exist. The Left-minded people, hating Fascism, were all for war.

The British Lion had roared and everybody was much impressed. Then it began to curl its whiskers and wag its tail. British prestige had been high. Germany had watched with astonishment and admiration. But something seemed to slip when Sir Samuel Hoare drew up a peace plan which would have given great slices of Ethiopia to the aggressor before his victory, which seemed to many minds at that time difficult and remote. Sanctions, they thought, would prove effective in the long run if the Ethiopians could only hold out.

There was an outburst of passion in England.

"It is not Abyssinia which has been betrayed," wrote one of the correspondents to *The Times*, which was filled with such correspondence. "It is we who have been betrayed."

Mr Baldwin came running into Downing Street. He pledged the government anew to a strong and faithful allegiance to the League Covenant. Mr Anthony Eden, that resolute young man, became foreign secretary in the place of Sir Samuel Hoare, who wept when he made his *apologia* to the House of Commons.

It was all very dramatic. The voice of England had spoken. But, as a friend of mine wrote to me from the United States: "England speaks the wrong words."

"You needn't pay any attention to these alleged Italian victories," I was told by an air commodore in his drawing room one day.

He had just flown over Abyssinia and had seen its jagged mountain ranges.

"The Italians make a little advance and then have to draw back. It will take them years to penetrate that country where black tigers lie behind the rocks."

"The Italian claims to victory are all bluff," said a young American in the same room. He had just spent six months in Abyssinia as a newspaper correspondent. "The rains churn up their roads. Transport is in a frightful mess. If the Ethiopians keep to guerilla warfare they will hold out for years."

Less than two months afterwards the Italian army entered Addis Ababa, and Haile Selassie fled from his country. Poison gas and air bombs had broken the spirit of the Ethiopians. They had fled in black terror. They had died in heaps.

It was a "glorious victory" for Italy. What price glory? It was the utter defeat of the League and all its supporters. Collective Security had failed. There was no law in Europe. The smaller nations knew now that the League would be impotent to save them if one of the big bullies got after them. It was, for a time, the end of all dreams of international law based on justice and supported by sanctions.

It was one cause of that shadow which had long been in the minds of European peoples—the shadow of fear over many frontiers which now deepened and darkened. It reached England.

4 *Hitler's Germany*

This Italian adventure gave a shock to Mr Stanley Baldwin, not easily shocked into any galvanic activity until something "really must be done"—and to his advisers in the Admiralty, War Office, and Foreign Office. The government was beggared now of all slogans for the public soul. It was no use talking any more about their faith in the League. The League had been badly battered and had gone into dry dock for repairs, if possible. The Disarmament Conference had dragged along its weary way to death. No use reviving that, they thought, wrongly, as I venture to think.

Another menace, which seemed to them more dangerous than Italy, more powerful, filled them with alarm. Germany, under the Führer, was breaking the clauses of the Versailles Treaty. One by one they were being repudiated with a violence of unilateral action by the strange, inexplicable man who had attained a power in Germany greater than any of its kings and had almost assumed divine authority over the German tribes. He was the author of *Mein Kampf*, a book which does not exactly breathe out the spirit of peace. He was a hater of Communists, Socialists, pacifists and Jews. His Nazi regime, his Brown Shirts and Black Shirts, expressed to the outside world the bully creed. His concentration camps for Communists, Socialists, pacifists and Jews were not places of conversion by loving kindness. His friends, occupying the highest offices in the state, did not inspire confidence in the other nations as men of high morality or high intelligence.

Some of the new leaders in Germany under allegiance to Hitler, to whom they rendered almost divine honours, were obsessed by fantastic ideas which seemed to non-German minds mad and false and very dangerous to European civilisation. All their talk about the "Aryan Race" was mad and false. Some of them wanted to revive a faith in the old German gods and the pagan spirit.

It was a kind of woolly Wagnerism applied to modern life. They exalted physical strength, instinct, force, against intellectualism and all the code of European culture derived from the Christian faith and the Renaissance. The old tribal law of Germany, the old tribal worship of the hero and the chief was recalled and centred in the person of Adolf Hitler. The suppression of all minorities, the merging of all parties into a totalitarian state under one ruler, one discipline, and one obedience, seemed an outrage to English and French minds, who hold fast to the rights of free criticism and free speech. That was *verboten* in Germany under Hitler's rule. A rigid censorship of the Press, the radio, the cinema, the theatre, the publishing houses, and every form of education and expression cut off the German people from communication of thought with other minds. The swastika became a symbol of oppression, brutality, and intolerance to all Communists, Socialists, Liberals and intellectuals in countries calling themselves democratic. The state of Germany before the coming of Hitler, desperately divided into armed camps and ripe for bloody revolution, was ignored.

The German people were being drilled intensively. They were being subjected to an intensive propaganda which blared into their ears, and into their minds, ceaselessly, under the direction of that human talking machine Herr Goebbels.

Worse still, to the outside world, German youth seemed to like it! They did not resist this discipline. They gloried in it.

Visitors to Germany were impressed by the physical splendour of German youth, by those endless parades of young men and boys under the banners of the swastika. They were impressed—and frightened. What would happen if one day Hitler—that fanatic, that barnstormer, that apostle of hatred against Jews and Communists and pacifists and intellectuals, touched a button on his desk and ordered the mobilisation of these young legions? They were ready to die for him. They had sworn to do so if he called to them. They were, it seemed, in a state of exaltation, eager for self-sacrifice. Those were reasons why Germany under Hitler was regarded with fear by peoples beyond her frontiers. That fear grew into an obsession. It obsessed the French mind. It has taken possession of many English minds, especially on the Left of political thought. The New Germany has become the Big Bogey of Europe to many minds in England and to nearly all its newspapers, who find it very frightful and, morning after morning, make the flesh of their readers creep.

The intensive rearmament of Germany, especially in the air, was revealed most fully at a time when the League had broken down, and when international law had become a mockery even in the minds of those who had had most hope in its ultimate authority. Hitler was denounced as one of the lawbreakers when he repudiated the Treaty of Versailles by rearming and the Treaty of Locarno by sending his troops into the demilitarised zone of the Rhineland. European correspondents of the American Press—an able body of men—watched all this with pessimistic eyes and reported that war was immediate in Europe. For the past two years they have expected the explosion to happen. Some of them are surprised—not without cause—that it hasn't happened yet.

"When is this war going to break out?" asked American people of a friend of mine named Curtis Brown a few months ago. They were staggered when he answered cheerfully: "There ain't going to be no war!"

The English Press does not share his optimism. Every day for the past two years many newspapers in this country have kept their readers' nerves on edge. Every crisis becomes to them a new threat of a world war. Every analysis of the world situation leads them to the conclusion that war is coming nearer. Their correspondents in many countries emphasise these constantly arriving dangers. Politicians repeat dolorously that the international situation is "deteriorating."

It deteriorated very intensively when the Spanish Civil War aroused passionate emotion on the Left and Right of all political groups. Spain became the Tom Tiddler's ground into which half-a-dozen nations poured aeroplanes, tanks, all munitions of war, and volunteers, for a trial of strength between Democracy, as it was called, and Fascism, as it was called, though in that tragic arena of blood, and heroism, and murder, and mercilessness on both sides—a disgrace to civilisation, an outrage against all Christian chivalry—there were many parties and many groups—on both sides—which were neither one nor the other.

Labour and the Communists and the Left Wing intellectuals clamoured for intervention on the side of the Madrid government, though it might have led to a European war. The

French and British governments stood fast on nonintervention with that peril in their minds. The Non-Intervention Committee was a pantomime which served this purpose.

Is it any wonder that in the early part of this year when England spoke behind closed doors, in old houses, in small flats, in college rooms, in little restaurants, in clubs, and in bed-sitting-rooms, there was a sense of fear that another war might happen and that we were drifting to a calamity which would be the death of civilisation and the ruin of the Western world?

5 *Who Wants War?*

A man spoke to me on the stairs of a London club, and we stood there for twenty-five minutes, I should say, while other members passed and said "Hullo!" or "How d'you do?"

Twenty-odd years ago this man, who now has grey hair and sad-looking eyes because he is disgusted with the state of the world, was a young officer in a Scottish regiment, and while he stood talking to me his mind went back to a day in 1914. That was after a melancholy remark he had made because of the dark shadow which was on his mind.

"We are all marching towards war," he said. "Who can doubt it? There's no ill feeling against the Germans. They have no ill feeling against us. But we are being dragged into a state of things which can only lead to another conflict. Democracy has no power over its own fate; there is no such thing as Democracy. It's at the mercy of those on top."

It was then that his memory went back to a day in 1914, at Christmas time, when there was a truce between the lines, and his men and the Germans went out into no-man's land to bury their dead and started talking to each other. It lasted for three days, that truce.

"Do you want to go on fighting?" asked this Scottish officer of one of the German soldiers.

He answered with the title of an English song:

"Home, Sweet Home! That's all I want."

They all wanted that, on both sides. If it had been left to them they would have stopped killing each other. They had no enmity at all. They hated the war. They could see no sense in it. It was the men on top who were going on with the war.

"This rearmament of ours," said my friend, who used to be a Liberal M.P., "is a sign that we have surrendered the League of Nations ideal. Now the government is in the hands of the armament firms, and Labour is supporting rearmament because it creates work and wages—until the slump comes, or the explosion. We missed the boat when there was a chance of getting a general limitation in arms. I sometimes think it would have been better if the supporters of the League had not been non-party. All parties gave it lip service as a beautiful ideal about which no one really bothered."

"Why not accept Hitler's offer of a Western Pact?" I asked. "Isn't that the first step to peace in Europe? With Germany in the League again . . ."

He didn't agree. He thought it would be playing Germany's game. Britain and France would be kept quiet while Germany made all plans to attack Russia.

"But what evidence have we," I asked, "that Germany intends to attack Russia? And why should Western Europe be laid in ruin because of our sensitive regard for the most sinister government on earth, which is that of Stalin and his executioners? Why not get onto friendly terms with Germany and bring her back into the League or, at least, as a good neighbour? We can influence the Germans much more by friendship than by hostility. After making a Western Pact we could do something about the Eastern frontier."

GAS! THE DARK SHADOW

He hated Fascism. He had no faith in Hitler's sincerity. But he groaned over the bill of costs for British rearmament and its enormous folly, as he thought it.

"Think of what all that money would mean in social services and productive plans! We could create a paradise. Now I despair."

There were others like him in every part of England, and Scotland, and Wales.

One optimist took tea with me, a charming man whom I met at the council table of the Charing Cross Hospital.

"I wish you would write an article," he suggested, "about the point of view of the younger crowd in every country, showing that none of them want war. It would be a great service, and I am sure you could get a lot of material from different countries. It's only the elder statesmen who have got this war complex."

I made a few mental reservations. It was true that even the young Nazis of Germany don't want another war. But they would march with the exaltation of self-sacrifice if Hitler called them. What about the young Italians?

And yet I believe he is right—this distinguished little lawyer, Sir John Stewart-Wallace by name—whose heart flows with the milk of human kindness and whose eyes reveal a schoolboy humour, in spite of his dusty lawbooks and his legal dryness. The young people of Europe are not panting for poison gas or eagerly awaiting the signal for their own blinding, and maiming, and agony of death. It seems to them no cheerful prospect.

6 *An Exhibition of Modern Culture*

I dropped into an exhibition arranged for public edification by the municipal authorities of Kensington, where once I used to live.

Now, when I walk through Kensington Gardens, I think of those peaceful days of my young manhood when I used to play with a small boy on the coast of that Sea of Adventure—the Round Pond—where thousands of small boys have watched their craft go out on distant voyages from which, on days of dead calm, they never came back. Those small boys grew up just in time, some of them, for a world war in which they were wanted, and they, too, so many of them, never came back.

Those ghost memories were in my head when I went through Kensington Gardens on the way to this exhibition at the Town Hall. It was an antigas exhibition to teach the people of Kensington what best to do in their homes if another war should come—its warnings seemed to suggest that there was considerable likelihood of its coming—when enemy aircraft would drop bombs filled with poisonous gases to blind, choke and kill the population of London.

By taking the advice kindly provided by the Home Office and passed on to the municipality of Kensington, it was suggested that precautions against this uncomfortable possibility should be taken in advance—today or tomorrow, if possible—and that by a few little gadgets—bits of stick, brown paper, gluepots and the glazed paper on cigarette boxes or chocolate boxes—Kensington families might avoid all disagreeable consequences of mustard gas or other varieties of poison vapour.

There was a little crowd in the exhibition, including old gentlemen of Kensington who were very much interested in this show and seemed to approve of its purpose thoroughly—"The nation wants waking up!" said one of them—and a number of ladies from Kensington Gore, Holland Street and Campden Hill (I guessed) who seemed to accept this chamber of horrors as complacently as they would go round Harrods to see the latest fashions.

"Most interesting!" . . . "It seems to me very necessary." . . .

"Now, isn't that a good idea?" . . . "So simple too! Really I think we must do something about it."

There were rooms of small size, representing bathrooms and bedrooms, converted into antigas chambers. Bits of stick had been tacked onto the doorways and round the windows. Wet blankets, or cloth of some fibrous stuff, made antigas curtains. The very latest types of gas mask suitable for Kensington ladies were exhibited on the tables. Lists of articles to be kept in a gasproof chamber before an expected, or unexpected, air raid were printed on big cards. They included domestic and sanitary utensils, a screen, drinking water, biscuits, toys for the children, playing cards for the grownups, and other items which might agreeably pass the time while the enemy was dropping bombs. It was really all very charming, to those whose minds work that way.

In charge of the exhibit were some young women in Red Cross uniforms. I ventured to speak to one.

"Don't you think it might be better to prevent a war rather than go in for this kind of thing?"

"Excellent idea!" she answered brightly. "How are you going to do it?"

"Doesn't this seem to you a surrender of reason?" I asked this good-looking girl with very steady eyes which looked frankly into mine.

"An acceptance of war, do you mean?" she asked.

"Yes. That's how it seems to me."

"There's only one kind of defence, really," she told me, looking over her shoulder as though she might be overheard; "that's by retaliation. I suppose if we're strong enough to retaliate we shan't be attacked. Isn't that the best hope?"

"What's the good of all this nonsense?" I asked. "Do you honestly think it's any good at all?"

She was very honest.

"It might save a few. That's better than saving none."

I wanted to have further conversation with her. She reminded me of a girl I had known before the war and in the war, a very brave young woman named Dorothy Feilding who had helped the wounded lying on Belgian battlefields, quite regardless of her own danger. This Red Cross girl would do the same kind of thing, I thought, in the streets of London if this horror came. She would try to save a few babies from being killed by poison gas, before her own body became mangled by high explosives which hostile aircraft would also drop. But I could see that she was getting bored with me, as she had every reason to be. She wasn't there to answer questions by a stern-looking inquisitor.

So this, I thought, as I wandered round alone, is what we are coming to! What a beautiful revelation of the civilisation we have reached in this year of grace! What a lovely introduction to life for young children who are to be instructed on the wearing of gas masks, instead of reading fairy tales, and who are to be told that in a year or two they may have to take their dolls into a blanketed room to escape from a poisonous breath creeping through the streets, while millions, who are unprepared, choke to death or are burnt and blistered! There will be the crash of heavy bombs, destroying many houses and burying their inhabitants under their ruins. There will be incendiary bombs, dear children, making bonfires in the sky and roasting thousands of people in their flames. You see, darling, the nasty Germans want their colonies back, but if you are very good, and wear your gas masks nicely, and play in those comfy little rooms with their cracks pasted up, our dear Lord will look after you, and possibly let you remain alive and see the ruins afterwards. Won't that be nice?

Great God! I thought, going round that exhibition in Kensington. So this is the best that mankind is doing with its intelligence! This is the latest exhibition of our Brave New World! Without any poison gas, I felt poisoned.

And a few days later I read a report about these Home Office recommendations for air-raid precautions. It was by a number of scientists at Cambridge and was published in a small book entitled *Protection of the Public from Aerial Attack*, published by Gollancz.

The experimenters, who included two women, converted four rooms—shop basement, villa dining room, council house sitting room, modern bathroom—into gasproof rooms according to the official handbook.

They found that gas penetrated bricks and plaster, cracks covered with brown paper and mushed paper, blocked-in fireplaces and sealed doors.

In one room gas, which outside would kill in two and a half minutes, would kill inside within ten.

In the bathroom—with steel-framed windows, tiled walls, concrete floor—gas would penetrate and kill within four hours.

Then they tested incendiary bombs—classified as a greater danger than gas or high explosives—and found that the sand-spreading advised was useless.

Welding thermit, a comparatively mild incendiary compound, defied all such efforts, burned under water, through metal, through sand, through floors.

"If we take a specimen raid of nine bombers, each carrying a thousand small bombs, nine thousand could be dropped on an area of two square miles.

"Allowing that in an urban area only a fifth of these cause fires, that means 1,800 fires. The danger of fires spreading over several blocks of buildings, making the centre of the conflagration quite unapproachable by fire brigades, is obvious.

"On hearing the warning people will rush to their gasproof rooms, and then when incendiary bombs set fire to the upper parts of their dwellings they will either run out and be caught by the gas or stay inside and be roasted alive.

"This is how they would act if they follow the instructions of the Home Office."

Gas masks tested were found useless against mustard gas and lewisite.

Protection for tiny children is shown to be impossible, and the report pictures children, sealed up in containers, screaming themselves into fits, with the mother trying to pump air to several at once.

Would fathers and mothers protect themselves and watch their children suffocate? they ask.

The full absurdity of all this is shown by a criticism of the Home Office advice: "Set aside a room in your house."

In England and Wales, say the scientists, 1,910,000 people are living already under overcrowded conditions. Another 6,759,000 would be overcrowded if they attempted to carry out the advice.

So 8,669,000 would find a gasproof room impossible.

As for evacuating big cities by train—a few bombs on the termini would stop traffic for days.

We had better concentrate on stopping that next war if possible, for if it comes, retaliation is no protection.

VII

Those Who Wear Wings

1 One of Our Air Pilots

I WENT to tea at a house in London where I am always sure of a friendly welcome and pleasant people round about the table.

It is like a country mansion with big rooms and big open fireplaces where, in winter, logs are burning. In summer the sun—if there is any sun—streams through the casement windows, and there is a garden behind the house with a lawn smooth and large enough for croquet, which the mistress of the house is pleased to play with her friends. Birds sing in the bushes. Once, I swear, I heard a nightingale, though if one has listening ears one hears very faintly the murmur of London traffic. It is fifteen minutes by taxi from Oxford Circus.

At that tea table, round which we sat in a homely way—there were some nice hot cakes thereon—I noticed two youngish men whom I had met before. They were, as I knew, "those who mount with wings as eagles." That is to say, they were pilots in the Royal Air Force.

There were some women at the table and laughter touched our talk. It was all very pleasant and very comfortable. This, I thought, is what civilisation means at its best: a pleasant room, a cheerful company round a tea table, conversation which is merry and open minded. One would not have to put a guard upon one's tongue, as one has to in some countries nowadays, or be afraid to express one's ideas on any subject which comes into one's mind. This was Liberty Hall. England itself is still Liberty Hall where one's mind is free.

One of the flying men sitting on my right picked up some phrase of mine. I have forgotten what it was, but I have an idea it was something about a recent visit I had paid to Germany.

"I suppose you know we're living in a fool's paradise?" he asked, with a queer ironical smile. "This country is in considerable danger, and nobody seems to know, and nobody cares a damn!"

He said something like that and there was an intensity in his voice which startled me, and a look in his eyes which I could not misinterpret. It was the look of a man who has something desperate on his mind.

"Don't you pay the slightest attention to him," said my hostess. "He has been trying to frighten me. If I believed a word of it I shouldn't be able to sleep a wink."

"No, no!" said the young airman, laughing good-naturedly, but a little uneasily, perhaps. "I'm not a scaremonger. But I hate eyewash and a false sense of security."

"Have another toasted bun," said the lady.

He had another toasted bun. The conversation went round the table in a lighthearted way. But I knew that the boy on my right was seething with something he knew and didn't like.

After tea four of us—all men—went into another room where there was another fire. They were the two young flying men and my host and myself. Three of us lit cigarettes.

"Did you see anything of what they were doing in the air in Germany?" asked the young pilot who had been on my right at the tea table and now was in a deep armchair with his legs outstretched.

FLIRTING WITH DEATH . . . .

I hadn't seen much of a technical kind. But I had spent a little time at the Flughaven near Berlin where there was great activity in civil aviation. Big aeroplanes, holding many passengers, had come in from different countries, keeping to a timetable with the regularity of railway trains. I had been impressed by the German genius for organisation. They were getting ahead of us altogether in the civil side of flying.

And I remembered a journey I had made through Germany when I had been startled by the tremendous propaganda which was being given to this development of aviation. At the entrance to small villages I had seen banners stretched across the roads.

Lift Up Your Eyes.
Our Future Is in the Air.
Help German Aviation.

In Berlin and other cities young German aviators had shaken collection boxes under the noses of the crowds. It was a kind of good-natured blackmail. Everybody had to pay tribute, however small. I remembered talking to a German woman in the market place at Stuttgart. She had told me frankly that she was afraid sometimes of all this intensive effort to put machines into the sky.

The flying man threw away his cigarette and spoke quietly but with a kind of restrained passion.

"Germany has developed her air force beyond all our calculations. She's doing it with an efficiency and organising power beyond the limited imagination of our people. Meanwhile our so-called statesmen and politicians hand out blather and eyewash to the nation. I don't know what you think about the international situation, but it seems to me . . ."

At that time it was distinctly unpleasant. We were still at cross-purposes with Signor Mussolini. Our prestige had fallen to a low ebb. Germany had repudiated the Locarno Treaty. The

Labour party was becoming militarist. No, the international situation was not agreeable.

The flying man thought it abominable. The League of Nations had proved itself impotent, he said, in a major crisis. Collective Security had failed in this Abyssinian affair, which was its supreme test.

"I'm not an alarmist," he went on, "but I suppose you would agree that some damn silly accident might happen, some combination of bandits might make trouble, or war might be forced upon us to defend vital interests. Germany might be our enemy again. Do you agree to that possibility?"

I hated to think so. It would be the end of everything which we find good or endurable.

"If war happened," said my flying friend, "it would come suddenly, perhaps without an ultimatum. German bombers would appear over London, flying high, at high speeds. Here before we knew they were coming!"

He looked me in the eyes and said something which made me feel rather cold, although the fire was still burning on the big hearth.

"We have no defence and no means of retaliation."

I couldn't believe that and told him so.

"What about our expansion scheme? The white paper! All this rearmament! Aren't we vastly increasing our fighting force in the air?"

The young airman laughed bitterly.

"Official dope! The expansion scheme is mainly on paper. It's faked arithmetic, put out by the Air Ministry to keep the nation lulled to sleep and ignorant of its appalling dangers. The higher control of the Air Force are the cause of all this mess, and their main preoccupation at the moment is to cover their past failures and deficiencies. Their concealment of these facts can only be done by going on with concealment. Men who have failed in the past—blind to the technical and tactical problems of air-fighting—go from important to more important posts, and this line of inefficiency continues without a break. Hopeless!"

He looked across at the other aviator.

"Am I exaggerating at all, do you think?"

The other man shook his head.

"The painful truth! Every experienced pilot knows it perfectly well."

The boy who wanted to get these things off his chest was silent for a little while and then sat forward in his chair.

"Germany has a pretty shrewd idea of what's going on," he said. "Do you think she won't exploit her advantage one day? Then where shall we be, say, in two years' time?"

He uttered another alarming sentence.

"Our Air Force can't strike a blow of any kind at Germany from England. We haven't a single bomber with the range that would carry it to Berlin and back, working under war conditions. Somebody ought to tell the truth about all this. How can one sit tight and say nothing when we are risking the life of the nation?"

The two air pilots went on talking.

2 *A Grave Indictment*

It was a terrible indictment which afterwards I heard from other sources of information. The present situation reveals that technically we haven't the aircraft, equipment or organisation which would give us the power we should need in another war. There is an appalling dilution of skilled personnel by hastily trained learners. Our biggest bombers have a short range, and are so slow compared with aircraft possessed by other nations that they couldn't hope to survive a long flight across hostile country, and do not possess the air endurance, at any endurable speed, to permit of them operating from home bases into a country as far away as Germany. The increase of the Air Force is based on the production of machines of these old-fashioned, slowgoing types of bombers.

"If we have a war forced upon us in the next few years we shall be powerless to retaliate in the air."

My host looked very grave but kept extraordinarily silent. I wondered about all this. I could hardly believe it. Perhaps the man who did most of the talking was fanatical on some theory, or disgruntled for some personal reason, or obsessed by the fear of a German menace. There was no doubt in my mind about the last point. He had no faith in German peace-mindedness. He gave them about two years—if that—before they strike. They were just playing for time, he thought. We should have to play for longer time than that, and even then we should be no match for Germany in the air, because all our policy was wrong, and under existing conditions of design and manufacture we should never catch up.

All this must be taken with heavy discount, I thought. This flying man is exaggerating his case and not making allowance for the government's plan of development. Anyhow, Germany is not going to attack us. Hitler offers a Western pact. Why don't we take it? The whole of the German people are deeply anxious for our friendship—I know that as a fact. In my mind I was busy with this thought of German friendliness. Supposing I was wrong? Supposing some new crisis happened in Europe which might cut across Germany's vital interests or ours and brought us to a clash? France and Russia. Spain. Austria. Czecho-Slovakia. There were many possibilities of danger, as I knew. Supposing the friendly feelings of the German people were suddenly switched off to anger? Supposing a little bell rang on

Hitler's desk one day, mobilising all his young braves? These questions stirred in my mind. Who could answer them with absolute certainty?

I left the house where those two airmen had been talking, and had a sense of dark doubt. I didn't believe in piling up armaments as the way to peace. I was a League of Nations man. Ever since the war I had written little words on bits of paper with the simple purpose of revealing the stupidity, beyond even the horror, of war and working for a reconciliation of nations and the re-establishment of civilised intelligence. Lately I had been on that Arms Commission with the hope in my head that it might help a little in checking the intensive competition in armaments by a general limitation under international control. It would be out of my mental frame to become a propagandist for more and better bombing aeroplanes. But the League system had broken down for a time. Collective Security had failed. The Labour party—utterly illogical—were breathing fire and blood against Fascist nations and, at the same time, discouraging recruiting and preparations for defence—or attack. Our ministers were talking to Germany like schoolmasters to naughty boys. Italy had become hostile to us. Our Foreign Office was associating its policy with that of France, but France was linked too closely for her own safety, and ours, perhaps, with Russia. Something might "slip." The sticking plaster holding European peace together might break somewhere. What then? What would happen to England if hostile bombers became active in our sky? What would happen to London and its nine million inhabitants? . . . What had that fellow said?

"We have no means of defence. Our Air Force is incapable of striking a blow against Germany from England."

"What's the matter?" asked a friend of mine whom I met on the way home. "You look as if you had heard bad news. Worried about something?"

"Worried about human stupidity," I answered. "This planet is not governed by intelligence. We're all going stark raving mad again."

He was very much amused.

"We've never been sane," he answered cheerfully.

3 *There Is No Defence*

I listened to a debate in defence in the House of Commons. Mr Winston Churchill, the right honourable gentleman below the gangway, as they called him, sat making notes while the talk went on. Presently he stood up and attacked the government for delays in expanding the Air Force. The government programme and pledges, he said, had broken down completely. We had been promised parity with Germany by a certain date. We were not approaching such equality with Germany with its present air strength of 1,500 front-line machines. He deplored "the years that the locusts had eaten."

As I listened to this debate I looked down upon the members of the House and the two front-line benches where ministers and ex-ministers sat in various attitudes of mild interest or mild boredom. The government men and their supporters, with few exceptions, seemed satisfied with Sir Thomas Inskip's report of progress. There was no sense of national danger sufficient to disturb their placidity of mind. They seemed to accept the inevitability of delay as though there were lots of time ahead, anyhow. Churchill's portentous phrases were what they expected from him but did not make them turn pale or hear from afar the noise of wings over Europe. Words! Political argument with—party bias. An interesting debate. . . . Who goes home?

All this had only touched lightly upon the difficulties and delays in expanding our Air Force. But after that debate I came into possession of facts—they seemed to me reliable—which revealed the reasons why the young airman with whom I had taken tea one day had no touch of breezy optimism but was gravely anxious. Those facts were given to me, I suppose, because I might have the power of the pen to stir up the nation to a sense of its unprotectedness in the air and to bring pressure upon the government to awake from its stupor. Those who were my informants acted, I am certain, from a high sense of duty to the nation and were ready to sacrifice their own careers that the truth might be known. The whole truth is not yet known, though some of it was exposed and admitted in another debate of the House on January 27 of this year.

Sir Thomas Inskip acknowledged very frankly that the original plan calling for the provision of 71 new squadrons of 12 first-line aircraft in each squadron, making 124 in all, had broken down in the timetable. Only 87 squadrons had so far been formed, though he anticipated that 100 would be reached by the end of March of this year. The remaining 24, "or at least 20," would be ready by July of this year. But not all of them would be real squadrons but only skeletons of one or more flight each, and Sir Thomas was not able to say that by that time they would be brought up to their full complement.

Mr Churchill urged that there was an enormous percentage of deficiency. If 124 squadrons were completed by March 31 it would still not give us parity with German strength at that date, nor anything like it. We had been solemnly promised that there should be parity. We had not got it. We had no right, he said, to assume that any quarrel would arise from Germany, but that was not the basis on which we discussed those military matters. We should have no parity during the whole of 1937 and he doubted whether we should have it in the whole of 1938. He again asserted the truth of the figure which he had given last November, that the German strength then was 1,500 front-line machines. It was, he thought, considerably more now. Actually, the Germans were believed to possess 150 formed squadrons of 12 machines each. That gave the figure of 1,800 front-line machines at the present time.

The debate put many cards on the table which had been held back, but by no means all of them. Many of these had been placed before the prime minister in a secret report by Mr Churchill, who found himself in the position of having a mass of information of an alarming character, as to lack of efficiency and failure in the very basis of planning and design, which he could hardly publish to the world without the revelation of secrets which might encourage potential enemies.

Curiously enough, I found myself in the same position. I had notes of a very technical and secret character which seemed to me too important to ignore or hold in my own knowledge. They were a grave indictment of official complacency, official inefficiency, and of a most distressing state of things in the Royal Air Force which would endanger the lives of our young pilots in time of peace and lead to inevitable disaster should there be war. But I could not bring myself to publish them in the Press in a series of scare articles. I decided to put them into the hands of the man who had taken up this subject and made himself the spokesman of the case for a strong Air Force. That was Winston Churchill, who might care to have my notes, though I might be "carrying coals to Newcastle." In his secret report he must have dealt with these facts, or some of them.

Meanwhile, in many countries—Germany, France, Italy, Russia, Japan, the United States—there was at the beginning of this year a ceaseless endeavour to increase the numbers of fighting aircraft, their range, their speed, the bomb-carrying capacity, and the number of their trained pilots and crews. The Civil War in Spain had been a testing ground for some of these new types, and on a small scale—though very terrible to the

GAS WITHOUT MASKS—THE HOUSE IS SITTING

manhood, womanhood and childhood in Spain—their power of destruction had been revealed. Man, who after long ages has mastered the secret of flight and given himself wings—"they mount with wings as eagles"—by which he is capable of rising very high not only into the blue but into new adventures of civilisation and splendour, is now terrified of this new power which he has created. For all this talk of ground defence against hostile aircraft is, I fear, mere dope to lull public terror. At the heights they go, at the speeds they go, there is no defence from the earth and very little in the sky. Over great cities enemy aircraft would find their way and drop their bombs. It would not be a decisive method of attack unless the morale of enormous populations densely crowded were overcome by mass panic and mass slaughter. That is doubtful. Man has inexhaustible reserves of endurance against all horror. He is incredibly brave when it comes to self-preservation and the last chance of survival. Men and women would dive into cellars, as in Spain, though many dead lay in the ruins. The survivors would crawl out to fight their invaders. War would go on; and whatever is meant by victory, when everything is ruined and much is dead, would go to those most able to stand the terror from the air with unbroken spirit. But why need these horrors come among nations proud of their intelligence? Why should this madness of mutual destruction replace the orderly settlement of disputes between nations all pledged to abstain from war as an act of policy, all fearful, all fully conscious, of its ruin—win or lose?

But what alarmed me most about the criticisms of our air efficiency was the awful thought that all this intensification of armament, now being carried out by our government, may be controlled by minds like those which were in charge of our war machine in 1914. Those minds of cavalry officers, promoted to high command by social pull, good looks and the camaraderie of a caste, were not exactly inspiring of confidence among the men who were condemned to die in a World War. The official history of the war does not break down the suspicion that they were unequal to the job in hand. Is there any new assurance that the men who are now in high command—in the Air Ministry, for instance—are of a different mental calibre from those who were Brass Hats in France and Flanders?

That is rather frightening.

VIII

The Red Dream

1 A Russian Fairy Tale

ALTHOUGH in England we are a lucky people compared with many others, there are groups of men and women among us, some of them with high brows, and many with low, who dream Red. The high-brows—I could name them—have a kind of religious reverence for an old ghost who in his lifetime, eighty years ago, masked himself behind a wealth of whiskers and wrote a book which has caused the death of millions by civil war, revolutions, murder, typhus, famine, and all brands of misery. The name of the hairy man was Karl Marx and the title of his book is *Das Kapital.*

I once tried to read that book and found it very difficult and dreary. But other people who have actually read it—most of those who worship at the shrine of Karl Marx have not read it—think it wonderful. Professor Laski, for instance, thinks it wonderful. I was dining opposite to him one night in a private party and he made a statement which astonished me.

"Before I studied Marx," he said to me across the table, "I could get no real basis of political and economic philosophy, but I found his work extraordinarily stimulating, and it gave me for the first time a sense of optimism."

I confessed that my unsuccessful endeavour to master *Das Kapital* had left me with a sense of profound gloom. For as far as I understood the main thesis of the author, it was that human society was moving towards an inevitable class conflict, because under Capitalism the poor were bound to get poorer and the rich richer until that immense gap caused a break of the whole system which would be followed by the dictatorship of the proletariat.

The old gentleman in the white whiskers and a Father Christmas beard was the apostle of the Class War. That doesn't seem to me a cause of joy. Yet one has only to look around one's own country, and others, to see that, apparently, his prophecy has not come true. Here in England that gap between the classes is not widening, it seems, but closing. Taxation gets after the big fortunes. The condition of the working classes is enormously improved since the date of that book. Our great industrialists—or some of them—have developed a social conscience. Nevertheless, those high-brows whose thoughts are coloured red still regard Marxism as the gospel of economic faith.

They have what seems to me a fairy tale in their minds. It is untouched by reality or by the cold evidence of truth. It has its origin in Russia. Their imagination is haunted by Moscow. The Soviet system of life seems to them the goal towards which humanity must move to establish peace and happiness on earth. At the very name of Russia one sees a look of softness in their eyes as though they were Catholic mystics who see the Beatific Vision.

I was struck by that one evening when I was invited to dinner by a charming friend of mine who "threw a party", as they say in the United States. It was a "stag party." Round the table sat fifteen youngish men, nearly all of them writers of books not without fame. I knew their names. I had read some of their books. I felt humble in their presence, for they were the daring lads—English and American—who are very advanced in their range of thought.

Charming young men, I found them. One of them had just written a book on Europe which was having a world-wide sale. Suddenly someone began talking about Russia, and, looking round the table, I saw the eyes of these youngish intellectuals go soft with that peculiar light which comes from inward ecstasy. Russia! Ah, what a country! It was making immense progress in industrialisation. It was beginning to lead the world in aviation and crowding the sky with bombing aeroplanes. The Soviet system was, of course, the ultimate ideal of humanity. That fellow Stalin! What a brain! Fascism, with its half-wit dictators, would crumple up before the assault of Marxian idealism. Nothing could check democratic ideology in the long run. Russia was solving the economic problem.

I did not intervene in this discussion. My knowledge of Russia is becoming distant—as far back as the days when twenty-five million people were starving (four and a half million died on the Volga), when everyone in Russia was hungry, when millions were dying of typhus. Perhaps things had improved since then. Some of these young men had been recently to Moscow as journalists. But as I listened to them I wondered why they seemed to believe in a Grimm fairy tale which leaves out the witches, the goblins and the ogres. How did they account, I wondered, for those trials and executions of the old Bolshevik leaders? Did they believe in those confessions of guilt? If so, then those who made the Russian revolution—their former heroes—were gangsters and gunmen without moral sense. If they didn't believe, then Stalin and the present rulers of Russia were murderers and torturers.

Did they honestly think that the condition of the Russian people was higher than in this country where they sat at table talking freely? Did they believe that liberty was there—any kind of free thought or free speech? Did they still believe that there was equality of class and equality of reward? Had they not seen the well-dressed and well-fed kommissars at the Mariinsky Theatre with their bourgeoise-looking women, and the Russian peasants, or labourers in the timber camps, not well dressed and not well fed, but miserable, and verminous, and hungry? Why this admiration for the mechanisation of Russian life—and the herding of peasants into collective farms, and the crowding of the sky with bombing aeroplanes, and the iron discipline of the ant heap? They used the words "Democracy" and "Liberty." Had they really seen such things in Russia? Or had they dreamed a fairy tale?

No doubt in Russia today there are millions of young people excited by the adventure of life and fairly pleased with it. The loud speakers, blasting forth propaganda, persuade them that they are greatly privileged to live in such an enlightened state. There is intensive education to make them machine minded and efficient—though they are nowhere near the standard of England, or Germany, or the United States. In railway stations and village halls they educate each other in elementary science, strictly censored, in elementary knowledge, strictly censored, equal perhaps to that doled out to English students in night classes since the foundation of Birkbeck College and free elementary education. All that is not too bad. It may lead somewhere, sometime. But is there in Russia any sign of a more beautiful civilisation, nobler ideals, a more spiritual vision of life, than in this bourgeois England? I do not find that in such books as those by Maurice Hindus, favourable to this system as he is. I find only descriptions of a dreary squalor in overcrowded houses, half-baked ideas of young fanatics, mean envies, jealousies and ambitions, a low-grade type of life compared with which our unemployed are lords of luxury. I do not find it in such a book as *I Was a Soviet Worker* by Andrew Smith, an American Communist who reveals that now, in 1937, there is still misery, filth, hunger, horrible vice, and horrible cruelty in Soviet Russia.

2 *Intellectual "Reds"*

At another party given by the same charming young friend of mine I sat opposite a man who is known throughout the English-speaking world as a fine scientist and thought-provoking brain. He dreams in Latin and is delirious in Greek. Presently he began to talk about Karl Marx, and the Russian revolution, and the creed of Communism. He seemed to see something fine and noble in what to others, like myself, appears to be a denial of intellectual liberty and the tyranny of Terror. This scientist, by some trick of the brain, was able to ignore the agonies and cruelties which have gone to make this Russian experiment of a new social system, or to weigh them lightly in the balance compared with agonies and cruelties inflicted on mankind by capitalism. He has persuaded himself that the results have justified all that suffering—results which appear in that low-grade civilisation now existing in Russia, that discipline of human ants, that tyranny of Cheka and Ogpu.

What is the mystery, or the secret vision, which causes such a mind as this—it belongs to Professor Haldane—to worship at the shrine of Lenin and pay homage to Stalin, that man of steel and blood? Professor Haldane has the courage of his convictions. He went to Spain, risking his own life to see how Spaniards kill each other. The B.B.C. gave him the air to tell us that always he would thank God that he was in Madrid on Christmas Day, where he saw brave men fighting and dying in defence of Liberty. He said nothing of the morgue in Madrid where lay the corpses of men and women shot each day by murder gangs. He spoke no word of pity, no word of horror, no word condemning that passionate vendetta which on both sides has disgraced the chivalry of Spain.

And yet Professor Jack Haldane has a fine brain, a gay humour, and, I am certain, a kindly heart. Other brains not so high as his, but quite intelligent—our little intellectuals—are seeing Red and dreaming Red, though they have never read Karl Marx nor walked across the Red Square below the Kremlin walls. They do not seem to know that Communism has been abandoned, largely, in Soviet Russia, which now has inequality of class and wages, recognises private property and the right of inheritance, and has established a corrupt and mean bureaucracy above a mass in human bondage.

3 *The Ardent Mind of Youth*

This Red dream touches the ardent mind of youth, here and there, in universities, training colleges, and bed-sitting-rooms. Undergraduates of Oxford gather in St Giles to hear Red stuff from London propagandists. A group of them formed their own Communist society called the October Club in honour of the Bolshevik Revolution in October 1917. Its membership was something under three hundred when it was dissolved towards the end of 1935 and amalgamated with the University Labour Club. The Federation of Student Societies which covered Red activities among all the universities has now been merged with the University Labour Federation. At Oxford and Cambridge there are ardent advocates of the United Front and passionate partisans of class war.

One of them—the son of an old friend of mine—honoured my wife and myself with a visit and was good enough to take tea with us. He is a very handsome young man with dark dreamy eyes in which at times there is a gentle smile. A poet, one would

TERROR BY NIGHT

say at first glance. But we didn't talk of poetry that afternoon. We talked of something more dangerous even than poetry. We talked of Communism.

He is a very intellectual young man and one of the leaders of the Extreme Left at Oxford. He and his sister, who was also up at Oxford for a time, are a remarkable pair in many ways. They have tramped about Europe, sleeping in German youth hostels and Austrian guesthouses. They speak German. They seem to know quite a lot about the European situation from firsthand knowledge, gained in places where youth talks loudly.

My wife and I gave the young man a fair innings and listened with amiable consideration. He did not believe in tolerance, he told us. Tolerance meant acquiescence in injustice—such as in the distressed areas—and the cruelties of the Capitalist system, which of course, he said, was beginning to break down everywhere. The younger people of his crowd looked forward to the end of all that by direct action and the removal of the old deadheads. Old age, he thought, had been too long in power. It wasn't their fault, of course, but their minds were incapable of moving forward and accepting any other system than the one into which they had been born.

"Everybody over the age of forty," said this humane young man, "ought to be shot."

My wife and I glanced at each other. We were, alas, over the age of forty.

"Their minds are too rigid," he explained gently. "One has to realise that nothing can be done in this country until that generation is safely dead. Then we can get busy, shaping things differently. Of course there will have to be a fight, anyhow. I am not one of those who believe that the system can be changed without bloodshed. Vested interests, the defenders of Capital, the diehard type of mind, the Fascist spirit, which is latent in snob minds, will have to be defeated—and they won't surrender without a struggle. I shall live to see the day when the barricades are up in London streets. One has to take a risk for an ideal. We shall have to risk our lives for the sake of humanity and the future."

"Supposing," said my wife very quietly, "that I happened to appear on the other side of your particular barricade? What would you do?"

Our distinguished visitor—that charming young man—took another piece of cake and flicked a crumb from his knee.

"I should shoot you," he said sadly but firmly.

It was an interesting conversation. I wondered how many followers this young man had at Oxford. When I saw him off from the front door, after listening a considerable time to his critical attack upon the Capitalistic system and his intellectual argument for the creed of Communism—once or twice I saw the little flame of fanaticism in his dark eyes—I apologised for being such an old-fashioned man as to disagree with him profoundly.

"It's quite all right," he said in a kindly way. "You can't help it. You're one of the old Liberals, of course. You belong to that era."

I belonged, in his mind, to the damned dead past.

4 *Impatience of the Younger Mind*

These young intellectual Communists are not to be taken too seriously, although they are influencing other minds, especially if they become schoolmasters and writers after college days.

What is the lure to them in this creed which, in every country where it works, leads to civil strife, murder and all cruelties? Is it due to a twisted morality in their minds? Is it some subtle poison of the brain? I think that among the younger intellectuals it is due to generous instincts—hatred of injustice, pity for the underdog, impatience with the slowness of social reform under parliamentary government, and disgust with the insincerities of the political game.

That emotion of sympathy with the down-and-outs, or the populations of the distressed areas, overwhelms their judgment and their sense of proportion. Because half a million people or so in this country are living in poor social conditions—which are getting better—they see red and are willing and, indeed, eager to drag down forty-eight and a half million people to the same equality of squalor. Because Parliament is incapable of rapid action, and the government twiddles its thumbs on the Front Bench while flagrant abuses cry out for redress, they ridicule the parliamentary system and proclaim the blessings of Soviet rule and the need of revolutionary action.

I can understand this impatience of the younger intellectuals. They went out to hear the stories of the Jarrow marchers and were angered. I don't blame them, for Jarrow is not a pleasant story, anyhow, and is no credit to a Conservative government, which, year after year, has left the men of Jarrow without lifting a finger to give them a chance of work. They played into the hands of sinister interests who blocked the only scheme—a new steel works—which would bring back life to Palmer's Yards. Even when the armament industry was in full blast, with rush orders, and arranged to lay down new steel works, it was not at Jarrow but at Scunthorpe—an obscure place in Lincolnshire—that they proposed to put down plant.

As the mayor of Jarrow, in great indignation, wrote to *The Times:*

> The Government's policy towards the Special Areas is a curious one. Surveys, Special Commissioners, public work schemes are all to the good, but surely these should be mere preparation for the introduction of permanent industry. On the eve of the introduction

of a Government Bill in Parliament to deal with Special Areas we read, only six months after the Jarrow scheme was turned down, of a new steel works in a small Lincolnshire town (which is not in a Special Area) which will employ between 2,000 and 3,000 more men than are employed at the present time.

These men will presumably be expected to come from other centres, leaving behind them a waste of social capital and necessitating doubtless the building of houses, roads, schools for their children, and other public works, and the provision of public services which they leave behind, whence they came, to be wasted.

That kind of thing makes men see red, even though the red dream is an illusion in its fairy tale, and here, if one tried to make it real, would lead to a river of blood and irredeemable ruin, more even than in Russia, which is less finely balanced in its social mechanism and more firmly planted on the soil.

Other voices call to the young intellectuals of our universities and to students in their bed-sitting-rooms where they look up from their books and hear the murmur of life in the streets; or go to a window and look across the chimney pots, and wonder at the meaning and mystery of life which they have to face and try to understand.

How is it, they ask, that there are so many anxieties pressing down on individual lives? There is no sense of security, no certainty of getting a job, even if an underpaid job. How can a man fulfil his life as nature intended? Where is his mate? How can he afford the luxury of love? He is shabby, overworked, uneasy in his mind, out of tune with life itself. Perhaps Marxism makes things easier, he thinks. In return for service to the state a man gets his food, clothes, amusements and lodging. No nagging landladies demanding arrears for lodgings. No class distinction of dress and snobbishness. No sense of insecurity. Free love, even if there is no free speech. A level of equality with one's fellows, without the damned injustice of prodigious wealth garnered into a few hands—the manipulators of money, the masters of machines, the Merchants of Death, the people with a pull, the jugglers with bears and bulls, while the mass of the population lives in dreary drudgery not sharing the fruits of their own toil. This Capitalism? "Oh, God!" cries the young intellectual, who doesn't believe in a deity but feels very moody on a Monday morning or inflamed with intellectual fervour on a Saturday night after three cocktails in another fellow's rooms. I can understand all that perfectly! As a French writer has said: "A man who is not a Marxist at twenty has no heart. A man who is a Marxist at forty has no head."

5 *A Young Man Thinks*

There is another reason why the young intellectual has leanings towards the Marxian ideal. His people at home look alarmed when he talks about it. It amuses him to alarm them.

His father is an instinctive Conservative and doesn't want a damn thing changed. He even grouses about the new buildings in London with many windows between bars of steel. He hates speed and thinks there ought to be a twenty-mile-an-hour limit on the roads. He detests aviation and says it is another menace to life. He still reads Charles Dickens, and Thackeray, and even —ye gods!—John Galsworthy. It's necessary, the young man thinks, to break up this Victorian mind, to ridicule the platitudes of this autocrat at the breakfast table, to show up the hypocrisies of ideas which the old bird thinks sacred and the stuffiness of the code which he calls "playing the game." Youth has the natural right, he claims, of revolt against the opinions of the previous generation. At the mere word of Communism the family blows up. How good to let in a little fresh air after that explosion! Besides, how can one join the ranks of the intellectuals in Bloomsbury, or Battersea, or Hampstead Garden Suburb without a touch of Red?

Then there is this menace of war. The young intelligentsia does not wish to be caught in some mantrap and blown to bits by tempered steel because Mr Stanley Baldwin says "our frontier is on the Rhine"; or because Mr Eden is playing a game of jigsaw puzzle with Mussolini on one side and M. Blum on the other; or because Herr Hitler has a grudge against Czecho-Slovakia—where is it on the map?—or because, having piled up a lot of armaments at great expense, it seems a pity not to use them with the blessing of the Bishop of London.

What is the good, asks the younger mind, of reading, thinking, scheming out a good life, working for the love of a nice girl, getting interested in art or music, when, in a year or two, Fascist bullies, or Colonel Blimp, decide to have another world war—or something slips by accident and makes the big explosion, to the astonishment perhaps of those who have been hoarding high explosives? That was the kind of question which caused a number of young gentlemen at Oxford to proclaim in the union: "We will not fight for King or Country." What they really meant was: "We will not fight for profiteers or die to play a Foreign Office game."

The H. G. Wells young man—1937 edition—reads the *News Chronicle* or the *Daily Herald*. Perhaps he goes up the Charing Cross Road, where there is a Red bookshop, and buys the *Daily Worker* and *Challenge* and little pamphlets on Communism and Peace.

Perhaps here is the clue, thinks Mr Kipps, to international comradeship across all frontiers. The United Workers of the World. The Dictatorship of the Proletariat. The working classes don't want war, he is sure of that. They don't want to have their bowels torn out by high explosives for some war arranged by a competition for markets between Capitalist nations. Perhaps the class war, he thinks, will have to happen first, before that union of democracies conducting their affairs by co-operation, and reason, and a sense of human brotherhood. The class war! Not too pleasant if it happens, of course! Karl Marx said it was inevitable. Perhaps Fascism and Black Shirts would win first. What about Russia with its Red Army—the strongest in Europe —and its Red aeroplanes? The Red dream is rather confusing just now. But young minds have their own sense of logic and jump the snags.

6 A Gruesome Show

In London recently I went to see an anti-Communist exhibition at Dorland House in Regent Street.

It was a gruesome show and not quite fair to Russian development since the early days of the revolution. Here were ghastly photographs of the starving children such as I had seen on the Volga in 1922. Here were the anti-God posters with their flaming hatred of priests and their ridicule of Christ.

Perhaps some of that has died down now. I was talking to a young Russian who told me that all over Russia there is a return, among many groups, to primitive Christianity, and that many of these groups are in the Red Army itself. Human nature even in Russia, even after all that propaganda, needs a religion and a faith in immortality. Even the successor to Djerjinsky, chief of the Ogpu and a sadist in his love of cruelty, is aghast at the results of the breaking down of family life and the criminal tendencies of young Russians brought up without a moral code. "Back to the home" is now a slogan in Russian villages encouraged by the Propaganda Bureau. The word has gone forth from Moscow to tolerate religion if it does not become political, so I am told.

What interested me most in this exhibition was the portrait gallery of the revolutionary leaders in the time of Lenin. It looked like a rogues' gallery. They had dreadful, almost inhuman, faces, some of these men. They were like masks out of which stared dead eyes. Perhaps the camera had not been flattering. Radek, the editor of *Pravda*, now in a prison cell, was very ugly, with a fringe of reddish hair round his flat face, but he had humorous eyes when I sat opposite to him in the Kremlin, and was not so frightful as his portrait here.

This room in Regent Street was like a Chamber of Horrors and was haunted by memories of Terror which have drenched Russia in blood for twenty years of recent history, unknown to the young intellectual who sees red or passes it off with a shrug of the shoulders because of czarist cruelties. It was, he thinks, an evitable chapter of the class war out of which will come a Brave New World.

In that exhibition one saw nothing of the new Russia with its industrialisation, its armies of young mechanics, its schools and laboratories. But even if all that had been shown I doubt whether life in the Soviet Republic would appeal to the working-man in England if he had to live under its discipline, which is not exactly our idea of democratic liberty in a new paradise on earth.

He would often be underfed. He would be spied on. He would live in filthy conditions with filthy food. He would see around him a mass of misery and the disease of vice even among young people.

7 *Free Speech on Tower Hill*

A wet wind was blowing on Tower Hill, and scudding clouds seemed low over the old Tower itself. About a thousand men, I guessed, stood about in small crowds on this open place during

THE ORATOR ON TOWER HILL

the lunch hour. They were grouped round different orators, each of whom was competing for an audience by his special brand of political conviction. One man dominated the rest, standing higher than the others on a raised platform and shouting louder. He had the biggest crowd and I hadn't been there two minutes before I knew that he stood for the Spanish Government of Caballero against Franco and his Fascist allies. He stood for the United Front, the Clenched Fist, and the right of free-born Englishmen to fight for Democracy in Spain or anywhere else.

Before I bent my attention to his argument I had a moment with old ghosts. For I was on ground once soaked with the blood of Englishmen who had died, by axe, or rope, or fire, for conscience' sake, for freedom of faith, or for their own intolerant fanaticism. Over there in the Tower of London men had been racked and subjected to merry tortures for their religious opinions or their political creed. Some of the noblest blood of England dripped onto stones inside those walls—saints and martyrs, poets and scholars, great gentlemen like Sir Thomas More and Sir Walter Raleigh. In damp cells and dungeons behind those walls lay rebels against the King's command, great noblemen who had allegiance to the wrong prince, women with white necks and weeping eyes, who went to the block when their time came because a King had tired of their beauty or found out their infidelities. Thumbscrews, and iron boots, and racks had tortured human flesh in the ages of intolerance, before the Age of Reason—has it arrived?—and democratic liberty.

In England we still have liberty. The orators on Tower Hill were, by their words, a proof of that. They could say almost anything, without the fear of a concentration camp or a Fascist prison.

Two City policemen, big beefy men, stood with their backs to a wall watching the crowd and the speakers but not listening.

They were there in case of a row. They were not there to check the flow of eloquence, however fiery or foolish. They were chatting together about professional incidents, one of which seemed humorous and caused a laugh to pass between them.

The crowd was made up mostly of city men, office boys, packers, porters, warehousemen, and such like. Where I stood on the edge of one group a sturdy middle-aged man, with a scarf instead of a collar round his neck, was eating monkey nuts industriously, and round him was a litter of empty shells. An old woman in the centre of the Hill was serving at a little chocolate stall and did good custom among spectacled office boys who had come here in their luncheon hour for an intellectual feast while they munched a few biscuits and sucked those sticks of chocolate.

The young man who had attracted the biggest audience was a tall, thin, muscular fellow with an Irish-looking face, gaunt and hollow eyed, with a shock of dark hair through which almost every minute he thrust both his hands with outspread fingers, as though to let his thoughts escape more freely from his hot head. He had a good voice which came from his stomach, as it should, instead of from his throat. His words rang across Tower Hill.

"Gibraltar," he shouted, "is the Achilles heel of the British Empire. Do our Tory diehards understand when they back Franco and his Moors, and do nothing to check the flow of arms from all the blackguard bullies of the Fascist nations, they are playing into the hands of Hitler and Mussolini—those two ruffians—and that if Franco wins with their aid they will close the Mediterranean against British ships when it suits them to do so, cut off our lines of communication with Egypt and India, and make Gibraltar utterly useless as a naval base?"

It seemed to me curious that a Communist, as I guessed him to be—certainly an orator of the United Front—should show such zeal for the British Empire, which in the past they have so often denounced for its "brutal Imperialism." But his hatred of Fascism was so intense that he was willing to appeal even to the imperialists to defend the anarchists, syndicalists and Marxists in Madrid.

His voice rang out over the heads of the crowd.

"We boast of our liberty, but is it not an outrage against liberty that Eden should ban any brave Englishman from going as a volunteer to Spain to fight, and, if need be, die, for those who are defending liberty in Europe? It is a unilateral action before the other powers have agreed to do likewise. Eden has betrayed Democracy."

"What about shooting civil prisoners in Madrid?" asked a voice in the crowd. "Is that your idea of justice and liberty?"

For a moment the orator high above his audience listened to this heckler in the crowd. He laughed scornfully.

"This gentleman talks about the shooting of prisoners in Madrid. What about the shooting of unarmed prisoners in Badajoz by Franco's murderers? And another thing! You all read the papers. You know I am not lying when I say that the first act of Caballero was to liberate thirty thousand prisoners—from the jails of Madrid—Spaniards imprisoned for their political belief in liberty—Spanish workingmen and democrats. You read your papers, don't you? Am I a liar or am I telling the truth?"

"You're a liar," said a man in the crowd.

There was a slight dispute on this point. It took the form of a heated conversation in the crowd itself.

"He's a liar," said one of them. "He isn't a liar," said others.

The orator thrust all his fingers through his dark hair and took a breather.

"This Spanish Civil War," he continued after that respite, "seems remote from England. It doesn't seem to touch our interests. But it touches us all very closely—every one of us—because it is the beginning, the trial trip, of that conflict which is going to be fought out in blood all over the world. It is a trial of strength between the Fascist powers and those who hold fast to Democracy and must one day fight for it. If Franco wins we shall all feel the results of that victory for tyranny. Our own liberties will next be challenged . . ."

He spoke well and interested this audience of city men, porters, packers, warehousemen, and casual labourers.

I joined another group gathered round another orator. Several office boys were listening to him with giggles and goggle eyes. The man who was eating monkey nuts was among his audience, standing among the shells. Squarely in front of him stood a well-dressed man who looked like a city clerk from one of the outer suburbs, and he interrupted the speaker from time to time in a polite and argumentative tone.

At first I could not quite make out the drift of this speaker's thesis. He was a Highland Scot, I should say, judging from his way of speech, and he had a lean face, with dark eyes and heavy eyebrows.

"What about the love of a woman for a man?" he was saying as I drew near. "Oh, very romantic! And I don't deny that there is such a thing. A woman will love a man—a man will love a woman—certainly. It's human nature. It has happened in history. It happens now. Married or unmarried, it makes no difference to love or loyalty. But when they get married what happens? The wife says, 'I want another shilling out of your wages.' The man says, 'I can't afford it, old girl.' She says, 'You've got to afford it.' That's when love flies out of the window. Why do women marry? For security and a man's wages. This marriage business is the cause of man's unhappiness and woman's."

"But your theory of companionate marriage," said the man

in the crowd, "what happens to it in the case of a child coming?"

I caught the drift of it now. That lean cadaverous fellow was an advocate for free love.

"In any case," he said, "there wouldn't be a child. I wouldn't take the risk of bringing a child into the world in its present state—with a war coming along pretty damn quick, and Capitalism arranging another Massacre of the Innocents. No sir! there would be no offspring of a six months trial. I say six months. In that time a man ought to know whether the woman suits him for keeps."

"But, Mr Speaker," said the man in the crowd earnestly, "accidents will happen, you know, in spite of your theory about rigid birth control."

"Wise people know how to deal with accidents," said the speaker. "I'll say no more about that! My point is——"

"But, Mr Speaker," said the city clerk—as I took him to be, "if everybody acted on your theory there would be no population at all. If nobody had children——"

"Well, I haven't made as many converts as all that!" answered the dark-eyed man, twisting his lean jaws to a frightful smile. "There will always be mugs. In any case . . ."

He had a grudge against Capitalism. He seemed to think that the support of family life was one of the forms of "dope" handed out by Capitalists to the starving proletariat to keep them enslaved.

"Family life!" he exclaimed scornfully. "Now, I ask you to remember your own family life. Was it a heavenly state, or was it damned disagreeable—a hell on earth—with family squabbles and family rows, and family tyrannies? What about the time when Ma is in one of her tantrums? What about those days when Pa laid down the law about staying out late or bringing home one's lassie? Family life? My God!"

One of the office boys sucking a stick of chocolate thought this extremely funny and giggled. He was enjoying his lunch hour prodigiously. But I wondered if it were quite good for this lad to listen to a discussion on birth control by a man who was trying to undermine family life on the Russian model. But there is free speech on Tower Hill.

I turned my steps towards another group. They were being addressed by a middle-aged man who belonged to some anti-Socialist league. He was in the middle of a quarrel with four or five men very close below him. Their heckling had made him angry.

"I demand free speech!" he shouted. "If you men come here you ought to give me a decent hearing. I'm trying to tell the truth. If you don't want to hear it others do."

"It isn't the truth!" said one man below him. "You're a dirty liar."

"And you're a supercilious fool," retorted the speaker. "You have no manners. I don't object to a reasonable amount of heckling but I won't stand for coarse abuse."

"You began the abuse," said the man below him. "You called me a cad. Now you call me a fool. You ought not to be here. You're just the paid agent of maiden ladies who are frightened of democracy. It makes me sick to listen to you."

"Gentlemen!" said the speaker, ignoring these last remarks and addressing the general audience, "on this Tower Hill there is the tradition of free speech on all sides. It is a valuable heritage. You see that it is denied to me and obstructed by those who mouth the word 'liberty' and under that name try to spread the poisonous doctrine of Lenin and his Russian colleagues. The recent trials in Moscow have shown the horrors of that regime, and——"

"Keep Moscow out of it!" shouted a voice in the crowd.

8 The Communist Party of Great Britain

Is there any real danger in this Red stuff which is being given as food to babes by Mr Harry Pollitt—that mild-mannered man who appeared before the Royal Commission on Arms—and his fellow members of the Communist party of Great Britain? Their own membership is something over eleven thousand, which isn't much in a population of forty-nine million. But they and other Red bodies do a considerable amount of quiet propaganda, in factories and arsenals and dockyards and barracks. It is partly paid for by subsidies from the Russian members of the Third International, called the Comintern. According to the Communist party's own reports in a leaflet quoted by the Anti-Socialist and Anti-Communist Union, it received in the first two years of its existence from outside sources £61,500, and from internal subscriptions £699. From the same source I quote another extract.

Mr Fenner Brockway, secretary of the Independent Labour party—one of the bodies which has recently agreed to form a United Front with the Communists—wrote to the *New Leader* as follows:

> The payment of subsidies to national Communist parties by the Commintern makes them the obedient instruments of the Russian Communist Party, which contributes predominately to the Comintern Funds. Take the position of the British Communist Party. Probably 70 per cent of its membership is unemployed. Yet the Party runs a daily newspaper and an elaborate monthly review, has a large staff of paid organisers, and conducts a planetary system of subsidiary organisations. Its subsidy from the Comintern must run into tens of thousands a year.

Vast numbers of the little leaflets distributed at factory and dockyard gates, in the distressed areas, and wherever trouble may be stirred up against the existing order of things, must be a waste of paper, ink and Russian gold.

The British workingman, employed or unemployed, is very conservative in his allegiance to law, order and tradition. He hates the idea of Red Revolution, which he knows would make an awful mess. In his inarticulate way he is intensely patriotic and won't stand for any "monkey stuff" about the King, or the Army, or the Empire. When the unemployed of Jarrow built a sports pavilion with funds provided by Sir John Jarvis and his friends they asked for a large Union Jack to wave from its flag-staff. Communist visitors in the distressed areas get short shrift from men standing unemployed round disused pit heads. I marvel why they are not more rebellious. Is it lack of spirit, or lack of intelligence? I am inclined to think it is a shrewd common sense and that humour which makes them laugh when a paid agitator screams wild words from a soap box. "'Ere, come off it!" they say. "Go 'ome and wash behind your ears." They are not tempted to use their sticks of furniture—paid for on the hire system—as barricades. They don't thirst for rivers of blood. They trudge off to the Labour Exchange to get their dole and hope that things will take a turn for the better. They have turned a good deal lately and there are more wages to spend. There is even money to save, judging from the latest figures of the savings banks, which are astonishing. Our craftsmen and mechanics and factory hands are getting higher wages than in any country in Europe. Their standard of living is higher. They are not going to risk it in Red ruin.

The Young Communist League is recruiting boys and girls in the slum districts, where Simon Tappertit may still be found. "Up, and up, and up!" writes the enthusiastic editor of *Challenge*. "Forty-five recruits this week; by the end of January we shall have made at least 200 new members, in the first month of the year. Actually this is not so very good. I mention it be-

IN BLOODTHIRSTY BLOOMSBURY

cause 100 of our best comrades are out there—in Spain—battling for Democracy and the honour of our movement. They will be overjoyed to know that 200 new ones have come forward to fill their places. Phil Gillan, who was seriously wounded in the University City section of Madrid and is now convalescent, will have his recovery greatly speeded up when he hears that while he has been away his branch has grown from 40 to 70 members."

These boys of the Young Communist League are being stuffed with all the old slogans of Red Russia used by the revolutionary leaders who are now mostly dead by orders of their comrade Stalin. Capitalism must be destroyed. Religion is the opium of the people. The workers must seize the means of production. The international class war must overthrow the tyrannies of imperialistic nations. World revolution is the way to world peace. Now they have new enemies, worse even than vested interests or the demon of Capitalism. They are Fascism and Nazidom. Hitler, Mussolini, and, in his little way, Sir Oswald Mosley—are recruiting agents for the Communist party of Great Britain, especially perhaps among the Jewish population, who have their own cause of hatred. Sir Stafford Cripps, learned in the law, knighted by the King, and Mr Maxton, of the Independent Labour party, have many strange types among their followers—overgrown office boys who listen to those orators on Tower Hill; undernourished students who economise over lunch and wander up the Charing Cross Road to read a flaming page or two in the Red bookshops; dreamers of utopias where all will be rich and all will be happy; hollow-eyed shabby men with glib tongues and shifty eyes who get paid by agents of the Third International; young Irishmen who remember Tom Paine and "The Rights of Man"; Jewish tailors who brood over the long story of persecution and pogroms; and youth with revolt in its mind or the inferiority complex which seeks revenge by way of Terror. There is also Professor Haldane. It's all very interesting, but not, I think, alarming as a threat in this year of grace. But if another world war comes even England may have a Red peril.

But the red dream is still dreamed by those who believe in fairy tales. It gets into the minds of young fellows over here, not only in St John's College, Oxford, and some of the students at the London School of Economics, but down by the London Docks in Bermondsey and Poplar, in Hoxton and Houndsditch. One hears its gospel preached on Tower Hill.

IX

The Sowers of Dragons' Teeth

1 The Fatal Past

IS IT ANY GOOD looking into past history—not long past—and retracing the fatal steps which, one by one, were trodden by our leaders as though they were blindfolded or sleepwalkers on the edge of a precipice?

Our present leaders, who, in most cases, are our old leaders, resent any inquisition into events further back than yesterday. They say: "Let the dead past bury its dead. We have to act today. We ask you gentlemen of the House of Commons, and men and women of England, to pass that £1,500,000,000 for the defence of your lives and liberties, so kindly look pleasant about it and pay—pay—pay."

Shall we let them get away with it quite as easily as that? Isn't it necessary to look back a moment or two to find out how it is that all the world is arming with feverish and frantic haste, and that we are going to spend upon the instruments of war that vast sum of money which, if it had been raised for social purposes—for the nation's well-being, health and beauty—would have been a great advance in civilisation?

One could go back profitably for one's mind as far as the Treaty of Versailles and those penalising clauses which were designed to keep a great and dynamic people in bondage to their enemies. There was no generosity of spirit which might have lifted humanity out of the ruins of that time and created a comradeship and co-operation between those who had fought each other.

We missed that chance.

We could—and perhaps should—re-examine ourselves and indict our leaders—and those of France—for demanding from a defeated nation unspecified tribute called reparations, rising to astronomical figures which we knew, or should have known, could not be paid even by the richest nation on earth, which at that time was the United States, and never could be paid by Germany, exhausted and ruined after the war.

We might do well to remind ourselves that out of the misery, humiliation and despair into which Germany was thrust by these claims to reparations and the French invasion of the Ruhr—we had no share in that—Hitler arose. As I wrote years ago, Poincaré was the father of Hitler. Our Foreign Office was the birthplace of General Goering.

But all that is rather boring. It is always rather boring to look back at missed chances and wanderings down the wrong roads.

Let us look at more recent history.

There was a Disarmament Conference in Geneva. Year after year it met to receive the reports of its committees and subcommittees and to talk about the limitation of arms down to a low level necessary for each nation's self-defence. Germany at that time was disarmed. That is certain, in spite of a lot of nonsense talked and printed about concealment of arms and secret drilling of men. Germany was disarmed, unable to defend herself against any combined attack, without heavy artillery, tanks, military aircraft, or munitions of war, apart from machine guns and rifles here and there. The League of Nations was under a moral obligation to arrange a general system of limitation in arms. It was possible to do so. In this country and others the people demanded with a passionate insistence that it should be done.

It was not done.

Year after year those dreary and false debates went on, about quantities and qualities, and every kind of technical argument designed to waste time and prevent progress. That play actor Paul Boncour was a past master at this game. And our own representatives at Geneva were equally obstructive and insincere.

It was our representative, Lord Londonderry, who demanded reservations regarding aerial bombing when there seemed some chance of agreement to prohibit that form of destruction. He has denied this, but his words stand on the record.

It was our representative, Sir John Simon, who, when the Germans were still in the League of Nations and pressing for equality of arms on any low level which might be agreed upon —an equality promised to them before the whole world—stood up and, with a glance at the French delegates, announced that the new regime in Germany under Adolf Hitler had so altered the situation that he proposed another period of probation for Germany—he suggested eight years—before they would be allowed to have this equality in arms.

The German representatives saw that all this was play acting, without sincerity, and without any intention of granting actual equality in armed strength to the German nation. Germany left the League of Nations. Germany decided to rearm. Who can blame her, without hypocrisy, for that decision?

We had missed another chance—the supreme chance at that time—of delivering the European peoples from their overwhelming burden of armaments and securing German cooperation in a system of law and collective security which would have given some reasonable chance of peace to Europe.

2 *Hitler Offers Peace*

When Hitler became chancellor and Führer of the German Reich he spoke more as a statesman and less as a barnstormer. He seemed to forget certain passages in his book *Mein Kampf*, though that was a best seller. He made before the German people and the world several offers of peace, in words which were unequivocal, emotional and idealistic. He was called a liar in the world Press.

He offered France friendship, saying that there was no further cause of quarrel between their two peoples. The French Press spat on his outstretched hand and increased their military strength. The British Press quoted the French Press.

Hitler offered to make a Western Pact between Great Britain, France, Italy and Germany, which would, he said, guarantee peace for a generation. It was not accepted. Russia was not included, and Mr Litvinov was annoyed, as were all his friends in France and England.

Hitler offered to limit the German army to three hundred thousand men. France increased her defensive system and ignored the offer.

France made an alliance with Soviet Russia, denounced by the French Right as the most sinister government in the world. It went beyond the covenant of the League in agreeing to instant action between them in case one of them were attacked. Germany regarded it as a new alliance against her, in line with the policy of encirclement—that old bogey which had led to 1914—with French influence in Czecho-Slovakia, Jugo-Slavia, Roumania and Poland. The Franco-Soviet Pact, said the leader of Germany and his propagandists, was a violation of the Locarno Pact and a new situation of which they had to take notice. I think they were right.

On March 7, 1936, Hitler tore up the Treaty of Locarno by sending troops into the demilitarised zone of the Rhineland, so repudiating a clause in that treaty which, in the opinion of many people in England, should never have been there, unless France also had had a demilitarised zone.

It was one of Hitler's "surprises" which shocked the world and created more fear in Europe. Public opinion in France was deeply alarmed. The French Press screamed. Belgium was staggered and dismayed. In England there was official condemnation of this unilateral action and treaty breaking, though public opinion was divided, and some even said: "The Rhineland is as German as Sussex is English. Why should Germany be deprived of sovereign rights over her own territory?"

But when steel-helmeted soldiers with guns and transport were riding through Cologne, Hitler made another offer of peace.

It was as follows:

1. The German Government declare themselves prepared to negotiate with France and Belgium, for the establishment of a bilateral demilitarised zone, and to assent to other proposals with regard to the extent and effect of such a zone, under the stipulation of complete parity.

2. In order to restore the inviolability and integrity of the frontiers of the West, the German Government propose the conclusion of a non-aggression pact between Germany, France and Belgium, with a duration which they are prepared to fix at 25 years.

3. The German Government desire to invite England and Italy to sign this treaty as guarantor powers.

4. The German Government are willing to include the Government of the Netherlands in this treaty system, should the Government of the Netherlands desire, and the other treaty powers approve.

5. For the further strengthening of these security arrangements between the Western Powers the German Government are prepared to conclude an Air Pact, which shall be designed, automatically and effectively, to prevent the danger of sudden attack from the air.

6. The German Government repeat their offer to conclude with

States bordering Germany in the East non-aggression pacts similar with that concluded with Poland.

7. With the achievement at last of Germany's equality of rights, and the restoration of sovereignty over the whole territory of the German Reich, the German Government regard the chief reason for their withdrawal from the League of Nations as eliminated. Germany is therefore prepared to enter the League of Nations again. In so saying she expresses at the same time her expectation that, in the course of a reasonable space of time, the problem of the colonial equality of rights, as well as of the separation of the League Covenant from the Versailles Treaty, will be clarified in the course of friendly negotiations.

These proposals were of vast importance to the peace of Europe. If they had been accepted and concluded, there would today be no need for those desperate burdens of rearmament which are crushing down upon all our shoulders, and all our souls, because of their inherent menace of explosion at the end of the race. The conclusion of Hitler's proposed Air Pact would have taken fear out of Europe—that most horrible fear of the bombing of great centres of population which has invaded the minds of millions in England and other countries. Germany's return to the League of Nations would have made possible a real system of Collective Security, which, without Germany, is an illusion and a menace.

There is no word of Russia here. But Russia also would have been safeguarded by the conclusion of such nonaggression pacts with states bordering on Germany. Russia is not on Germany's border line, and to get at Russia Germany would have to pass through states whose territory she was ready to declare inviolable.

The hostile critics of Germany said: "How can we rely upon any pact made by a nation which has violently repudiated those already made?"

But is it impossible for us, or France, to understand the motives and the limit of Germany's action in repudiating a treaty forced upon her by defeat, starvation and revolution? All that Hitler had done—and it was much—was to regain for Germany sovereign rights over her own territory, free from foreign control or interference, and to stand equal with other powers. If we English folk had been defeated in the World War, deprived of our sovereign rights over our own land, and made subject to the dictates of foreign powers or a hated treaty, we, too, should have struggled to release ourselves and regain our ancient liberties. We should have acclaimed any leader who would have restored our pride and broken our bonds. We should have gloried in the patriotism of English youth who, after humiliation, bitterness, misery and demoralisation, rallied up to the traditional spirit of England and said to all the world: "Our English soil is free. We have torn up our treaty of shame: We stand, as once we stood, independent and unafraid." So would France have been glad of a leader and a spirit which would do such things after defeat and bondage. Have we no imagination, no touch of generosity, no sympathy with a nation which breaks its fetters? I dare to say that Hitler, in these acts, was heroic in his liberation of the German folk from foreign control and inequality of justice. If we refuse to admit that in the case of Germany, we are false to all our history and all our code of fair play. I think that our statesmen, and French statesmen, and our Press and the French Press, were stricken with blindness in not pursuing these proposals which offered Europe a new foundation of peace and escape from the darkening shadows of another world war.

To the man in the street and the third-class railway carriage in England it seemed a pretty good offer. Instead of testing the sincerity of Hitler by accepting the principles of this peace proposal and inviting German delegates to a council table, the German envoy—Herr von Ribbentrop—was put into the dock by the council of the League of St James's Palace.

I stood there listening at the open door of the room in which the council of the League sat at a horseshoe table. Behind me was a long corridor hung with tapestries. The eighth Henry had given his fat hand to Anne Boleyn, his "truly beloved", as oft he wrote to her, and led her down this passage to his banqueting room. The initials of that royal pair are carved on the stone fireplace, not chipped off when Anne Boleyn's head fell on the block and another lady took her place in the Court of St James's. Long afterwards the second Charles, with his haggard face and dark eyes, had walked up this corridor and stood laughing with his pretty ladies at the door against which I leaned. The ghosts of English history crowded round me and I was more aware of them for a minute or two than I was of the Americans, Italians, Germans, Frenchmen, who stood close trying to get a glimpse into that room with the horseshoe table where the delegates of many nations sat in judgment.

They condemned the action of Herr Hitler in repudiating a treaty, freely signed by unilateral action. The Belgian minister spoke with deep emotion, as though the Belgian people were again threatened with invasion because German troops were on their frontier. Each speaker spoke solemnly and sternly of this violation of international law. Herr von Ribbentrop's defence was ignored and dismissed. It was a painful time for Germany's envoy.

The verdict was inescapable. The German government had broken the Treaty of Versailles in repudiating a clause without discussion. It was—standing alone—another breakdown of international law and another step to European anarchy.

There was no mention of Hitler's peace offer nor of his hope of rebuilding the structure of law now that he had regained the sovereign rights of Germany over all her territory. No one closed with that offer.

Mr Anthony Eden, acting with French advice—French politicians were hot with passion—addressed a questionnaire to Germany. It was unfortunate in its tone to the leader of a nation unwilling to be dealt with as a doubtful and disorderly character whose word could not be relied on without guarantees.

On January 30 of this year—four years after his appointment as chancellor of Germany—Hitler addressed the Reichstag and the world again.

In the course of his speech he announced that the government would take over the control of the German railways and the Reichsbank as the final freeing of the state from the provisions of the Treaty of Versailles.

"The Versailles Treaty is at an end," he declared. "It took equality from our people and degraded us to an inferior status. German honour has been restored."

Then he made a promise which, if believed—and it was not believed—would relieve the fear of his neighbours and remove the dark shadow which lies heavy over Europe.

"With the achievement of equality the time of so-called 'surprises' is at an end. As a nation possessing equal rights Germany will loyally co-operate in solving the problems preoccupying other nations."

Was he lying when he said that? I for one do not think so.

He declared that it was quite out of the question to think of a conflict with France, and he regarded her soil as sacred and inviolable, as he had given assurance to Holland and Belgium to regard their countries as inviolable territory.

Was he lying? I do not believe that.

"I have already tried to bring about a good understanding in Europe," he said, "and I have, especially, to the British people and its government, given assurances of how ardently we wish a sincere and hearty co-operation with them."

Was that a lie? If so, he must be worse than Ananias. But I am convinced that he spoke with sincerity.

Certainly he denounced Communism and deplored the fact that Mr Eden, the foreign secretary of Great Britain, seemed to think that it was something in Moscow which did not regard the outside world.

"For us," he said, "it's a plague against which we had to defend ourselves in a bloody struggle. Bolshevist doctrine in one of world revolution and economic destruction."

In the past that was so—who can deny it?—though now Russia seems to be returning to Capitalism. But Russia's action in the Spanish Civil War seems to show that they have not yet abandoned their support of revolution in other countries.

That speech seemed benevolent in intention and in promise. Why not believe it? Why not put it to the test? Why not make use of German desire for our friendship, which not only Hitler proclaims but which is acknowledged by every traveller in Germany?

Yet on the very evening of that speech, our B.B.C. was very quick to give a comment dictated, surely, by some member of the government or the Foreign Office. It was critical, contemptuous and hostile in tone. The French Press ignored the assurance that Hitler would respect the sacred inviolability of their soil. They wrote as though he had insulted them. Their comments were quoted by the B.B.C.

Another chance of peace was lost.

In Munich, on February 17 of this year, Hitler addressed a body of international ex-service men, and he spoke the following words on the very day when our House of Commons passed the government's vast rearmament scheme, caused undoubtedly by their conviction that Germany might force another war on Europe:

"A new war would have catastrophic consequences for all

THE LABOUR CORPS

nations. Any disturbance of peace at home would endanger Germany's reconstruction work, but a menace to external peace would utterly destroy Germany's gigantic efforts for recovery.

"The German people no longer entertain the slightest ill feeling over the war. Nothing remains but great respect for our former opponents."

Is it wise to go on disbelieving the words of Hitler when, by believing them, we might get Germany to come in with us as the guarantors of peace?

What was the consequence of abandoning hope that Germany had peaceful intentions?

It was the announcement on February 16, by the issue of a white paper, that the British government would spend £1,500,000,000 in the next five years on rearmament.

I moved about London that day in underground trains, in clubs, in the streets. Everywhere I overheard those figures: *Fifteen hundred million!* They would have to be paid for sometime. One voice in the crowd came to me.

"Who is the enemy? Who is going to attack us?"

"Someone has gone mad," said a young man over the luncheon table.

"It's a gesture against Hitler," said an elderly man—a famous writer—who used to be a Radical in his ardent youth and even in his mature middle age.

"Of course it's all the fault of the pacifists," said another writing man who has jumped to fame as a novelist. "We ought to have kept up our strength and kept Germany down. We ought to have taught Mussolini a lesson and cut the Suez Canal."

I thought of that old story of the man who sowed dragons' teeth which afterwards sprang up as armed men. Our leaders were busy sowing dragons' teeth as soon as the bugles sounded "Cease Fire!" to a world war.

3 *German Visitors*

On the evening of the day when the government was speaking darkly of danger which forced upon them the painful duty of spending fifteen hundred million pounds on armaments—Germany was on their minds though not on their lips—a number of English men and women, not without distinction, sat down at dinner in a London restaurant with a number of German men and women who were visitors or residents in England.

Being in this company, I tried to distinguish the Germans from the English by the look of them. It wasn't possible, I found. We are very much like each other as blood relations, to some extent, far back in history. I made my bow to the Countess von der Goltz and exchanged laughter with a merry lady named Frau von Dewall whose eyes are always laughing.

"Strange!" I thought. "Here we are quite friendly with each other. None of these Germans want to go to war with England. We don't want to go to war with them. What's it all about—this feverish rearming?"

One of the Germans gave a little explanation of it as far as his country was concerned.

"We're a continental people," he said, "with a frontier which needs a certain defence in an uncertain world. Our rearmament has no aggressive intentions. It's to preserve our independence. After all, we have some rather powerful neighbours. Take Russia. How many times do you think Germany goes into Russia on the map? Five or six times, you may say. No, forty-five times! It makes us think. But, in any case, our plan of rearmament is nearly finished. We don't want to go on too long in that business. And it's not in Berlin that has come a refusal for a general limitation of arms."

Another German told us about the way in which the Hitler

regime had dealt with unemployment. Previous to 1933, when Hitler had come into power, there were seven and a half million unemployed. To provide them with the dole cost £750,000,000 a year. (I think his arithmetic must have gone astray here.) Previous governments which changed their Cabinets every six months had utterly failed to solve this human problem. They had borrowed foreign money at high rates of interest and spent it on unproductive works. Massed populations in industrial areas had sunk deeper into misery and worklessness. They were seething with Communism and revolt. The student classes were equally hopeless and workless when they were ready for business life. There were no jobs for them. Germany, with thirty-six political parties and five private armies, was ready for a frightful revolution. So he told us, and it was true, as I know by my own knowledge of Germany at that time.

Hitler and his Nazis had changed all that. They had put six and a half million men back into productive work—a small percentage only, said the German visitor, in armament factories. They had made great roads which had increased the value of the adjoining land upon which semiagricultural settlements had been built. They had drained marshes; and done good work in forestry; and created many new industries, not centred round the old industrial areas but distributed throughout the country. Each man who had gone back to work had created work and wages for three other men, by increased demand for food, boots, clothes and all necessities of life. The national loans for this productive labour had already been profitable, Germany was paying its way and not plunging into the ruinous policy of inflation.

All that sounded to me very much like a scheme once put forward by Lloyd George and turned down contemptuously by the national government, as being fantastic in its conception and cost—though looking back on it it would have cost less than this present scheme of rearmament which will have nothing to show for itself in the end but masses of guns, shells, bombs and other unpleasant-looking things unproductive of anything but death, if ever used.

At the head of the table was an Englishman by name of Lord Mount Temple.

He had a great admiration, it seemed, for the German Labour camps at which every young German spends six months learning an outdoor life, the use of the earth, and the value of God's trees, and other things worth knowing. They were taught a pride in labour. Young fellows from one district of Germany were shifted to camps far away in other districts so that they learned to know their country and fellow countrymen.

"I would to God," said this Englishman, "that we in this country had some system of training in outdoor life and labour, and some such spirit of teamwork for the state."

I confess my own mind thought of the gangs of young derelicts who get free food on the Embankment each night, and of young idlers on the dole who have no work to do and get demoralised.

A young woman, very easy on the eye, as the Americans say, by name of Peggy Boyle, sprang to her feet and praised the German interest in eugenics. They were doing wonderful work, she said, eliminating disease, and the mating of the unfit, and the type of mental degeneracy which filled our homes and asylums.

A young man next to me passed a remark.

"It's very difficult to get at the truth of things, isn't it? Is Germany undernourished? Have they a lack of fats? One reads that in our newspapers."

"There's no sign of food shortage," I told him on good authority and my own observations. "German youth seems to me quite well nourished."

It was all very interesting. But the chief interest to me was this gathering of the Anglo-British fellowship in frank and friendly conversation on the very day when our country was being burdened with an enormous debt for munitions of war to protect ourselves against the German bogey, which affrights the mind of our statesmen, and gentlemen of the Labour party, and many others.

As the young man said on my left:

"It's very difficult to get at the truth of things, isn't it?"

X

The Bogey of Europe

1 The German Riddle

IS IT ANY USE pretending that Germany was not in the mind of our government and its supporters when they demanded £1,500,000,000 for rearmament?

There was no pretence about that from the Left wing of Labour.

"Labour regarded Naziism," said Sir Stafford Cripps, that grim advocate of the class war, "with all that it implied in aggressiveness, brutality, and the suppression of freedom, as Public Enemy Number One in the world today. They had no quarrel with the peoples of Germany, and they would have no desire or need to create great armaments against them if they were convinced of the pacific intentions of their rulers. They did not believe in Herr Hitler's protestations of peace."

Winston Churchill had made the flesh of his readers and listeners creep by the figures he produced out of his hat relating to Germany's intensive rearmament, and by his lurid interpretations of Germany's aggressive spirit. Ramsay MacDonald was impatient with me when, at a private luncheon one day, I tried to put in a word for Germany, in which I had been travelling. He knew all about Germany, it seemed. He had no illusions. Stanley Baldwin, Neville Chamberlain, the experts of the

Foreign Office, seemed to be convinced that Germany was preparing for war in which we should be involved.

So did friends of mine for whose intelligence I have enormous respect. Idealists like Julian Huxley, with whom I talked about this in a country lane, were shocked that I should seem to forget —though I didn't forget—the persecution of Jews, the bully spirit of the Nazi creed, the brutalities of the concentration camps. When I expressed my belief in Hitler's sincerity in his words of peace, and in the ardent wish of the whole German people to establish friendship with us, these friends shook their heads.

"How can we be friends with a nation," asked Julian Huxley, "which denies free speech, suppresses all liberty of thought and culture, and behaves with such mean cruelty to their Jews and pacifists?"

"How can we be friends with people," asked an American friend of mine—he is the London correspondent of a great American journal—"who accept every concession as weakness, and when they are given something ask for something else? It's like buying off the Danes. They will never be satisfied. How can you deal on terms of intelligence and reason with people who deny intelligence and reason? The present generation in Germany is educated to believe that England is decadent, and that there's a Jewish conspiracy to overthrow the world, and that instinct and brute force should take the place of the intellectual mind. How can you argue with people like that? Hitler is a madman. Goering is a moral degenerate. The Nazi philosophy of life is a challenge to Europe. Of course they want to make peace in the West—to keep England and France quiet while they attack Russia. . . . You Liberals have the idea that people can't be so bad as they're painted. You think that they can be converted by kindness. You can't convert the beasts of the jungle to a gentle Liberalism! Hitler hasn't withdrawn *Mein Kampf*."

These arguments are difficult to dispute, especially by people who believe, as I do, in free speech and tolerance of thought, and who hate cruelty and brutality. But what causes me a certain doubt now and then in the sincerity, or the logic, of those who hate the Nazis is their admiration, or tolerance, of Russian Communism and its leaders. Where is the logic which makes them believe there is more liberty and less cruelty in Russia than in Germany, more human happiness in Russia than in Germany? Don't they know, the Left wing idealists, that the German revolution under Hitler was bloodless compared with the streams of blood which ran in Russia, and that, whereas a few scores were killed in the German struggle under the leadership of Hitler, millions perished under Lenin and Stalin? Do they, at this time of history, believe that the Soviet system is in favour of democracy, or that the Russian people govern themselves?

Are the German people hunted, miserable, oppressed and terrorised? A visit to any part of Germany will answer that question. It is true of the German Jews. They have a cause of terror. They are unhappy. Many of them have been brutally and meanly treated. I have a deep sense of pity for those who were good citizens, good Germans, and people of talent and culture—though not all of them were that.

But among the German people as a whole it is ludicrously untrue to say that they are oppressed or terrorised. The younger generation, passionately devoted to sport and the outdoor life, with marvellous opportunities in both those forms of pleasure, are remarkably cheerful. They go about singing in crowds and laughing in crowds. They are healthy and bright eyed and very pleased with themselves. There seems to me more happiness in Germany among the younger people than in England. There is certainly more happiness in Germany than in France, which is anxious, strained and dejected.

We do not like many things about the Nazi regime. Perhaps

there are many things which they don't like about, let us say, French corruption or British self-complacency. But it is impossible to say truly that Hitler rules his people by terror. Most of them adore him. He has given them work and wages, self-pride again, unity, a sense of hopefulness in the future, and a belief in the spirit of duty and service. Those are not negligible gifts, though political liberty is not among them, and though the propaganda of Herr Goebbels is very, very boring to all intelligent Germans, of whom there are many.

It seems to me foolish—senseless, indeed—that the hatred of our Left wing for Fascism and Naziism is so intense that they are ready, and almost eager, to wage war against it in the name of "Collective Security", or for the defence of "Democracy", including Anarchy, Syndicalism, Communism and Sadism.

Is it not because of this hatred of Hitler and his colleagues that the Labour party supported our government's programme of colossal rearmament?

I can hardly think otherwise. For I see creeping even into England that religious fanaticism which is tending to divide the world into two rival creeds—called "ideologies" in the new jargon. On one side are the believers in Marxism and the Dictatorship of the Proletariat—which means the dictatorship of fanatics who will wade through the blood of the bourgeoisie—to which most of them belong—for the sake of their creed; and on the other side the Fascist minds who deride the old Liberalism and desire to enforce a common discipline and the suppression of all minorities.

But there is something more important than our dislike of Fascism in Germany. It is our dislike of another world war.

That German bogey—is it so frightful in its menace of war that we should burden ourselves with a terrible incubus of debt and munitions and go forth to slay it?

A few weeks before writing these words I talked with a German Jew who took tea with me in my club. Being a Jew and an intellectual, he has no love for the Nazis. He complained that life in Germany was intolerable to him. He is afraid even to go to the theatre lest any careless word of criticism should be overheard by another playgoer who, seeing that he was a Jew, might make things very unpleasant for him. He feels intellectually isolated, as though living on a desert island.

"Culture," he says, "has departed from Germany."

He cannot talk freely or discuss philosophical ideas. He has no sense of security. At any moment he may find himself forced out of business. From such a man—a German Jew—one does not hear views favourable to the Nazi regime.

"Do you think Germany is preparing for an aggressive war?" I asked him.

"No," he answered. "Those people want to impress the world, but they don't want to fight it. All this marching and drilling in Germany is to keep the people from thinking, and to keep them excited with a sense of doing something, even if it's only moving about. Everybody in Germany—all the young people—are kept moving about, and flag wagging. If once they sat still and began to think, it might be dangerous! As a matter of fact, Germany can't fight an aggressive war. Where are her allies? Italy? Who trusts Italy? No, much as I detest fellows like Goering I don't believe they have any idea of making war."

I thought that was interesting and important from a German Jew of high intellectual distinction.

2 *Who Wants War?*

At a luncheon party I met a tall, handsome, charmingly mannered man, who was Baron Marschall von Bieberstein. He regretted something I had written about Germany in one of my novels.

"Your last chapter," he said, "was on the wrong note, if I may say so! I wish you had written it in a more optimistic tone. For instance, it would have been good if you could have ended with the description of a scene which I saw recently in London. It was a meeting of front-line fighters of Germany and England—the veterans of the last war. We sat at table with each other. We were the men who had fought each other twenty-odd years ago. There was no sense of hostility or restraint. We were conscious of our comradeship. There was a wonderful spirit at the table. I was deeply moved and prayed to God that never again in history may our two peoples fight each other."

He spoke with emotion and, I am certain, with utter sincerity.

We tend to believe over here in England that the whole of the German people are in a mental slavery under the Nazi regime; and that the ideas of Aryanism and Paganism, and the denial of intellectuality and reason, and the exaltation of brute force and instinct, preached by some of the extreme men like Streicher and Von Schirach, penetrate the German mind and make them incapable of thought or reason. That is not one's impression in Germany. The German people as a whole retain their character, their individuality, their private right of criticism, in spite of Press censorship and propaganda.

The students in all the universities—80 per cent of them I am told—are critical of the Brown Shirt leaders, whom they regard as Jacks-in-office, working for self-interest.

There is one man I know who has a very close and continuous knowledge of German life in all its aspects and classes. He belongs to the Society of Friends and for fifteen years or so has been working quietly among the Germans, in Berlin and other parts of Germany, speaking on behalf of political prisoners, befriending the poor, using his influence for peace wherever possible. Now and again he has got into trouble.

The Black Shirt police have arrested him and accused him of being a Communist. On his denial of this they have made another accusation.

"At least you must confess that you are a pacifist!"

"I am a lover of peace," he had answered. "That is my creed as a Quaker."

That seemed to startle them.

"Well," said their spokesman, "we are all that, of course! We are all lovers of peace. But not pacifists! Everybody must be ready to defend his own country. Otherwise he is a coward or a traitor."

They shook hands with him very politely and let him go.

"How do you size it all up?" I asked after an interesting conversation. "Is there any truth in this German bogey which frightens so many peoples?"

"Germany doesn't want war," he answered.

"Not even with Russia?"

"They don't want to attack Russia. But they're afraid of Russian influence in Germany—Communist propaganda. Over here we are inclined to pooh-pooh the danger of Communism in Germany. People think Hitler is using it only as a scarecrow to frighten his own folk and to keep up discipline. But there's real fear of Communism in Germany. No doubt a good deal of it has gone to ground, but there it is seething underneath. We mustn't forget that Germany had a hard struggle with Communism, and but for the coming of Hitler it might have gone Red and had an orgy of blood. The Germans themselves don't forget that, and they are quite honest in regarding Russia as a tremendous menace against which they have to protect themselves."

He spoke for some time of what Hitler had done for the economic life of Germany and its restoration to self-pride.

"A great deal has actually been done for the unemployed, and there's something very fine in the abolition of class consciousness in the Labour camps. The young people have been inspired to believe in the dignity of work, and in the nobility of service, however humble it may be. The craftsman and the peasant have an equality of pride with the 'white-collar man.'"

"Is there any criticism of the regime?"

My Quaker friend laughed.

"Plenty! Many of the younger men want less Nationalism and more Socialism. But there is no criticism of Hitler, whose sincerity and will for the well-being of the German people are unquestioned by them."

"What about their feelings towards England?"

"There's a general admiration of England—a wish for closer friendship. I've found that everywhere, even among the leaders of the old Stahlhelm. Rather an amusing remark was made to me the other day by an important man. 'We ought to hate England,' he said, 'but we can't and don't!' As a matter of fact, though it sounds silly to say so, Germany wants to be loved—especially by England! They have been so long ostracised, and attacked, and surrounded by hostile critics and open enemies. If only somebody would love them!"

"Sometimes they make it difficult!" I said. "This Jew-baiting puts people's backs up here more than anything. If only they would drop that!"

"Talking about war again," said my friend the Quaker, "I feel convinced I'm right—though not perhaps 100 per cent!—when I say that Germany as a whole dreads the idea of another war. But the younger people get depressed about it sometimes. They talk about Fate—*Das Schicksal*—as though some mystical power might force them into war against their will. One finds articles against war in the most unexpected places, certainly not intended for outside propaganda."

Words of peace are spoken by Germans who cannot be accused of throwing dust into the eyes of the world for sinister and dreadful purposes.

In the State Opera House of Berlin, on February 22 of this year, at a great demonstration in honour of the old German army, Field Marshal von Blomberg, war minister of the new Nazi Germany, spoke under faded war flags carried by regiments in the World War, against a background formed by a monstrous iron cross which commemorated the valour of two million German dead.

"Forget hate!" said General Blomberg. "Show that you are worthy of these sacrifices. Do all in your power to prevent war happening again. Thus do we interpret the call which comes to us from those graves of the World War."

Words like that come from Germany again and again—and I believe them. I believe that our politicians have made a false bogey with which to frighten the British folk, and that the enormous burden of armaments which has been imposed upon this country is dangerous, unnecessary and ruinous.

It is acknowledged by all our travellers to Germany, as I have said, that the German people—whatever their leaders may be saying or thinking—are friendly to us. But is there any friendliness in Germany for the French people; or any in France for their former enemies?

Judging from the French Press, one would not imagine that there could be one Frenchman willing to believe in Germany's offer of friendship. But here is an account by a French ex-soldier —Gabriel Dufour—of a visit paid by himself and some of his comrades to those people across the Rhine.

"From the time of our first welcome—with touching cordiality, at the Strasbourg bridgehead—my comrades and I were the subject of enthusiastic demonstrations throughout our stay. At Baden-Baden, Wildbad, Heidelberg, Esslingen, Freiburg, and

Stuttgart, we were received by a friendly, joyous, and even exuberant population. Let us make some notes from the speeches of our German hosts:

"'We soldiers of the war generation have always felt a profound admiration for the French. We will not allow certain people to push us once more into a catastrophe of which we should again be victims. What could be the advantage of such a killing? We have understood that not hatred, but mutual esteem, was the honour of the soldiers of the trenches. French comrades, please say that on this side of the Rhine there lives a people which loves peace, fathers and mothers devoted to their children, for whom their hope is that they should not know the horrors of war. We pray to God to give us strength to carry through this task to the end.'

"At Stuttgart the members of the ex-soldiers' organisations had been asked to offer hospitality in their homes to the French comrades. On the evening of our arrival the applicants waiting to claim their Frenchmen were numerous. There were only forty-four of us. How could everybody be satisfied? It was impossible. It was touching, but true, that I saw German people going away alone with tears in their eyes. As we left Stuttgart a crowd surrounded our motorcars and showed its enthusiasm by shouting over and over again: 'Vive la France!'

"Some of our Great Patriots call this childishness, comedy, good enough for fools. . . . Well, I don't. I am firmly convinced that if these people are right these demonstrations could only take place by a monstrous collective hypocrisy. These German people seemed to me sincere, retaining, like us, a horror of the war they had been through. In our journeys of hundreds of kilometres, making contacts with German people in town and country, with intellectuals, workmen, and peasants, my comrades and I gained the impression that Germany sincerely desires peace."

These friendly greetings between ex-enemies are, alas, no guarantee of peace, because the common folk are at the mercy of rulers who play a game of jigsaw puzzle in the diplomatic world, and the people have no control over their own destiny. Their opinions and feeling fail to find expression in a sinister Press, which is utterly insincere, and deliberate in its policy of inflaming hatred and passion. How can the peoples of Europe, wishing peace, escape the doom which they feel is dragging them all to war?

3 *A German View of War*

It is enormously important to us, and all other peoples, that we should get a real understanding of the German mind, at its best and at its worst, in its attitude towards war and peace. Many are afraid that words spoken in favour of peace by Hitler or his lieutenants may be for propaganda purposes, or for the hiding of sinister ambitions. It is therefore extraordinarily interesting to read something, which no one could suggest was written for outside propaganda, revealing the inmost convictions of the inner circle of Nazi chiefs. Such a revelation appeared, on January 14 of this year 1937, in a paper called *Das Schwarze Corps* (the Black Corps). It is the organ of the S. S. or Schutzstaffel (Defence Staff), who are the Black Shirts under Himmler, the personal guards of Adolf Hitler, and the quintessence of the party organisation. The title of the article is "Our Opinion about War."

In this screed one may find the clearest statement of the National Socialist philosophy about war, written without camouflage for party consumption; and it contains at the beginning phrases and ideas which might be quoted to prove that Germany glorifies the war spirit. But if one reads further one gets a different point of view.

"For eternal peace," it begins, "perfect harmony is needed in the heart of the individual. That is Utopian. Human hearts will remain restless. This restlessness of the individual will affect whole peoples. There will be further wars."

The nobler aspects of war are enumerated: comradeship, grandeur of contact with danger and death, courage.

Then there is reference to the cheap illusions about war in the younger mind: playing with danger, the highwayman touch, the liberation of animal and half-animal instincts, in short, all that used to be described by the expression "Frisch—fröhlicher Krieg (the merry game of war)."

"Any soldier who went through the last war," says the writer in the *Das Schwarze Corps*, "will tell you that there is no more unholy expression than that. We all want to raise the cultural level of the world. As it is raised, the inclination to war is reduced. This is not decadence, for soldierly virtues can also be developed in times when there is no war. There will always be struggle in the world; but it need not be a struggle of men against men. There is enough without that to claim the devotion of unnumbered hosts of the finest men. The attempt to abolish war may be ascribed to the fact that with increasing culture men attain gradually to harmony, without, however, being able to reach it completely in measurable time.

"If you ask any old soldier" (this article continues), "he will tell you: No. I do not love war. The soldier does not love war, though he does his duty, and will always do it, should it come. The soldier loves life, perhaps even more than all those who have never seen, or suffered from, war themselves. All of us—Germans, French, English, Italians, and whoever else took part in the war—are still too much under its shattering spell to take the thought of it lightly—an attitude that has often been the cause of so much evil in the past.

"We Germans have, thank God, struggled through to our

own standpoint; one that would have seemed almost dishonourable before the war: not to praise war as the most beautiful thing in the world. We shall never take part in war out of the desire for war. The soldier does not love war . . . And he will not infect, or educate, the younger generation, who have not yet seen it, with love for war.

"That he has often promised himself and others. Those tens of thousands of soldiers—English, French and German—also promised this, as recently they did at Douaumont, when they swore to work for peace."

The writer reverts to the thought that war may be enforced by Fate and that, if this Fate commanded again, the soldier would again do his duty.

"Yet the soldier will try to keep peace. He will continue to say: 'Peace above all!' though he recognises the justification of that old phrase, Si vis pacem, para bellum. For the rest, let us hope, and desire, and work, that harmony in the individual heart throughout the whole world may grow to the end that, at last, the world may obtain eternal peace.

"Does the soldier love war? All, all of us soldiers of the nations, do not love it."

That article might have been written by General Sir Ian Hamilton, who knows war and loves peace. It might have been written by General Smuts, who hates war and loves peace. It appeared in the organ of the S. S.—who are Hitler's bodyguards, and Himmler's Black Shirts! It seems to me remarkable. No word of it reached any French or English newspaper.

4 *The German Claim to Colonies*

The chance of good relationship between Germany and Great Britain has not been made easier by the German demand for the return of her lost colonies. It is rather the tone in which that has been made than the question itself—difficult as it is—which has aroused the anger of those who regard Germany as our potential enemy. In a speech by General Goering on October 26, 1936, he said harshly that German colonies had been "stolen" from her. This was repeated by that glib-tongued man Herr Goebbels. The Führer, himself, in his book *Mein Kampf*, repudiated the desire for the possession of African colonies but has now made their return a matter of national urgency and prestige.

In *The Times* and other papers there has been a considerable amount of correspondence on this subject, and many leaders of opinion in this country, like Lord Noel Buxton, Lord David Cecil, and Lord Allen of Hurtwood, have expressed sympathy with the German claims on the score of justice, good will and appeasement, as well as for economic reasons, giving Germany access to raw materials. On the other hand, many writers have criticised and challenged the reasons given by Germans themselves for the return of their old colonial possessions.

The argument of Dr Schacht, the German minister of economy, and president of the Reichsbank, is that colonies are indispensable to Germany because from them she would obtain the raw materials that she needs. Fats could be supplied from what were previously German colonies; rubber could be cultivated in what was German East Africa and the Cameroons; wool, cotton, flax, hemp and jute were actually found in the German colonies, and metals and minerals were, no doubt, to be found there.

This argument is countered by the criticism that only a small part of the world's raw materials are produced by colonial territories. Most of them come from Europe, the United States and Asia. Africa accounts for only 3.7 per cent. Were Germany to recover her former colonies, they would not secure for her a supply of such vital raw materials as copper, petrol, cotton, wool or iron.

It is argued by Germans that the greater part of trade in mandated territories goes to the mandatory power. But, as a matter of fact, it does not work out like that, and a very considerable part of the trade of the former German colonies is still with Germany. The Cameroons take 50 per cent of their imports from Germany and send her 80 per cent of their exports. In Tanganyika German trade in 1933–36 amounted to over two million pounds sterling in exports and imports.

Germany's popular cry that she needs these colonies for the surplus population is made rather ridiculous by the small numbers—twenty thousand or so—who settled in these lands previous to the war.

Nevertheless, Germany wants them back, and there is incessant propaganda stimulating the national grievance on this account. It is, above all, a question of national pride, and that is the most dangerous and difficult mood with which to deal. It is especially difficult to settle generously and in justice at a time when Germany is accused of aggressive intentions in which lurk a menace of war; and when those who believe that charge are hardened against any concession which would seem like surrender or weakness on account of fear. Germany, they say, would use Tanganyika as a submarine and aeroplane base, which would imperil the Cape-to-Cairo route, and alarm not only South Africa but India and the Far East.

The difficulties of handing back the mandates to Germany are very great and hardly realised by Germans themselves. Whitehall has no power to decide upon their return. South Africa, an independent Dominion of the British Commonwealth, would utterly refuse. How then could we enforce any decision to hand back German East Africa or the Cameroons? Some of these mandates over the former German colonies are held jointly by seven different countries, including France, New Zealand, Belgium and Japan. It would not be easy to get a general consent to the handing back of these countries.

Once again the errors of the past come up like ghosts to endanger the present. I agree personally with the German argument that the seizure of these colonies after the war was a violation of President Wilson's Fourteen Points, upon which Germany put her faith as solemn pledges to her for a future peace settlement. It violated Wilson's pledge that peoples and territories should not be handed about like chattels from one power to another. Utterly false, according to a man who knew German East Africa as few others—Sir Harry Johnston—was the war propaganda that German administration was bad. He told me that it was a model administration, and other witnesses bear this out as far as Tanganyika is concerned.

It is necessary, surely, to find some way out of this trouble, which is psychological in Germany as well as a claim for material advantages. "Paris vaut bien une messe", said Henry of Navarre. European peace is worth a concession to Germany, deprived of any opportunity of colonial development by an Empire which has vast possessions, unused and undeveloped.

We cannot hope to keep that Empire from challenge and attack if we shut its gates to crowded nations, deprived of easy access to raw material and forbidden to settle in these empty spaces. Unless we adopt the policy of the open door it will be forced open.

Our own government, by its spokesman Sir Samuel Hoare, first raised the hope of a better distribution of raw materials and a freer access to their sources. The most intelligent minds in this country who are looking at world problems without party bias, or political fanaticism, are agreed that much of the tension underlying the general expansion of armaments, and the drift towards war, has its foundations in economic and industrial conditions, and especially in the breakdown of trading relations between the peoples of the world.

"We believe," said the signatories of an appeal to our government on behalf of the open-door policy, "that measures of reconstruction altogether new in scope and magnitude—aiming at the solution of economic problems—offer the best, if not the sole remaining, hope of escape from the gathering threat of war."

They urged upon the government the need of doing all in its power to hasten investigation under the League of Nations into the question of access to raw materials, and to take the necessary action to carry out the conclusions reached.

This appeal, supported by the most distinguished list of representative minds in Great Britain today, of all professions and callings, advocated the removal of quotas and the lowering of tariffs between the British Empire and other groups of nations.

It urged a return to a policy of the open door for trade in all dependent territories under British control, and a revision of the mandate system which would replace a purely nationalist control of such areas.

German threats over her colonial claims will be heard coldly by public opinion in this country. They will harden resistance to any concession, even if based upon justice or fair play. But if Germany were to return to the League in support of European peace and a general limitation of arms, I have no doubt at all that some revision of the mandates for colonial territories could be made, to the advantage of Germany, and this country, and the Dominions if the British Commonwealth would be in favour of the friendliest possible arrangement, ensuring to Germany great opportunities for her trade and industry and open gates for German settlers. Whether it will be possible to restore German sovereign rights over Tanganyika and other African lands with the consent of South Africa, I have grave doubts. That is one of the curses bequeathed to us by those who made a peace and forgot the future.

But is it worth a world war, or bloody strife between us and Germany? That question is answered by its own absurdity. I am assured by a German diplomat who knows the mind of Hitler that he will never make this claim a cause of war.

5 *The Way of Understanding*

According to information I get from people who know Germany well, as well as from my own observations in Germany in recent years and months, the German people are very much like ourselves in feeling under a sense of doom that, in spite of a general desire for peace, war may come. Recently they are under the impression that the tension is not so severe, after a very critical period during the Spanish Civil War and the charge against Germany of intervention in Morocco. The situation in political circles is still regarded as grave, though not hopeless. A vast majority of the German people prefer National Socialism to Communism, but an even larger majority would welcome a modification of the present regime, especially as regards personnel. There is general dislike of subordinate officials who exercise a petty tyranny. There is still a fear, I am told, in many German minds that there may be civil war, in spite of apparent unity and loyalty.

They complain bitterly of being "misunderstood", especially by England—regarded by some hostile observers as the selfish hypocrite who can never see other people's points of view and is therefore always unfair. Fairness of treatment is what Germany cares about, above all else. England should make allowances, they plead, for blunt men untrained in diplomatic usages, with no experience of foreign politics, who are now directing the

Reich. They should also make allowance for the difference of tone and phrasing between a dictator proclaiming to the masses and a parliamentarian addressing his constituents. Germany is centuries behind England in political development and is touched in some ways—as they believe themselves—by the dynamic spirit of the Elizabethan era—youthful, virile, adventurous. In this mood Germany is unlikely to accept any conditions of inequality and will only act as an equal partner with other great powers. The way to overcome mistrust is to get Hitler's signature to a definite agreement upon outstanding problems. It would be kept, I am assured by those who know him.

"Germany," said my friend the Quaker, who knows that country as well as any man amongst us, "seems to be struggling along fairly well under its burdens—political, economical and financial. But there is a feeling amongst nationally minded people that life in Germany is a hard struggle with no attempt to ease it by other peoples whose burdens are lighter. The result is a dissatisfied state of mind and the temptation to use the power now possessed to make things a bit easier for themselves. Nothing would induce them to throw away this lever they have forged, after the years of humiliation and helplessness without it. Each of our countries seems so confirmed in its own point of view that perhaps nothing can be gained by argument; besides, it is largely a question of feelings on both sides, not of reason at all. Naturally we don't like dictatorships, Jew-baiting, and so forth. Perhaps still more we detest the blunt unpolished methods of intercourse. Germans dislike our Pharisaism, our inability or determination not to understand them. They worry themselves to exasperation about this and think the only possible remedy for present difficulties must be some concession by England—not realising that concession can only come from understanding, and that they make no effort on their side to help in attaining it.

Hence we reach deadlock. It seems to me, puzzling over this problem, that the only solution may be mutual and simultaneous concession. Perhaps something of the kind is not beyond the powers of diplomacy. The difficulties are enormous. The reward, however, is the peace of the world."

There is still time to establish friendly relations with Germany and to arrange a limitation of arms, especially in the air, which would do something, and much, to relieve the darkness of that shadow of fear which casts a gloom over Europe and the minds of young people. All this hideous nonsense of gas masks and gas-proof chambers for women and children is a disgrace to civilisation and a mockery of humanity itself, besides being utterly useless if war really came. Let us abandon that way of folly and reach out a friendly and cordial hand to Germany without any nagging words or mental reservations.

Let us make a pact of peace and understanding with the German people who—strange as it may seem—like us and want our comradeship. They offer it also to France, and, with France and us, Germany would be a guarantor of peace in Western Europe. That would be something to save the bodies of our young men and to avoid the calamity of a world war. Through friendship with Germany the Eastern frontier could be safeguarded, better than by hostility with Germany.

France's military alliance with Soviet Russia is no guarantee of peace. It is no step forward to Collective Security. Our own military understanding with France is not a perfect guarantee of peace or a gesture of faith in international justice. It is the old balance of power again, directed against Germany and her allies, which led to war in 1914. It will lead to war again if we decide that Germany will and must be the enemy. What madness is that, which is shared by a Conservative government and the British Labour party, and all the little intellectuals of the Left?

XI

Men and Ideas

I. THE YOUNG IDEA

1 The Undergraduate Mind

I HAD an invitation to lunch in the rooms of a young Fellow at Cambridge, and he had promised to bring one or two bright representatives of the undergraduate species for intelligent conversation. It seemed to me an excellent opportunity of getting a hint of the young idea in one of its strongholds.

Arriving early in Cambridge, I wandered around the university city, refreshing my mind with its beauty and walking into the sanctuaries of its ancient spirit. It was a wintry day in early spring—and it can be as cold as death in Cambridge—but the crocuses were out in the meadows along the Backs, and a few undergraduates strolled over Clare Bridge in short jackets and grey flannel bags, as though summer had come again. That was a sign of hardihood, disproving the charge of "softness" brought against the younger generation of today by elderly critics who know them not. I noticed that they stood now and then to look at the crocuses, with their glint of gold in the grass, and let their eyes rest on the glory of King's College Chapel and the scene about them, with its green lawns below Trinity and the stone bridges mirrored in the water below them. This beauty spoke to them, as I could see. They did not ignore it, and I thought that, whatever their character and experience might be, whatever life brings in the future struggle, which may be grim and sordid, something of this loveliness must always stay with them.

"What do you think of the present crowd of undergraduates?" I asked the landlord of a little old inn into which I went for a cup of coffee.

He looked at me with sombre eyes.

"I'd hardly like to size them up," he told me. "I can only say that they're sloppy. That's what they are—sloppy!"

A moment later he seemed conscience stricken by that harsh judgment.

"Perhaps I shouldn't have said that," he amended. "Seems unfair. I dare say my father thought I was sloppy. I dare say my grandfather thought my father was sloppy. It's like that from age to age."

Against the walls of the colleges and under their gateway many push bikes were stacked in rows. Now and again some of the undergraduates came out, mounted these machines, with a gown flung over one shoulder and a pile of books tucked under one arm, and rode off in the teeth of the wind—which was east.

I watched them with a foolish envy. I wondered if they knew their own luck in being young, and having life in front of them, and being here as students at one of these old colleges whose stones have been mellowed through many centuries of time. I felt incredibly old as I passed these lads who call themselves men. And I thought how futile it was to seek their ideas about life and the problems of this time in which they live. The Young Idea? How can they have any clear-cut ideas about anything? Each generation has to work out its own experience and fumble for its own half-baked philosophy, enabling them to get through adolescence, and to acquire the necessary shell case for the protection of their sensibilities, and to furnish their minds with the maximum, or minimum, of knowledge demanded by the fashion of thought in their time, in order to take their place in the world. Generation after generation of young men have come to King's College, or Trinity, or Pembroke, or Clare, or St John's, or Emmanuel, with the same dreams and hopes. They have faced the same perplexities and the same mental conflicts as their predecessors. What is this mystery of life? all of them have asked, age by age. How can the individual best fit into his social surroundings? How can he ensure self-preservation? How can he develop his own soul and body, and subject himself to the right measure of discipline and conformity? What is his relation to God? How shall he comport himself with his fellows? Sex, religion, the political arena, the ideal state—how far shall he go in unorthodoxy, in rebellion against his elders, in new adventures of thought? What is the right balance between self-indulgence and austerity, study and pleasure, the demands of the body and those of the spirit? Youth cannot escape these searching questions.

"What's my best way to Emmanuel?" I asked one of the undergraduates after I had emerged from the cold magnificence of King's College Chapel, where I had stood, utterly alone, under the fan tracery of its high roof, and looked down the far vista of its grey walls carved with the rose and portcullis of a Tudor king.

"I'm walking that way," said a friendly young man, who smiled at me through a pair of round glasses.

"What's your college?" I asked.

"Trinity. It's my third year."

"Do you like it?" I enquired, for the sake of conversation.

"I've been quite interested. I shall be sorry to go down."

"I suppose most of the undergraduates lean a bit to the Left," I hazarded after some remarks about the climate in Cambridge and things in general.

KINGS CHAPEL, CAMBRIDGE

"Yes, those who think about politics," answered this young man, glancing at me as though wondering what I might be. "Most of them don't—so they may be reckoned as Conservatives, perhaps. They're too busy with other things, including getting their degree. Personally, I'm keen on politics, theoretically, at least."

"How do you size up the situation?" I asked.

He glanced at me again, and his eyes were smiling behind his glasses.

"Pretty rotten! All these millions for armaments are not exactly a joy forever. What beats me is the way in which impoverished countries like Italy and Germany can spend such vast sums on their armed forces. I suppose they just create new money. It seems to work all right."

"I've come to the conclusion that money is an illusion," I told him. "It's fairy arithmetic, made by mysterious people called Bankers."

He nodded.

"The old economic theories seem to be knocked edgewise. But I expect two and two still make four."

He had been walking at a stiff pace.

"There's the gateway of Emmanuel," he said politely. "Good morning!"

There was nothing sloppy about that young man. He had good manners and perfect self-possession.

I passed through the gateway of Emmanuel, where a group of "hearties" took the air—cold enough to make one's teeth rattle—before their midday meal. They were unlike the ghosts of their predecessors who had stood under this same gateway some time ago: sober-minded young men with the corners of their lips pulled down in the Puritan style, to show their godliness—though God loves laughter, I dare say—before entering the ministry; still more unlike, at least in outward habit, earlier dwellers on this plot of ground, who were Augustinian friars. The dining hall of the college is built on the site of their chapel, and only a few bits of wall, and a little garden, remain from the scene which was here before Thomas Cromwell and fat Henry's officers grabbed the monastic lands.

The young Fellow of Emmanuel waited for me in his sitting room. Though a scientist, he had, I noticed, a good-looking piano in his room; and he himself looked more romantic than a scientist does as a rule, having the eye and mind of an artist. If I had stepped back into the eighteenth century, as one may slip a century or two in Cambridge so easily, I imagine I should have seen in this room a young Georgian Englishman like this; for he has an old-fashioned look and could step onto the stage untouched for a character in a drama of that period.

Presently we were joined by two undergraduates who showed no hostility to my presence; and over the luncheon table talked extremely well, and with a complete lack of affectation.

Now this lack of affectation is, I think, characteristic of the present generation of young manhood, who have reached or are reaching the twenties this year. As far as I have come across them, they talk simply and sincerely, avoiding the epigram which destroyed so many of their predecessors, and not attempting to shine by any false glamour of intelligence. Another thing I notice about them is that they do not seem ill at ease, or particularly bored, with men of my years. They seem to give us credit for a certain tolerance and understanding. They do not condescend in their talk to a man of middle age or deal with him as though he were in the final stage of senility. They don't seem to be conscious of any vast gap between themselves and their elders but behave as though there were no difference of age to bother about. That makes them extremely pleasant to elderly folk nowadays who are unduly sensitive to their own years and have a kind of wistful gratitude when youth is kind to them. Never once did these young men call me "sir", and I felt flattered by not having this distinction of age thrust upon me. We talked on terms of equality. I find that is general nowadays, and I believe it is because middle age has dropped its pomposities, and youth has drawn near to its fathers in sympathy and understanding, untrammelled by the need of false humility or sham respect.

The undergraduate who sat opposite me at lunch took an active part in the debates at the union. He was well informed about political affairs, but I noticed that he never gave away his own position and discussed the political view of his contemporaries with a finely balanced mind, useful to anybody sitting on a fence, and with a sense of humour.

He agreed with the undergraduate who had shown me the way to Emmanuel, that many of the politically minded men at Cambridge leaned to the Left, some of them rather heavily. There was a pretty strong body, he told me, who belonged to the United Front—about three hundred. Many of them proclaimed their simple faith in Communism, subscribed to the Left Book Club, and invited Mr Gallacher or Mr Harry Pollitt to address them from time to time.

"Is there any opposition at these meetings?" I asked.

There had been lively opposition now and then, but rather in the past. There had been one considerable riot with free fights in the hall and calls for the police, but during the present year nothing of the kind had happened. The opponents of the Left assembled to call out "Shame!" but found men like Harry Pollitt talking with such apparent mildness that it was difficult to make a row. Mostly they kept away. They were much more interested in other things, and Cambridge was filled with other things—more than could be crowded into term time.

We talked about Germany. One always talks about Germany when discussion gets down to the international situation.

The undergraduate on my right had been in Germany during

a recent vacation. He spoke a bit of German. Among his impressions were the friendliness of the ordinary German folk for England and their apparent resistance to ideas which came to them by way of propaganda. He had never met any German who believed in the new Paganism. The German Catholics seemed very solid in their religion. German Protestantism was putting up a considerable fight for its rights.

"Any sign of a food shortage?"

He said there was a shortage of eggs where he had been. Apart from that, he hadn't noticed anything much in the way of undernourishment, but he wasn't quite sure about some of the Labour Camps. He had seen groups of fellows from one camp who didn't seem in good shape. They looked thinned down and as though they might be on a poor diet.

"Are your contemporaries apprehensive about a new war?" I asked.

They were cautious in their answers. They admitted that there was a certain gloom on the subject among minds at Cambridge who took an interest in such questions.

The young man who was a member of the union had his facts and figures handy. He knew all about the terms of Hitler's offer of peace following his remilitarisation of the Rhine. He quoted the clauses.

"But can you believe Hitler?" he asked.

I ventured to say that I believed in him when he said something three times; and that seemed to surprise the company.

These undergraduates had no fanaticism. They had studied the various brands of pacifism, including that of the Rev. Dick Sheppard. One of them, who revealed a spiritual point of view and was particularly interested in religious ideas, confessed that, in his opinion, the Rev. Dick Sheppard put the case against war in the most logical and unanswerable way if one happened to be a Christian. But he—or perhaps his friend—admitted the difficulties. It was possible to adopt passive resistance for one's own actions—it might lead to one's own martyrdom—but it might mean delivering over millions of others to the wild beasts—without their willingness or consent.

We discussed the idea of Collective Security. We discussed the attitude of the Labour party to rearmament, and their hatred of Fascism, which, they agreed, might lead us into another war if they came to power.

Never once did these young men flame out into any passionate affirmation of faith or show any grim fanaticism for a political creed. They were trying to find some reasonable solution of these problems and relying upon intelligence as the best way of escape from threatened calamity.

I did not like to discourage them by suggesting that over wide tracks of the world's map reason had been discarded, and that racial urges, national fetishes, totems and symbols were in the ascendant. I did not even hint that the forces of evil and darkness might be winning against those of beauty and light. I listened with respect and admiration to these undergraduates of Cambridge who spoke from minds steeped, I should say, in the Liberal tradition of enquiry, tolerance, and belief in man's progress towards the Age of Reason.

Switching away from these subjects, I asked the member of the union whether most of the undergraduates were keen on their studies or whether they were up to have a good time.

He was amused by that question.

"Quite a lot—perhaps the majority—study just enough to scrape through with a second. They hope to get a degree, which is just good enough to give them the right standing for any future job or to keep their social end up."

"And do they get jobs now? It must be better than five or six years ago."

"Still difficult for men who haven't specialised."

"I'm going in for engineering," said one of them. "On the whole there are still opportunities in that line."

Knowledge, I understood one of them to say, was not necessarily power. A Cambridge degree was not an open sesame to employment. When one went down . . .

I could see that he was not sure what life might offer him when he went down. Everything was very uncertain. The news one read in the papers did not make for certainty. The war, for instance—when was it coming, if it was coming?

I took the young Fellow to tea in a teashop which looked like a baronial hall in the Dark Ages, though we had some very nice tea cakes which would have put King Alfred to shame.

"What do you think about all this?" I asked.

He guessed that I meant such problems as war, and pacifism, and all that we had been talking about.

"I'm a bit of a heretic on the subject of war," he confessed. "My study of animal life tells me that man is a fighter, and that groups of men will always fight other groups for primitive reasons—as primitive as the vital urge."

"What goes on in the minds of these undergraduates? We reached no conclusions today! There were no revelations."

"They're all bewildered," he said. "They hear so much which is utterly conflicting. There's no clear line for them anywhere. They're all groping their way. Aren't we all? Is there any spiritual or intellectual leadership nowadays? Everything is in the melting pot, isn't it?"

We talked about art and literature, until I had to rush for a train, which I missed. On the way back I read several university reviews and tried to get a glimmer of what was working in the undergraduate brain. I failed. They did not give themselves away in these sheets. They evaded the serious issues, very rightly, no doubt. They were disappointing in their lack of illumination.

2 *Senior Scholars*

"What do you think of the present vintage of youth?" I asked an elderly man who was my host at table in an old house in an old town.

I was asking a man who had had great experience of boys for forty years past. During all that time, once a week, in this old house, he has entertained the senior scholars and Old Boys of a school founded in Tudor days by Edward VI. Sometimes he gets people to talk on them on different subjects, and that was why I was dining at his table. Last Christmas, he told me, he had fifty letters or so from those Old Boys who remember these weekly evenings as pleasant hours in their lives. Some of them are now grandfathers and some of them fathers of the present generation.

He answered my question.

"A very good lot, I think! They're more thoughtful than the prewar boys. They think more about the problems of life."

There were two other men at table, both rather younger than myself, I think.

"We didn't get the same chance in our days," said one of them. "Nobody cared what we thought about, and, anyhow, we didn't have the same opportunities. No wireless. No intelligent conversation with our elders. We were regarded as young hooligans, and that was all there was to it. Besides, world problems didn't press down upon us so closely. We never gave a thought to such things before a world war and the disintegration of Europe."

I was taken into a long room of noble proportions where thirty boys or so had gathered. I was supposed to give them a bit of a talk, and this I did after hearing from them that they wanted me to talk about foreign affairs. They were a nice-looking crowd, I thought, as now and then I glanced at their faces. They listened with decent attention and didn't seem bored. But I was more interested myself when I asked for questions and offered to answer any that might be put to me. They asked some very good questions about Germany and France, and the chance of avoiding another war in Europe. Then my turn came to ask them questions, and their answers were worth hearing, because I could tell instantly that they were talking sincerely.

Two of them had been recently in Germany, going from one youth hostel to another, talking to young Nazis, getting to know the German people.

"How do you sum it all up?" I asked. "What kind of impression did the young Nazis make on you?"

One of the young men spoke for his fellows.

They had seen much to admire in Germany. They found the younger Nazis very decent fellows and very friendly. They admired the physical fitness of German youth but didn't think we in this country should stand for so much drilling and marching about.

"Don't you think we might do, perhaps, with a bit more discipline?" I asked. "Discipline is disagreeable, of course, but aren't we getting rather slack? What would you say to some kind of military training on the Swiss model?"

"Why military?" asked one of the boys. "Why not physical training without a military aim to it?"

"Our fellows are too individualistic," said another boy. "They wouldn't go into camp under compulsion, but they might go if they thought it was by their own free will."

"Did you find any hostility to England in Germany?"

"Hostility? Good heavens, no! Quite the contrary."

"Or any menace of war against anybody?"

There was a moment's silence. The young man who had been in Germany was thinking over his experiences.

"They're afraid of being attacked," he said. "They think all their rearming is for self-defence. Some of them thought that Russia and France would combine against them, and that England might have to go in again. They're obsessed with the idea of all that."

I asked a question of the whole company of boys which rather startled them.

"Do any of you get worried at all about all this talk of war? Does it get on your nerves, or anything like that?"

"No!" said several boys together.

"Yes," said one boy sitting near me.

Another answered more fully.

"In my opinion, we don't think enough about it. The ordinary fellow doesn't pay the least attention to international affairs, and they don't mean a thing to him. He goes pottering on. He's much more interested in the cinema or the cricket news."

I didn't say "Thank heaven!" aloud, but I thought that inside myself.

Before I left that evening the young man who had been in Germany came up to me rather shyly.

"May I ask one final question?"

"Yes, rather!" I answered, hoping it wouldn't be too much of a poser.

"Which side do you take in this Spanish Civil War? Do you sympathise with General Franco or the Spanish government?"

"I can't take sides," I told him. "I hate to think of the cold-blooded slaughter at Badajoz. And I can't forgive the Spanish Reds for their frightful cruelties and murders. One can't take sides in Red Indian warfare. Thank goodness, we've kept out of it."

"Perhaps it's because I'm young," he said, "but I sympathise with the Reds, as you call them. They seem to me to have justice on their side."

He repeated his first words with a little laugh.

"Perhaps that's because I'm young!"

I was told afterwards by my host that the boys had stayed late, talking excitedly about all the problems that had been raised in our discussion. So they hadn't been bored, and I was glad of that, because it is so easy when one isn't young to bore those who are.

"Come again!" said my host, who for forty years has had these weekly meetings in his house.

I envied him for that experience, and for some reason I thought of a pleasant little book I had read called *Good-bye, Mr Chips*.

3 *Air Pilot*

A young airman of ours was good enough to talk very frankly to me about certain ideas in his own mind and in the minds of his comrades of the Royal Air Force, as far as he knew them. We were having a snack lunch at a table on the edge of a swimming bath, into which a portly old fellow had just flung himself from the diving board with a considerable displacement of water.

"I don't believe in this Collective Security racket," he told me after the inevitable drift of conversation to world affairs. "We don't want to fight for any crusade—the Lord forbid! Fighting other people's battles for the sake of some combination of powers against another combination, and calling that Collective Security, seems to us a bit of a paradox and sheer nonsense."

He opened up a ham sandwich to put in some mustard and,

after absorbing it into his system and washing it down with draught ale, continued his little monologue with occasional encouragement from me.

"Of course this Collective Security idea, with an international police force and all that, is pretty good as an ideal towards which we ought to work. But it's the hell of a long way off, don't you think? Meanwhile, nothing would induce this country to fight except direct attack. Anyhow, that's my opinion, and I hear a lot of chitchat to the same effect from all the fellows I happen to know."

He was a cheery-looking lad and curiously sure of himself in this world of uncertainty and doubt. He spoke with a kind of quiet and good-tempered confidence in his own convictions. He had thought it all out.

"No nation wants to go to war nowadays," he told me. "Some of us walk around a bit in Europe. We talk now and again to foreigners in their own countries. People of our generation are all against war. I'm certain of that. It's beyond all argument, in spite of the filthy stuff—the daily spate of lies—in most of our newspapers."

I felt encouraged by this young airman's conviction about the general will to peace.

"What about Germany?" I asked.

He didn't blink an eyelid about Germany, although so many of our statesmen were in a state of blue funk about the German air force.

"Perfectly sincere in saying that their rearmament is in self-defence. Don't we say the same thing? Why should we always be abusing the Germans because they don't want to be kicked in the pants by France or any other nation and take steps to regain their independence and self-respect?"

"Aren't they in a rather dangerous state of exaltation?" I asked to draw him out. "They all seem ready to fight and die for the Fatherland and Adolf Hitler. Mightn't this spirit of eagerness for self-sacrifice lead them into any kind of war if their leader touched a button on his desk one day?"

The young airman shrugged his shoulders. I understood him to say that he didn't think Hitler would touch the button. He wouldn't be such a fool, he thought. But so far as he himself was concerned, and he spoke also for his friends, the desire for martyrdom was nonexistent.

"We don't join the Air Force in a sacrificial spirit," he told me firmly. "We're not panting to die for King and Country. We don't want to die, damn it. Why should we?"

He called for another pot of ale.

The portly gentleman who was enjoying himself in the swimming bath fell with an awful smack on his stomach from the high dive. A young Adonis entirely divested of costume was weighing himself on the machine.

"Our fellows join the Air Force," said the young airman, "because if any war does come along—arranged by the old gentlemen who have gone gaga—they'll be experts and have a place, instead of being among the sheep led to the slaughter. Also, they want a career and think it's useful to learn a craft. The Air Age hasn't come yet, but it's coming. Even our short service of four years will turn us out with some pretty valuable knowledge and experience. I mean to say, one ought to know how to fly nowadays, in order not to be left behind. Don't you agree? . . . Well, cheerio! *European Journey* is the best book you ever wrote, if I may say so."

I was glad to hear him say so. It astonished me that he had ever read a book of mine. I felt extremely flattered.

A remarkable young man, I thought him, because of his decided views and frank expression and Galahad look. Besides, I feel a sense of awe in the presence of a boy child who has won his wings. I shall never be able to fly.

II. THE MAN WITH THE BEACONS

1 Massacre of the Innocents

Every day in this overcrowded isle five hundred new motor-cars are put on to the roads.

That is to say, five hundred new lethal weapons of great velocity are put into the hands of butcher boys, grocers' young men, university students, retired old gentlemen whose eyes are getting rather dim and who are rather hard of hearing, young girls with high spirits and long legs, businessmen who drive to town each morning (and back again each evening) and if they have chauffeurs, after a nice little gamble in base metals or armament shares, tell them to "step on it."

The owners of these lethal weapons of great velocity put them onto roads which were made for the steady pace of a Roman legion, and afterwards for the quiet pace of fat-bellied horses, and farm wagons, and Canterbury pilgrims, and peasants slogging slowly from the fields, and children picking wild flowers in the hedges, and cattle heavy with their milk, and sheep going to the markets.

Many of these roads of England—except those down which the Roman legions marched—go winding through the country-side, taking curves and corners like the walk of a drunken giant or of a poet with a song in his heart. The lanes are narrow between the hedges, with hardly room for two farm carts to pass each other. Few of them have footpaths for those who go on shanks' nag. But they were very safe thirty years ago, and three hundred years ago, except for a horse that shied at a scarecrow, or a governess cart going at the furious pace of four miles an hour. Children could pick wild flowers without the menace of death. The poet might walk down these winding lanes and make a rhyme as he went, without expecting to lie dead and bleeding before he could get a rhyme for "love" or "dove." If the schoolboy were five minutes late for his tea his mother did not turn pale and go to her cottage door with panic in her heart. If the husbandman came home even an hour late, because he had stopped for a glass of ale in the Three Horseshoes, his wife did not expect his corpse to be brought to her on a stretcher.

Now the grocers' young men and the butcher boys and the tradesmen with motor vans, and the young girls with high spirits and long legs, and the young gentlemen of the universities, and all the rest who buy, swop or hire these new lethal weapons, which are motorcars, rush along the roads and the winding lanes in a great hurry for God knows what, and leave a trail of dead and wounded round about England.

There is a massacre of the innocents in the great cities. School children are particularly marked down for death or maiming. Their chance of survival is thinning out. It's their own fault, say the motorists. They will run out into the roads, the little devils! They will suddenly dart in front of a car going the slow speed of thirty miles an hour—far less than an express train, and a speed very hindering to business, and modern progress, and the ardent spirit of youth. If these children's parents won't look after them and give them a clip over the ear when they run out into the roads like that then, says the motor trade, they must get run over. There is nothing to do about it. They get run over in great numbers.

In London and the big cities mothers of elementary-school children, especially on roads like Westway and other death traps for young life, have a panic when little Betty, or little Bill, is five minutes late. So many little Bettys and little Bills have been brought home lately dead, or dying, or grievously injured.

The figures are startling and appalling if one is not dulled, as so many are, to this particular form of slaughter. During a year in this free and happy land about six thousand are killed and about two hundred thousand injured on the roads—as heavy a casualty list as in a great battle on the Somme during the war.

It is, of course, one way of reducing the population of an overcrowded country. And, of course, it is only an inevitable aspect of that modern progress of which we are all proud. We must go on "progressing", even if we don't know the direction in which we are moving—even if it leads to hell itself. Because, after all, "Progress" is "Progress", even if it rushes over the bodies of children, and elderly men who get absent minded and step off the curb without looking, or young lovers who go wobbling about on bicycles, and other folk who have no road sense at all —not remembering that roads are now railway tracks for engines without rails.

Now and again, of course, one has a stab at the heart, in spite of the joy of Progress, when some brilliant young man is smashed up at the crossroads, or when some beautiful young woman, famous perhaps on the stage or screen, is killed by a car dashing out of a side road at forty miles an hour. It seems a pity. But these things will happen—won't they?—in this age of speed and progress.

The motorists go cutting in, taking chances, clinging to the crown of the road, putting a bit of speed on because there's a cocktail party at the end of the journey, seeing what the little old engine can do if it's pushed, taking a wide curve round a high-hedged bend without worrying whether something may be coming from the other way. One can't expect a motorist to crawl along like a funeral hearse! Besides, those damned pedestrians and cyclists ought to be more careful. Do they think the roads are made for them?

Who cares? Who worries? Whose business is it to slow down the pace of life or reduce the number of casualties? After a moment's shock when the figures are published now and then, after raised eyebrows because the number of dead has gone up this time, the man in the corner of the third-class carriage turns to the sports page or his crossword puzzle. Who cares about those statistics of death and accident on the roads of England—unless one's own child or wife is among them.

2 *The Man Who Cares*

There is one man who cares. It's his job, and he's keen on it. He made up his mind when he took it on that he would do something to reduce those figures and make the roads safer for everybody using them, including the motorists. He would do it by cajoling, warning, pleading, by any kind of means which would teach people to use these lethal weapons with more care, and better manners, and some human kindness. He would use what powers he had to improve the roads, and put up safety devices, and mark out crossings for pedestrians, and put on some kind of a speed limit in built-up areas, in spite of all the opposition which he knew he would get, and got.

He is the man with the beacons. He is that man Hore-Belisha of the golden globes—much derided—and the winking lights—much cursed by drivers—and the silver studs across the streets—much ignored—and the radio voice which speaks to the public now and then before bank holidays, warning them that they will be dead if they don't behave themselves, or that other people will be dead before next Tuesday if they don't drive with a certain consideration for their fellow beings.

He does these radio talks well, like a friendly soul talking to each individual who may be listening. He is persuasive, simple, direct, and without pomposity. He has saved a great number of lives worth saving—thousands since he took up his job.

He happens to be a friend of mine, and at lunch recently in

THE BELISHA BEACON

his little house which was built a century ago for one of Queen Victoria's maids of honour—she lived in it until she was ninety—he told me something about his difficulties in this adventure of lifesaving.

He complained of his limited powers. Most of his ideas have had to be carried out not by authority but by persuasion and moral pressure—against people who don't want to be persuaded and make a lot of fuss about it. They are the local authorities who have power over the roads in their own districts. There are 122 such bodies in London. The whole of England is divided up by local authorities who have their own ideas, and stick to their own rights, and are not easily induced to adopt any big unified scheme or any reasonable recommendations.

"Take these by-passes," said my friend Hore-Belisha. "What can I do about all this ribbon development? I have no authority to stop it, and the local authorities allow all those houses to be crowded along each side of the road for twenty miles out of London—ruining the countryside—so that one wants a by-pass to by-pass the by-pass. Each little house has its own garage and motorcar. Out they come to join the stream of traffic. Every day more cars are on the road. The speedway meant for fast-moving cars is cluttered up with local traffic."

He spoke of the conditions in London, increasing the dangers and congestion every time the local authorities give permission for the building of another monstrous block of flats. On a space which once held a row of houses with one family in each there are now huge buildings in which three hundred people are crowded. They all become motorists. The London street is choked with their cars. The whole thing is a menace.

The question of parking becomes one of the big problems. It is destroying the amenities of London life when quiet residential squares, like Hans Place, become crowded with cars all day long because their owners are shopping at Harrods.

But the minister of transport has done something about all this by getting an act of Parliament passed on behalf of the government, giving certain powers to local authorities. Under this act it is illegal now to build, or make means of access without consent, within 220 feet of either side of the middle of any classified road. Sixty thousand miles of road are henceforth preserved as sanctuaries from the desecrator, if the authorities will use their powers—and they won't get grants unless they do. Another act which the minister of transport got through before last Christmas makes him highway authority over all trunk roads (4,500 miles) from April 1. This is a breach with the principle of locality which has prevailed in England. It went through without a division.

Every month and every year the problems the minister of transport has to tackle become more difficult to handle. He is fighting all the time against the increased pressure of traffic, and his only satisfaction is that by all his signs and safety devices he has checked the upward rate of casualties.

The number of persons killed or injured during each of the last three years, and the number of casualties per 1,000 vehicles registered, were as follows:

Year	Killed	Injured	Total	Number of persons killed or injured per 1,000 motor vehicles registered
1934	7,343	231,603	238,946	98.8
1935	6,502	221,726	228,228	88.4
1936	6,561	227,813	234,374	84.7

Numbers of mechanically propelled road vehicles:

1934	2,416,908
1935	2,581,027
1936	2,768,606

These figures show that there has been a continuous reduction in the number of casualties in relation to the numbers of motor vehicles registered, and, while it is, of course, impossible to estimate the number of lives that have been saved by the Man with the Beacons, the figures show that his efforts have had a great effect, taking into account the constant increase in traffic, and that the ratio of killed to injured has appreciably fallen.

His latest scheme for lifesaving is his raising of 800 specially trained traffic men who will act as mentors of the roads and not as traffic cops out for more summonses. He hopes that it is only the first recruiting of a body who will be raised in all parts of the country. But that hope is again dependent on the willingness of local authorities to co-operate and make their own roads safer.

We have to pay the price of liberty from dictatorship which has its advantages now and then. There is no Mussolini here to make an urban district council tremble in its shoes and pale at its gills when an order comes from the great man.

This Man with the Beacons is a human, friendly, dynamic and humorous fellow, and his career has been astonishing in its quick rise to Cabinet rank.

His father died when he was nine months old, and he was left with a widowed mother who struggled to give him an education, and to whom he owes, he tells me, everything in life. After the war, when he was still a young man, he went up to Oxford and then looked round for a career. What about the law? What about politics?

There was a general election in Devonport. He went down with a carpetbag to Devonshire, where an old gentleman named Sir Thomas Kynoch Coke sat in his own stronghold. Young Hore-Belisha held some meetings and at one of them he was told that his political opponent had referred to him as "a little chit of a fellow." The blood of the Hore-Belishas was roused. Passionately he reminded his audience of sailors, and stokers, and dockyard men, that he was not such a little chit of a fellow as Napoleon when he crossed the Alps, or as Sir John Wolfe when he stormed the heights of Abraham, or as Nelson when he won the battle of Trafalgar, or as Pitt when at twenty-three he was prime minister of England. He went back to ancient Greece and Rome for little chits of fellows. "And let me tell Sir Thomas Kynoch Coke," he shouted, "that five million little chits of fellows defended England in time of war and that a million of them left their bones in France"—or words to that effect.

He won the election with a handsome majority and was startled to find himself a member of Parliament without visible means of subsistence. He went into Fleet Street, once called "The Street of Adventure" by a certain novelist, and presently got a job in the Board of Trade, followed by one in the Treasury, and afterwards was appointed to the Ministry of Transport.

He had to decide whether he would conform to conventions and play the game with the old school tie, according to the code of old gents on the Front Bench, or do his job with a dangerous zeal which might seem rather "pushful" to the elder statesmen.

He decided to go all out on this job of lifesaving, by every means of publicity, and drastic experiment, and forceful pressure, and persuasion, and beguilement. He went to the radio and got into direct touch with the great public. His traffic signals aroused ridicule, contempt and annoyance. Everything he did raised a storm of criticism from the motoring world and the papers which gets its advertisements. But he got the figures of mortality down. He kept the casualty lists from mounting. Needless to say, he was called a self-advertiser, a mountebank, and a dangerous fellow, upsetting the stately humdrum of ministerial dignity. But he saved the lives of children, and old people, and cyclists, and all manner of folk who but for him would now be dead. Not a bad job!

He won his spurs. He was called to Cabinet rank in the office he had made for himself. He is one of the few younger men who stands out as a future leader. He is worth watching, and I happen to know that behind all his much-criticised pushfulness there is a spiritual outlook on life, and a disregard of personal ambition, and a rather boyish and wistful mind, which loves beauty, and passionately hates the spread of ugliness—the horrible destruction of beautiful old buildings in London and other cities—and is keen to check its sprawling advance upon the loveliness of England.

III. STUDENTS OF HUMANITY

1 Architects of a Brave New World

I went into a great building off Kingsway to take lunch with a little man with a high-powered intelligence, considered dangerous by people who don't like his particular type of mind and its results in printed or spoken words. His name is Laski.

As I stood in the hall, waiting for him to take me to his room, I was passed by numbers of young men and women who were all in a great hurry to fill up empty spaces in their system. It was, as I have said, the luncheon hour.

I scanned them as they passed. Among them were two Japanese, a young Chinaman, several Indians, and a much larger number of young men who might have been Americans, or English, or Germans, or Danes, or indeed any kind of European. Many of them wore glasses. Most of them looked undernourished but were probably thinned down by thought, or an ill-balanced diet, or hunger for truth and knowledge.

Girls came along with broad brows, and serious eyes, and clothes not worn for allurement. I know their type. I have seen them in Berlin University, in Columbia College, New York, in King's College, Strand. They were students, and students look very much the same in most countries of the West.

This place was and is one of the intellectual powerhouses of the world. It is, for this country and many others, the Intelligence Department of that Brave New World towards which we are all advancing, whether we like it or whether we don't, and which may reach a higher phase of civilisation if its blueprints are not destroyed by catastrophe before the design has been put in hand. It is the London School of Economics.

Each year brings three thousand students here—regular, occasional and intercollegiate. Of these, something over five hundred come from forty different foreign countries, including about one hundred from China. The numbers from Germany are declining slightly, dropping from 115 last year to 84 this year. The Americans send a strong contingent. France sends very few, as all Frenchmen believe that their country is the intellectual centre of the world and dislike crossing the Channel, which makes them sick.

The regular students are those who take full day or evening courses and read for their degrees. The occasional students take special courses in subjects which particularly interest them. The intercollegiate students come from other colleges in the federation of London University for special subjects. There are also research students from this and other countries. There is an increasing number of women students, though it still leaves the school with two-and-a-half times as many men as women.

Those are dry figures, but they represent something which is very remarkable in the life and thought of this country and those other forty foreign countries from which the students come.

For this school is not merely an institution in which the younger mind assimilates a certain amount of knowledge for its culture or intellectual satisfaction. It is a dynamic place. It deals with facts and problems bearing down upon human life today, however remote may be their origins in the distant past. Its professors, and lecturers, and students are all keenly at work, analysing the causes of things now happening to all communities and classes in this planet.

They specialise in the history of that whimsical and murderous animal called Man.

They are examining modern civilisation in every country of the world, by every kind of statistical standard, by graphs and curves which record progress or decay, booms and slumps, epidemics of the body, and madnesses of the mind.

They study the output of natural wealth and its distribution or restriction; who goes hungry and why; where the gold comes from and where it goes, the mystery of money; the effect of tariffs, quotas and subsidies on world trade; the birth rate and death rate, and the future state of world populations if the decline in the birth rate is not checked; the accessibility of raw material and the effects of maldistribution upon political systems and social unrest.

They track down the blind forces moving beneath the surface of the human scene.

Research in the great building includes the whole history of Man since his first gropings to some kind of association with his fellows, all through this story of trial and error, achievement and failure, endless conflict, endless agony, and endless folly, with here and there a gleam of reason or a touch of genius.

There are lecturers in all the laws which man has made for his discipline, or his fanaticism, or his peace and comfort. They even lecture on international law and make out a case for its existence, though it is not apparent to the naked eye of the man in the third-class carriage reading the *Daily Express* or the *Evening Standard.*

They lecture on every "ism" which was invented by human brains to attain the perfect form of government which they endeavoured, and still endeavour, to impose upon their fellow citizens for their own good, even though they must wade through blood and terror to make them happy.

These students hear lectures now upon Communism, Fascism, Naziism, pacifism and other creeds which are at present in debate; though the fanatics of each faith are unaware of the scientific analysis by which they are being probed and measured by the students of the L.S.E.

Professor Gregory, Professor Plant, Professor Robbins, have been lecturing on Contemporary British Problems of Economics. They think they know a lot about it, and it might be helpful if the two Front Benches of the House of Commons took a few courses under them. Then they, too, might begin to know something about it.

Professor Ginsberg and Professor Mannheim are lecturing on sociology, and Mr Marshall has been giving twenty lectures on the social developments of modern England. It is the story and analysis of all that has happened in this land to get a decent way of life for the common crowd—not yet fully achieved but, on the whole, not too bad compared with other tribes.

There is a statistical department where large numbers of young men and women learn to measure up almost everything from birth to death in all the populations of the world, and in every class of economic problem, by cold little figures which have no mercy on sentiment, imagination or oratorical vagueness. They ought to tell the exact truth about almost everything, except that even figures may be awful liars—which is rather worrying to those who tend to rely upon them.

Here, then, is a powerhouse of human intelligence, as far as it goes, and not negligible in its influence upon our modern world of thought. It is the G.H.Q. of statistical information, under the direction of men like Sir William Beveridge and Sir Josiah Stamp. It is a workshop of planning for the present and

AN INTELLECTUAL POWER HOUSE

future. It is an information department for those who want any facts to back up their theories. When ministers of state want special information they send round here for it, and get it.

Many of the debates in the House of Commons on such subjects as the birth rate, or the nourishment of school children, are conducted on figures and facts provided by this powerhouse.

The French government applies to it for information, though French students are rare in its lecture rooms.

The dreamers of a new China make their plans from the study of Chinese students at the London School of Economics.

The world that is coming, if it comes without a crash, will be permeated with the ideas and visions derived from the 200,000 volumes stored in the library of this school. Here are the blueprints and the brains which will help to make that Brave New World—to which older and traditional minds, like mine, look forward with apprehension and horror.

2 *Left-Wing Laski*

But I have been too long in getting to that lunch with Professor Harold Laski.

Of all the brains in the London School of Economics his is, perhaps, the most nimble, audacious, card indexed and disturbing. It is, perhaps, also the most influential, because many thousands of young and forward-thinking minds read Laski, quote Laski, and bow their heads three times when his name is mentioned. In China they know him. In India they have his books on their shelves. In Japan his essays are hidden by students who do not accept the faith of their fathers. In the United States every university knows Laski as well as they do Sinclair Lewis, and when an article appears by him in *Harper's Magazine*, as often it does, young fellows from Columbia College to the

University of Washington read it with a belief in revelation.

He gave me lunch, and I knew that I was sitting opposite a man who wants to change our social system in a way which I should find extraordinarily unpleasant, which would probably deprive me of my house and garden and selfish pleasures. It would drag down many of my friends to ruin. It would destroy the last relics of individualism and create a human ant heap under one law and one discipline in this land of so-called liberty (we have quite a lot compared with other folk), and would leave the older traditional people derelict and broken in an uncomfortable world.

He is a charming little man.

Watching him across the table, I thought how absurd it would be to think of him as one of those dark and sinister men who want to raise the Red flag and dabble it from time to time in human gore! Behind his round spectacles he looks very young and boyish, though he is in the forties. A smile darts into his eyes and lights up his schoolboy face. He talks simply, unaffectedly and brilliantly. I had an idea that he must have been a wonder child in his cradle. At twenty-four years of age he was negotiating important affairs between such men as Haldane, and Milner, and Lloyd George. During the war he had a chair at Harvard. He has absorbed vast stores of facts, all of which are perfectly arranged in his mind and perfectly remembered. He has one of those deadly memories which slay the inaccurate thinker and loose-mouthed orator.

Once, I am told, he was in debate with a certain statesman who misquoted a sentence from Karl Marx. Laski smiled—his boyish smile—and said: "That's not quite right." Then he quoted a whole page from Karl Marx in German. An awful fellow to meet in open debate!

He told me a good deal about the work at the London School of Economics.

"What goes on in the students' minds?" I asked as we passed groups of them. "Do they have a sense of apprehension about a coming war? Does the spectre affright them?"

He nodded.

"It certainly does! They feel that it is futile to go on studying, and making plans, and dreaming dreams, if at the end of it the shambles is waiting for them. They can't do anything about it. Who can?"

He spoke of the extraordinary development of the school during the past thirty years or so, when it was first started in a very small way.

"Most of these students," he told me, "come from a class not endowed with the wealth of this world. This place is an Open Sesame to them. They are all very keen. Something must come of all this intelligence unless it is frustrated by war."

He took me up into his room and talked of his early experiences in the United States as student of international law and political science. His hero was an old man named Holmes, the son of Oliver Wendell Holmes, who wrote *The Autocrat of the Breakfast Table* and other lovely books. He showed me a facsimile of the old man's notes of the books he had read year by year. At ninety or thereabouts he was still an insatiable reader. He had read more books in a year than most men read in ten.

Laski gave me a book of his own: *The Rise of European Liberalism*, and I have been reading it with admiration and annoyance. It is a brilliant study, stuffed with historical research. It has almost (but not quite) undermined the foundations of my faith in the Liberal ideal. His thesis is that Liberalism was restricted in its purpose and ideal to gaining liberty, free from all restraint, to acquire and safeguard property, to make profits, to increase trade and commerce for the merchant and middle class, without consideration for the toiling masses, kept low in wages and social conditions so that they should not interfere with the traders, the money-makers, and the small gentry. He quotes evidence in support of this from the eighteenth-century idealists—the makers of the French Revolution, the Code Napoléon, and the writings of Voltaire and other men who have been regarded as the apostles of democracy.

That is a harsh view of Liberalism which Laski softens in a passage or two, and it is one which I find hard to accept, having been steeped in the Liberal tradition which has coloured all my thoughts and feelings. But Laski makes out a good case as counsel for the prosecution of the Liberal idea. I should hate to challenge him in open debate.

He and Gollancz run a Left Book Club which has, I believe, been very successful. If it isn't one of the most subversive influences in this country I am much mistaken. It challenges our social system and the whole structure of Capitalism, not easy to defend with all these profiteers about and so much callous wealth—from every side. It is distinctly Red in its hue of thought and I dislike that colour, which reminds me of blood.

But Professor Harold Laski disarms one by his glinting smile, his good nature, his intellectual charm. One of his friends gave me a line on him.

"Harold J. Laski is one of the acutest minds on the Left side of England; and he is well over to the Left, though not as far as Moscow. He is resolute for freedom of the mind. That is to say, whether a government is Right or Left, Laski is sure to be an inveterate rebel. Our own Labour party knows that. Labour people are always nervous when Laski is actively about, because he is hard on all soft and indecisive stuff, and snipes blithely but unerringly. His mind, as well as being acute, is as cheerful as a boy's who knows he can face the dons with wider and better knowledge. In fact, he used to do that at Oxford when he was an undergraduate.

"He still looks an insignificant boyish figure. He surprises people when they learn he is a professor in constitutional history. What they are chiefly aware of is a pair of large round spectacles and a mischievous smile. He has a habit of waiting inconspicuously while ponderous bigwigs are letting loose large solemnities; building up, we will say, their massy eloquence; and then coming in with a quiet voice, and that smile, to bring down the lot with a funny anecdote devastatingly relevant. So there are those who hate the little man. His tactics in debate are diabolical!"

The librarian of the London School of Economics in charge of those 200,000 volumes and a vast number of pamphlets, reviews and other printed matter is Dr Dickenson, the son-in-law of the greatest master of English prose today. I mean, of course, H. M. Tomlinson, who writes like an angel, being one, though God knows he doesn't look like it.

"I suppose the minds that come out of this school are on the Left?" I asked Dr Dickenson, disguising my apprehension of the Left if it goes beyond my mild form of Liberalism and my hatred of all violence.

"Inevitably," he said. "They are young. Their minds look forward."

"The Extreme Left?" I asked with some anxiety.

He reassured me.

"There is a small Communist group here but it doesn't amount to much. The majority are followers of the Labour party, but there is a strong Liberal society and a stronger Conservative club. Many of the governors are Conservatives. The mind of England is represented in all its angles and all its traditional conservatism, in spite of the natural instinct of the younger mind to be in revolt against conventions and the established system, whatever it may be."

So there it is, this remarkable workshop of intelligence. I am inclined to think that it is more important than Oxford or Cambridge in making the England of tomorrow. I do not disguise my own anxieties as to the sort of England it will be, but I hope for the best. There is a lot of room for improvement.

IV. THE NEW COMMONWEALTH

1 The Huntsmen of Peace

There are many minds appalled by this horrible menace of war. They refuse in their souls to accept the possibility of its apparition. All over England there are Peace Societies, pouring out words and propaganda against the futility and wickedness of war. But they are preaching mostly to the converted and not reaching out much to other nations whose leaders are scornful of the peace ideal and raise their hands in salute to a forest of bayonets above the heads of their well-trained youth.

There are many kinds of pacifists and busy peacemakers who believe that they are having a race with time and the devil. Most of them have no plan. They hate war, but how can they stop it? They uphold the League of Nations with a sense of despair in its impotence. They reaffirm their belief in Collective Security, though it broke down hopelessly over Abyssinia.

Some of them, like Canon Dick Sheppard and Aldous Huxley, adopt the policy of nonresistance, whatever enemy may attack. They advocate the resignation to martyrdom of the early Christians who put up no fight against Caesar and his gladiators, and surrendered their bodies to the wild beasts. From a Christian point of view that may be the only consistent attitude as far as one's own body is concerned, but they would be sacrificing other people's bodies to the beasts—the bodies of our babes and millions of helpless people under our protection, to say nothing of our liberties and our moral code. The beast would triumph and would have many victims.

There are other types of mind to whom this drift to war is equally abhorrent, but they have different ideas for averting it.

One of them is a man whom one would not easily imagine as an idealist with a plan of peace, judging him by personal appearance or outward characteristics. For people obsessed with this ideal are, as a rule, "sicklied o'er with the pale cast of thought"; but this man has a ruddy skin and a soldierly look. The pacifists are caricatured as wearing their hair long and being thin chested and anaemic. But this man, who has devoted twenty years of his life and fortune to the prevention of that "next war" and all others, is a hunting man with blue eyes which have scanned many a field where the hounds are out, and he has a hearty way with him and a fine joyous laugh.

I once travelled with him years ago on a long railway journey. We were both on the way to Geneva to attend the Assembly of the League of Nations as observers and supporters of that attempt to establish co-operation among peoples who had been killing each other in great numbers not long before.

My travelling companion was known to his friends as D. D., which is short for David Davies. He is now Lord Davies, but it makes no difference to his laugh.

In the railway carriage, I remember, as we rushed across Europe, he talked a good deal about his ideas for an international police force which would act, if need be, as guardians of the people, but at other times he pulled out a little red book in which he kept the names and records of his hounds. Those names were sweet music to his soul and made him break out into song—mostly hymns—which he trolled out like marching songs so that they became quite cheerful, and would have pleased St Francis of Assisi, who used merry tunes for his glad praises of Christ his beloved.

I believe the saints would have liked this cheery Welshman, because he has the heart of a boy, and a gay spirit, and great courage in the service of the Prince of Peace.

I saw something of his courage in those early years after the war. His plan of peace seemed fantastic to many cynics. They ridiculed it, but he didn't take umbrage. He became a passionate propagandist of his idea for a new commonwealth of nations, submitting their differences to a supreme court of equity, and defending world peace, not by independent armies, but by an international police force.

It would have been so much more pleasing to him to go on keeping his pack of hounds and living the life of a country squire, but he became a student and a writing man. He wrote many pamphlets and had them published at his own expense and distributed to people who, in many cases, no doubt, pitched them into the wastepaper basket. He wrote long books which cost him a lot of time and a lot of study, and study must be a strain on a man who loves the cry of the hounds and the whistle of the wind. He plunged deep into the peace plans of ancient philosophers and medieval scholars, and startled high-brow gentlemen who thought they knew everything but had missed these. He was the disciple of an idea which has been moving in the mind of thinkers looking out upon a world of anarchy and warfare since the first oases of civilisation; an idea which lapsed from time to time, and was forgotten, and then reappeared.

It was restated rather well by one of his own countrymen—few people have heard of Richard Price—in the eighteenth century.

"Let every state with respect to its internal concerns be continued independent of all the rest: and let a general confederation be formed by the appointment of a Senate consisting of representatives from all the different states. Let this Senate possess the power of managing all the common concerns of the united States, and of judging and deciding between them as a common Arbiter or Umpire in all disputes, *having at the same time under its direction the common force of the states to support its decisions.*"

D. D., as we used to call him—it's hard to get out of the habit—has founded a society to study this idea of a commonwealth of nations, sovereign and independent in their own systems of government, but obedient to the decisions of a court of justice and equity on all disputes between themselves, and enforcing the law, if need be, by a police force which, in the last resort, would be used against any nation acting in a criminal way against its neighbours and in defence of the law.

All that, of course, goes beyond the Covenant of the League of Nations as now existing, because there is no recognised international law, and no international police force taking the place of private armies and ready for immediate action in case of need.

2 *Lions and Lambs*

The New Commonwealth, founded by my cheery friend for the promotion and study of this peace plan, started in a very small way. Now it has branches in many countries, including Germany, and has attracted distinguished minds of many political shades of thought.

Its membership is extraordinary in this country. The president of the British section is Winston Churchill, that stormy petrel who is now a convert—he says—to the principles of Collective Security. Socialists like Snowden, Attlee, and Philip Noel Baker are vice-presidents with such anti-Socialists as the Marquess of Crewe, Duff-Cooper (secretary for war), Viscount Astor and Sir Robert Horne. Pacifists like Sir Norman Angell and Lord Cecil, and that sturdy old champion of international peace, the Right Honourable George Barnes, support this New

Commonwealth idea with General Macdonogh, who was our chief of intelligence in the war, Major General Sir Frederick Maurice, and Major General Sir Ernest Swinton.

Commissioner Lamb of the Salvation Army, and Dr Hertz, a Jewish rabbi, are in the same list of vice-presidents as the Archbishops of York and Wales, the Bishops of Chelmsford, Durham, Lichfield, Liverpool, and St Asaph, and the Dean of Canterbury. The head of Imperial Chemicals (who makes quite a lot of high explosives) is on the same roll-call as that child Beverley Nichols, who wrote a very passionate book against that class of business. Vice-Admiral Gordon Campbell, V.C., is there, with Allen of Hurtwood, who was a conscientious objector in time of war. Great lawyers, scientists, economists and industrialists are fellow members of that organisation called the New Commonwealth which has its headquarters at Thorney House, Westminster.

It has an influence beyond its numbers on English thought today and is worth joining, I think, by anyone who wishes to support some constructive plan of law and order in this European jungle of passion and anarchy. It is the ultimate ideal—the goal towards which humanity must move or perish. Is there time to get there before reason is overwhelmed? To pretend that it exists now under the magic phrase "Collective Security" would be folly beyond words.

I went round one day recently to see the founder of this society—that man of Wales who has a dream in his mind and a laugh in his heart, and a desperate purpose to do something to save the young manhood of the world, and this civilisation, such as it is.

He gave a Tallyho! at the sight of me and raised his hand in a high salute.

"Here's a good story you might like to hear," he said. "It comes from Wales."

It was a good story, but not for this page, having nothing to do with world peace.

Presently he sat down at the table and gave a kind of groan.

"What do you think of things?" he asked. "Better or worse?"

He was not pleased by news which had reached him from Germany and Spain. I had asked to see him for ten minutes, but we talked for two hours, and the gist of it I put down here, leaving out our conversational interludes. It states his case rather well.

"There's no doubt that we're steadily drifting towards war," he said. "Our descent down the slippery slope is littered with the debris of lost opportunities and broken pledges."

He gave a list of them.

"There was America's repudiation of the League. When the United States withdrew from its membership, the moral authority of the League was seriously impaired and it has never recovered from this initial setback. The seizure of Vilna, and the invasion of the Ruhr, followed by the bombardment of Corfu by Mussolini, demonstrated to the world that the members of the new International Authority were governed by expediency rather than by the principles of equity and justice.

"The rejection of the 1924 Protocol, mainly at the instigation of Great Britain, blocked the development of the League and prevented it from assuming the responsibilities of an International Authority. Locarno was a sorry substitute.

"The rejection by Japan of the recommendations of the Lytton Commission, and the failure of the League to apply financial and economic sanctions, still further undermined its prestige and authority.

"The Italo-Abyssinian debacle robbed the League of the last shreds of its influence and convinced the smaller nations that they could no longer regard it as the sheet anchor of their existence and security."

He added some more items of this Catalogue of Failure in recent history.

"The demilitarised zones of the Rhineland and the Dardanelles, which we all hoped would be valuable precedents for a preventive policy against war, are now being refortified. Then there's Danzig—a free city under the protection of the League. During the last few weeks it has been thrown to the wolves, and the supporters of the League find themselves in concentration camps and prisons.

"Lastly, the Disarmament Conference has ended in failure, with the result that each sovereign nation has now entered a rearmament race, bound sooner or later to end in a titanic struggle, unless, in the meantime, saner counsels prevail and a bold attempt is made to abolish international anarchy and to substitute in its place the rule of law."

In spite of all this he hasn't abandoned all hope of the League and doesn't despair of the League ideal.

"It still lives, maybe in an attenuated form, but we ought to remember that it has prevented more than one war and done many useful jobs. There's no reason why it shouldn't acquire fresh strength and vigour if its members are determined to profit by past experience and apply the lessons derived from its failures to the future development of an effective international authority. What other hope is there?"

3 *The Reign of Law*

"We must get back to the reign of law," said my peace-loving friend, after we had discussed the need of tolerance in international affairs—tolerance of other people's ideas and systems of government.

"How do you define that mystical word Law?" I asked.

He said that it possessed three attributes. First, that it must be supported by public opinion; second, that it must be capable of modification and amendment by means of a peaceful procedure; and third, that it can be enforced if necessary by the imposition of sanctions.

"International law in its present form," he said, "does not possess these attributes; therefore it is not law at all. It's merely a fiction, because no peaceful procedure exists at present to alter the law and there is no organised sanction to uphold it. There's no machinery for the revision of treaties to bring them into conformity with changed conditions and to express the dynamic principle in international relationships. War—the duel—has been, and still is, the instrument of change, and so long as we acquiesce in this arrangement we are bound sooner or later to drift into war."

He developed his argument about the necessity of an international police force to enforce and uphold the law. Treaties, he said, can be torn up with impunity whenever a nation decides to denounce a pact and believes it is strong enough to do so.

"During the last two years Germany has repudiated most of her obligations under the Treaty of Versailles. From the strictly judicial standpoint she was hopelessly in the wrong. Hitler had no right to take unilateral action in denouncing a treaty which, rightly or wrongly, was an integral part of the public law of Europe. On the other hand, as there was no peaceful procedure to adjudicate upon Germany's grievances, it's difficult to see what other course was open to her. How could she secure relief from what she considered to be the unjust terms imposed upon her, to which she had only agreed at the point of the bayonet?"

What he kept emphasising was that the idea of equity or justice never seems to enter into this so-called system of international law, and, so long as these ideas are excluded, it is idle to suggest, he thinks, that there can be any real commonwealth of nations or that we can avert the drift towards war. Consequently, he thinks, we are driven to the conclusion that in order to establish the rule of law, two things at least are essential—first, a peaceful procedure for the settlement of all disputes, including what are described as political issues—and second, an adequate and, if possible, an overwhelming sanction to deter an aggressor from the crime of war, to uphold the sanctity of treaties, and to guarantee that the changes in the law recommended and decided upon from time to time by an international court of justice shall become effective.

"But war is war," I argued, "even if it is waged by an international police force. As Dick Sheppard says, a Geneva bomb would kill just in the same way as a German bomb."

My friend saw no sense in that remark.

"No one suggests," he answered, "that because a country refused to carry out a decision, its inhabitants should be immediately attacked or bombed by an international police force. A man who refuses to pay his fine is not visited and instantly bludgeoned by a policeman because he is a defaulter; he is merely escorted to prison. Similarly, nations can be completely isolated by the imposition of diplomatic, financial and economic sanctions, which is tantamount to sending them to prison. But these sanctions will also be useless unless behind them, and in the background, the military resources of the Commonwealth of International Authority stand properly organised and equipped, ready to intervene if need be, and to go to the assistance of any nation which is the victim of aggression."

He pointed to the experience of the Italo-Abyssinian War.

It seemed to him to prove conclusively that financial and economic sanctions will not suffice, alone, either to deter a nation from going to war or to extinguish the conflagration once it has started. The threat of military reprisals by Mussolini against individual members of the League, especially Great

Britain, who were prepared to apply the oil sanction sufficed, he said, to strangle that proposal.

Had there been a powerful international police force, supported by all the members of the League, that threat, he thought, would have never been made; in fact, in his belief, there would have been no war at all. It was, he said, the absence of any police force, organised before—not after—the crisis had arisen, which brought about the collapse of economic sanctions, destroyed the authority of the League, and contributed to the humiliation of the British Empire.

All this leads him to the conclusion that there can be no real security for peace unless provision has been made for these two vital institutions: an equity tribunal and an international police force, because until they have been established, he maintains, the rule of law cannot become operative.

"Well, to sum it all up . . ." I suggested.

He summed it all up.

"It's for this reason that the New Commonwealth Society has come into existence to preach the gospel that all disputes must be settled by recourse to reason, instead of brute force, and to proclaim the principle that the only right or moral use of force is the policing function. It endeavours to concentrate public opinion on the necessity for these two institutions as essential to the successful working of the League.

"Of course, it's not intended that they should supersede the existing machinery. On the contrary, we regard the League of Nations as the foundation upon which to build, and we suggest that both these institutions should be grafted on to its present organisation.

"I'm sure we all agree that war—the ancient practice of trial by battle—ought to be abolished. But people are tired of listening merely to the denunciation of war, of its horrors and sufferings, its immorality and futility. What everyone wants to know is this: How are we going to put a stop to it? How are we going to prevent it?

"The answer of the New Commonwealth is: by expressing our determination to abolish it in terms of institutions and organisation, and this, I believe, can only be accomplished on the basis of justice. At present these institutions don't exist, with the result that the collective will to peace is thwarted and baulked. The inevitable consequence is that nations, instead of preparing for peace, are preparing for war."

This argument—which I have given at some length because I think it is a well-reasoned statement of a great idea—seems to me convincing on general principles. But I cannot see, I confess, any immediate hope of its adoption by nations like Germany and Italy—though miracles may happen even there, especially when miracles are aided by economic pressures and by the enormous dangers of general ruin which would overtake all nations alike if war is the only argument. But I am desperately afraid that this idea of Collective Security may be used by a group of nations before it is collective and before it is secure.

As Winston Churchill, that realist, said in a speech to the New Commonwealth—it was a great gathering of the most distinguished minds in England—"We don't want to proceed under the name of Collective Security like a flock of sheep advancing to the butcher." But as he also added: "What alternative is there to this plan and purpose of the New Commonwealth?"

The Labour party has been using the words Collective Security as a magic incantation and urging the government to found its policy upon that basis. But at the present time, without the United States, Japan, Germany and Italy, it has no basis and no reality. To pretend that it has reality now would be to involve this country in wars which we should have to fight mainly alone, or with Russia and France in another "World War." We must build the New Commonwealth on a broader and firmer basis than that.

But the New Commonwealth holds up the standard of faith in justice and equity, and the defence of law by international police. It's worth working for, I think.

Younger men looking to the future ought to join it. Its ideals will happen one day.

V. THE SQUIRE OF CHARTWELL MANOR

1 A Man of Kent

I went one day down to Kent to see a man who by his genius and character is in direct line of descent with the political leaders of English history—Fox, Pitt, Palmerston—and further back than that to his own ancestor, the Duke of Marlborough, and the contemporaries of that great soldier and adventurer in the days of Queen Anne. It was, of course, Winston Churchill.

I had a particular and, for me, extraordinary reason for going to see him. I had been given, as I have told elsewhere in this book, a number of facts about our Air Force which revealed a very unsatisfactory state of affairs, to say the least of it, from the point of view of national defence in the event of a war happening within the next few years. It seemed inconsistent in me—I was conscious of the inconsistency—that I should be the carrier of this information, believing as I did that the piling up of armaments by all the nations, in fierce and fearful competition, and especially the crowding of the skies with fighting and bombing aeroplanes, was bound to lead to the enormous calamity of another great war unless the leaders of Europe recoiled in time.

But I was under a pledge to hand on certain secret facts to

Winston Churchill, and there were other reasons, less urgent, why I wanted to call on him. He paints pictures in oil colours and I wanted to see what kind of work he did. And I wanted to have a talk with a man whose books I have read with immense admiration for their quality of historical writing, and whose career—with all its faults and all its failures—will be written in history also as that of the most brilliant and dynamic figure of our time.

I was a few minutes late in arriving for lunch, because on a first visit to his house of Chartwell Manor, near Westerham, in Kent, where he has lived for many years, it is not easy to find the way. I pushed a little bell at the side of a heavy oak door, between two elaborately carved columns in a great square brick house of Georgian, or Queen Anne, style.

"Mr Churchill is waiting for you," said the servant, and I found him waiting, not impatiently, in a room where he was painting with a friend. He seemed to have a hundred brushes, and I was filled with admiration and envy. But lunch was ready, and while he washed his hands his friend—a distinguished physicist—led me to the room where we were going to eat.

It was an immense room, like a dining hall in some old monastery, very plainly and barely furnished, except for a few paintings on the walls by the master of the house. In a few moments he came to join us at table and gave me one quick smiling look as he sat down.

"The last time I met you," he said, "was during the war at an old château in France."

"A long time ago now," I remarked.

"Yes. And all of us have grown older since then."

I remembered him perfectly as he looked at that time, very young for his years, very alert, and quick in movement. Now he was heavier, stouter, older. But I knew that I had changed even more, though not in bulk.

"Tell me what you know about the Air Force," he said.

I told him the facts which had been given to me and which I believed to be reliable. He listened attentively and surprised me by doing so. I have noticed so often that men who have held high positions do not listen much. They like to do all the telling and all the talking. But I soon found that I was bringing coals to Newcastle. Churchill had all the facts. There was very little he didn't know about the technical deficiencies of our aircraft and organisation.

"I have made it my subject lately," he said. "And of course I get information from all sources. I don't weave these things out of my imagination. I will read you out the private report I made to the government on this subject. I think you will find I have covered most of your points."

He certainly had, and I was impressed by his memory and mastery of such technical problems as the range, weight, carrying capacity, equipment and speed of various types of aircraft. Now and again he turned to his friend, the distinguished physicist, for confirmation of his statements, and that quiet man opposite nodded and said: "That's right."

Then he spoke of the general world situation, and was not pleased with it, but was not quite hopeless about the possibilities of avoiding another great war.

"If we can get over the next two years there's a chance that we may keep the peace. The present dangers may be averted by the internal breakdown of dictatorships and a general relaxation of tension. Meanwhile, strange as it may seem, I put my faith in the League of Nations!"

He laughed for a moment, as though conscious that this might be regarded by some of his critics as an unbelievable statement.

"I'm all in favour," he explained, "of Collective Security against any aggressor nation."

I reminded him of the private speech he had made when he said that it would be foolish to adopt the collective security of a flock of sheep advancing on their way to the butcher.

There was a smile in his eyes at the remembrance of this phrase.

"Quite so! But we may get a combination of nations backing the idea of Collective Security—so strong that even Germany would hesitate to attack. I don't see any other alternative as a working policy for us. Isolation is out of the question. Therefore, we must collect with us all the nations who are prepared to resist any other big power if it becomes aggressive or wants to play the bully. There's already a formidable reaction against Hitler's Germany."

I ventured to talk a little about the desire of all Germans—or nearly all—for friendship with us, and told some of my experiences of the warm welcome which any Englishman gets in any part of Germany.

"All that could be so easily switched off to another direction," he answered. "Germany, of course, is anxious to be friends with us if we undertake not to stand between her and what she believes to be her destiny; and if we give her everything for which she asks."

Coffee came and Winston Churchill lit a long cigar which he smoked in a holder so that it looked even longer. We lingered at table talking over many aspects of the international situation and the possibility of war in the air. He did not believe that a decisive victory could be obtained by enemy aircraft. People will endure it, and the survivors will go on resisting, as they are doing in Spain.

"But I'm not one of those who believe that another war is inevitable," he told me. "I still have hopes that we may get time to make some reasonable form of peace."

He spoke of his efforts on behalf of national defence.

"I've done my best to warn the government and the nation of our deficiencies—in the air especially. If they won't do anything about it I have at least a clear conscience, and at my age one takes a philosophical attitude if one has done all one can. Come and have a look at things outside. You had better put on a pair of goloshes. It's a bit boggy here and there."

2 *The English Balbus*

I put on a spare pair of goloshes, kept for his guests, and followed him through his fields and grounds. He has an enchanting place beyond his manor house, with lovely woods above a valley which is on a plateau five hundred feet up. He has altered nature to suit his own purpose and pleasure, using some springs and watercourses to make three little lakes—and not so little either—where a variety of ducks and geese and swans and waterfowl, some of them of foreign breeds, give life to a picture which is good. I could see that his heart is in this place and that he loves every stick and stone of it, and the birds and fish he has placed in its waters.

He has been a great builder here, using his inexhaustible reserve of energy—untired by politics, the stupendous strain of the war days, the writing of books, and journalism, and the painting of pictures—as a bricklayer and plasterer. I stared in admiration at a big swimming pool he has made, lined with green cement. But that was nothing compared with my astonishment and homage at his prowess as a builder of walls.

He has built mighty walls surrounding his fruit and kitchen gardens. They stand straight and strong, with good red bricks, and every one of those bricks in many of the walls was laid by his own hand, though he has had help with others. He has built his own studio, and into that I went to see some of his paintings after our long walk round, when he strode ahead across the wet fields, talking a good deal.

Astonishing man! He has all the talents. These pictures, of which he has hundreds, were good work, far beyond the reach of a talented amateur, I thought. They showed a touch of genius. He has a fine sense of colour. He knows how to draw. There was atmosphere and light in these studies of Morocco, and the Riviera and the English countryside, and still life of glass and pottery and flowers. Every stroke of his brush is decisive. I thought of my own little efforts in this adventure of colour and felt abashed.

"It's a very absorbing hobby," he said. "One forgets everything when one's painting. I often think how tired one would get if one had to stand for half an hour on parade, but one can stand at one's easel for two hours without a sense of fatigue. And one forgets one's mealtimes, and all the cares of life, and every other thing, while one is trying to get something down onto a bit of canvas."

"Well do I know!" I agreed. "I become completely immoral when I try to paint. That's to say, I neglect every duty and nothing else matters."

He turned to me presently with a laugh—we were on the way back to his courtyard—and said something which shocked me for a moment.

"You're one of the goody-goodies, aren't you?" he asked.

This was a bit of a blow after his friendly hospitality.

If he had called me a wicked fellow, or a bandit, or a man lacking in moral sense I should not have been so hurt.

"A goody-goody," I asked hotly. "What do you mean by that?"

"One of the pacifists," he answered. "Like Dick Sheppard and his crowd."

"I'm a stern realist," I told him uneasily.

He laughed good-naturedly but didn't believe me.

"All I want," I said, "is to push off this war we've been talking about."

"Well," he said, "I agree with you! That's all I want too. Only I believe we must be strong in order to keep the peace."

He gave me his hand cordially.

I went away with that phrase making me laugh to myself and yet rankling. How awful to be called a goody-goody! And how very untrue as far as I am concerned! For, alas, I have none of the simple faith, or the spiritual courage, of the Rev. Dick Sheppard, who believes in nonresistance to armed force and is convinced that the only way of stopping war with aeroplanes, poison gas, and other scientific means of slaughter is by the utter refusal to take part in such murderous adventures, and to lay down one's arms, whatever enemy is on the warpath.

That is a counsel of perfection which I cannot follow, because it would mean not only one's own martyrdom in the arena by the wild beasts—and that is not an easy thing to suffer in these days of little faith!—but it would mean also—wouldn't it?—the loss of all liberty, the surrender of civilisation, the massacre of the innocents among all peoples under our protection, and the victory of the beast over the greater part of the world, before—if ever—the beast became tamed and converted by its own victims. Who has the courage and faith to go that way of sacrifice? Who will ask others to make that surrender and accept that martyrdom? Who will do so in this age of cruelty?

Churchill had touched on that at lunch, I remembered.

"The extreme pacifists don't realise," he said, "that modern weapons are the one means of protection against attack by superior forces. If we were to abandon guns and high explosives and go back to swords or knives, or sticks and stones, man power would have it all its own way. A big bully nation would advance upon the little peoples and overwhelm them. There would be no security—and no means of defence—for those who wish to live in peace and get on with their jobs."

Churchill had given me a pinprick by his mocking phrase, meant good-naturedly. He believes, and has always believed, in big navies and big guns. Now he believes in a big air force. But his mind seems to be moving in the direction of a union of European nations acting together for the support of law and order and general peace. He is—under the stress of this menace to our own interests, ideas and need of self-preservation—prepared to revive the League of Nations and to support its principles of international justice, which so far have failed.

VI. ALLEN OF HURTWOOD

There is a wooded heath in Surrey called Hurtwood. It was very lonely once and only bad men—outlaws—knew its tracks through tangled undergrowth to a few clearings between old oak trees. Now it has been found out by lads and lasses who go walking with bare knees and shorts—the girls like Rosalind, in another wood called Arden, who wore her breeches bravely—and come this way to one of those youth hostels—Holmbury or Ewhurst—where they drop their packs and fry sausages for supper and sit round a hearthside, tired and talkative. I have seen them in those glades of Hurtwood and liked the look of them. I have seen some of them hesitate at the corner of a track which looks inviting because it leads to the brow of the hill and an open view. But there is a wooden signboard which says: To Hurtwood House; so they pass on and strike the road to Peaselake or take another path where in April the cuckoo calls and on any day in any month a fellow named Pan pipes a note to the spirit of modern youth.

On the last day of January of this year I went down the way

TO HURTWOOD

with the sign to Hurtwood House and wondered what sort of place the woodland baron who dwells there had built for himself. He must live in a rare quietude, because on working days few people come this way, and the squirrels and other small creatures have a merry time to themselves. On this January day the thrushes were shouting as though spring had come, and rabbits scuttled about the tree trunks.

The woodland lord—he is Allen of Hurtwood—hasn't a baron's castle here. He calls it his "little home" and it's not very large, but its architect had an eye for a far view, like the man who lives in it. It has an odd way of approach at the end of the long track. One goes down a number of steps, and then one goes up a number of steps—like the thirty-nine of John Buchan—to get to the front door. I wasn't quite sure of that front door until it was opened to me by a good-looking young man in a white jacket.

"You have a fine view from here!" I said to show that I was a friendly visitor. He answered with enthusiasm, though I have heard it said that one "can't live on a view."

"Yes! Wonderful, isn't it? On a good day one can see the sea and the Isle of Wight."

He showed me into a room with this view from the window but I saw neither the sea nor the Isle of Wight, because mists were rising from sodden fields after a week of rain. But even through the mists I could see a good countryside and above them a lot of sky.

This room with a view was inviting. It belonged—one could see at a glance—to a civilised man and a pleasant personality. Here was a big open hearth with a fire burning—the first sign of civilisation—and the walls were clad with many books which looked as though they had been read and were not in fine bindings stuck up in a row at so much a yard. At the end of the room was a piano and on the window sill a violin. Truly, here was one of the little sanctuaries of civilisation in the heart of a woodland whose roots go back to the time when the only men hereabouts were hiding and hunted men, rough, no doubt, and brutal.

I knew something of the history of the man for whom I waited half a minute. He had been in prison three times, but for no wickedness, unless judged by Colonel Blimp. He was one of the conscientious objectors against war when almost the whole world was at war, and it needed, perhaps, more moral courage of a kind to refuse to "Join Up" than to trudge up to the trenches under shellfire with all the lads. Anyhow, he must have had a horrible time. He was a young fellow in those days—about twenty-five, as far as I can reckon—and recently down from Peterhouse College, Cambridge. He had joined the Labour party and was set to found its first daily paper. He was a Labour delegate to Russia in 1920 and sat face to face with Lenin and talked with him. Not long ago he sat face to face with Hitler and talked with him. How strange to meet a woodland baron who has talked with both those men—each with some power in him, some flame of the spirit, which gave him mastery over millions of human beings and established a new social system—at the opposite poles—by which they live.

Lord Allen of Hurtwood came through the open door and greeted me. Years ago some book of mine had pleased him and he told me so. That was a pleasant beginning to conversation, but even if he had hated everything I have written I should have been attracted by him and been glad to sit by his fireside. He has a poet's face, finely cut and thoughtful. He also has a charm of manner which nowadays is perhaps a little rare, except among old people. When he talked, after filling a pipe, I knew that here was a man who loves the things that make life sweet, and hates cruelty, and injustice, and stupidity, and ugliness, and the things that make life bad for civilised minds.

He talked without intolerance, without any doctrinaire rigidity of opinion and principle, utterly without the narrowness of the party mind. We talked together mostly that day about the thing which one has to keep on talking about lest we should all stumble into a mantrap and even to the dark pit into which all good things would be hurled. The subject of our conversation was—how to prevent, or to push off, that menace of war which is overshadowing the mind of Europe.

It was the day after Hitler's speech in the Reichstag, which to my mind offered a new hope of peace, though the immediate reaction to it in England had been a critical and carping comment by the B.B.C., surely dictated by some mind in the Foreign Office, which is rigid in its refusal to look beyond its traditional policy of alliance with France and a balance of power against Germany.

We spoke of Hitler—that Man of Destiny—and Lord Allen said that he had perhaps a dual personality, ruthless and violent on one side but, on the other, not incapable of generous views, warmth of emotion, some touch of spiritual fire.

"I met him first," he said, "when he was new to power—reserved, a little lacking in confidence, rather like a man in a dream. But afterwards, two years later, when I talked with him again he had changed. He was much more sure of himself. His personality had broadened. He was more statesmanlike, and I was surprised when we talked about naval limitation, or foreign diplomacy, how much he seemed to know of the practical side of the problem and how much a master of detail he had become."

Lord Allen spoke of our missed opportunity when a year earlier Hitler offered to rejoin the League of Nations on the basis of absolute equality of status. He was willing to limit his army to 300,000 men. He was willing to agree to a limitation of aircraft, to less than equality with his neighbours.

"If we had taken Hitler at his word then," said Lord Allen, "we should not be going ahead with this fierce competition in armaments without any sense of security or finality. Emphasis was put by far too many of us upon the breaking of the Locarno Treaty and the return of German troops to the Rhineland, rather than upon the possibilities Hitler offered of a new basis and of peaceful arrangement within the League. That questionnaire put to Germany by our government was surely a grave mistake. It was wrong in manner. It was utterly tactless. It was bound to put up the backs of German leaders who were questioned like naughty schoolboys by an austere master, almost sure of their wickedness."

"French anger and pressure may have influenced our Foreign Office," I suggested.

Lord Allen agreed.

"Quite likely! On that Sunday night French politicians were ready to march. It was touch and go with them."

"And now?" I asked. "How are we going to break down the suspicions and fears of France? Hitler has guaranteed the inviolability of French soil but, judging from the comments of Pertinax and other journalists in Paris, one would imagine that he had insulted them. Our Press hasn't been much better."

Lord Allen thought M. Blum, the French premier, would be more statesmanlike. He was a philosopher with courage. He believed also that Anthony Eden would get away from Foreign Office rigidity and answer Hitler without any nagging conditions or pinpricks of argument.

"What we ought now to do," he said, "is to take an initiative in favour of a *general* settlement, and to give up trying to reach the peace of Europe by hectic attempts to settle first one crisis and then another as they emerge. We ought to offer to negotiate with Germany for the first time on all subjects and from the starting point of equality of status. There has never yet been an invitation which asked her to join in such a discussion, for every previous invitation has arisen out of some isolated crisis, like the occupation of the Rhineland, or has taken as a jumping-off ground some one problem, such as access to raw materials. This haphazard procedure can no more lead to a settlement than did Sir Edward Grey's effort in prewar days as he clutched at each passing critical event. We must ask for Germany's friendly co-operation and establish European peace upon lines which would not merely enforce the status quo but would remove humiliating inequalities and allow for treaty revision, adjustment of colonial administration, and alterations of frontiers badly drawn at Versailles and Trianon. Up to now Hitler has claimed to have the right on his side, and indeed he has often had it. He has never, so far, struck outside the frontiers of his own country. If he were to refuse this offer of co-operation, he would put himself in the wrong before all the world and especially in the eyes of America. I do not think he is foolish enough to slip into that mistake. I think the offer to negotiate a new and just settlement from the starting point of equality might be more formidable and embarrassing to a nation having ambitious designs than the threat to mobilise force against him as an aggressor."

"Treaty revision raises a crowd of dangers," I reminded Lord Allen. He knew them all but was convinced that if there were no revision of treaties a greater danger would arise, the end of which would be war. "The offer to consider treaty revision must come first," he urged, "but no concessions must be offered as an isolated bait to an aggressor. All revisions must only be part of a general scheme, including limitation in arms, mutual guarantees of security whilst negotiations are in progress, and culminating in Germany's return to the League. . . . British public opinion would make concessions to achieve a final peace settlement of this kind which they would never grant as Danegeld to the aggressor. But remember that you cannot divorce the problem of treaty revision from the need to protect the peace whilst you are negotiating. You may need to emphasise first the one and then the other, but they are both equally important. It was Lord Cecil who said that in dealing with these two subjects diplomacy was like trying to shut a drawer which would not go in. It is useless trying to get the whole thing in at once. One has to press a little first on one side and then on the other, and then in the middle."

Lord Allen still believed in Collective Security as the only way of protecting the peace of Europe and Britain's own safety, but he thought that the British public was now nervous lest this idea, which, when the League was complete in membership, might have *prevented* war, would in these days, when its membership was broken, possibly *lead to war*. The public feel that Collective Security is only a sure way of preventing war when it has preponderant power and when its use can be made predictable before a crisis.

"I am," said Lord Allen, "under present circumstances, very doubtful whether we shall carry the public with us in making any more declarations defining our intention to take part in collective force, unless such declarations form part of a general statement of Britain's peace policy covering all outstanding disputes, grievances and unsettled problems.

"The public has an uneasy conscience about the existing law they are called upon to protect. They feel that no nation can be expected to respect the law, unless all are equal before the law. If, therefore, we are to press for this vital necessity of the modern world, namely Collective Security, it must be one item in a declaration covering the whole subject of Britain's peace policy for Europe, and we should ask all nations to protect the truce while negotiations are proceeding. I would rather put collective force behind a truce leading to a new peace settlement than behind the existing status quo."

I put a question to him which I phrased rather clumsily.

"Do you think there is any chance of the Labour party behaving in a reasonable way? It seems to me that their hatred of the Nazi regime is so intense that they are ready to back a war with Germany and almost eager for it, while at the same time they have a kind of fairy tale in their minds about Russia which they still regard as a beautiful utopia of democracy! Haven't they become militarists, wanting this country to take sides for Communism against Fascism in any part of the world where those two forces come into conflict?"

"That is only partially true," said Lord Allen, who was once an intellectual of the Labour party. "This attitude of mind is a handicap to reasonable conciliation with Germany. It would get us nowhere except to war. But in my judgment the Labour party is as suspicious of Communism as it is of Naziism. It is prepared to deal with either Russia or Germany as a sovereign state, irrespective of the regime under which they are governed. The trouble is that Labour is disposed to underestimate the dangers of Russian revolutionary propaganda in Europe and allows its hatred of Naziism to blind its judgment with regard to fair dealing with Germany.

"But the real snag about the Labour party at the moment is rather different. It alienates British public opinion by the bellicose manner in which it presents its socialist programme. Were it to introduce once more into its advocacy something of the spiritual note which inspired confidence in its early days, then I think it would win support and have a chance of becoming an alternative government. Failing this, I doubt whether it will again achieve office in our lifetime."

We talked round about this problem until presently I switched off to another aspect.

"What about Hitler's demand for the return of the German colonies? Isn't that one of the great snags? Even if we were willing to give back Tanganyika—and I suppose we're not—South Africa would be dead against it."

Lord Allen puffed at his pipe and looked into the fire burning on his hearth.

"Something might be arranged elsewhere. Curiously enough, I have been studying maps on this very question this morning. . . . There is no doubt that the colonial question is vital to the peace of the world, but I do not believe its solution is so difficult as all that. It is certainly fantastic for Britain and the other colonial powers to insist that the world is for all time parcelled out and that no adjustments can now take place. To argue in that way is to make every European problem 'a counter in the deadly game of prestige.' I am convinced that if the present colonial Powers insist upon retaining the sovereign control of any undeveloped territory, they cannot deny a similar right to Germany. Togoland or other areas in Western Africa might provide an opportunity for dealing with this subject with less difficulty than would arise in the case of Tanganyika. But surely the real answer to this colonial problem is to set in motion developments which would lead to all African undeveloped areas being ultimately administered under some form of international trusteeship rather than by sovereign ownership or sovereign mandate. I recognise that this is by no means an easy task, but it is one in favour of which I think Britain should now declare herself. She should invite other Powers to co-operate at once in setting up the first stages of the necessary machinery to reach this goal. In any case, this offer must only be part of a general plan of peace, with Germany co-operating within the League in return for helpfulness and recognition of Germany's, and other countries', rights and interests."

So we talked. And I was impressed by a mind groping for

THE SPIRIT OF ENGLAND

some intelligent arrangement, some appeal to reason instead of passion, some plan inspired by a vision, which might thrust away the spectre of another war in which nothing much would be left of decent life or any kind of beauty. He was willing to move a step at a time, to take advantage of immediate opportunities without trying to enforce everything at once and so lose all. He had a dislike, which I share, of doctrinaire obstinacy and fanatical adherence to a rigid principle for whose sake all the world must be laid in ruin.

Here, I thought, is a good brain and, behind it, moral courage, and something even better than that, which is pity and tenderness of spirit, in a world of growing cruelty and spreading intolerance, and also a desire to apply the sympathy of understanding in international affairs.

He still has faith in British democracy as capable of giving a lead to the world but wants a more dynamic leadership and a revision of the parliamentary system which would speed up and revitalise its power of action. These ideas are elaborated in a book of his, called *Britain's Political Future*, which is extraordinarily interesting, though here I can only quote one passage in its preface, which gives the keynote to the book and is a good ending to my conversation in his house:

A number of distinguished visitors from abroad were recently discussing world problems round my fireside. They came from many nations. Some were exiles, others were about to return with heavy hearts to face personal dangers. A few were young and were trying to convince themselves that, notwithstanding many cruelties and horrors, their countries were making new discoveries of great political value. All were agreed, however, upon one subject: it was good to be in Britain. Here for a little while they could speak freely. This country seemed to them like a place of refuge in a great storm. Could she, they asked, lead the world once again in the art of government? Could she achieve a new social order without the violence and tyrannies they had all endured? . . . I said that I believed British Democracy would stand the test. I prophesied that if we met in a few years' time, we should find more happiness and more freedom, combined with a more highly developed social order, than in any country in the world.

A brave prophecy!

XII

The Spirit of England

1 The Anxious Days

In this year of grace of which I write, England has many anxieties. It has been a year of ordeal, following the death of King George V, whose Jubilee called out for a time, partly because of sun-soaked days and warm darkness, a touch of the Elizabethan spirit—the merriment of Shakespeare's pageant of life—when youth danced to the tune of piano organs or any kind of music in the glamorous nights of London streets, and beacons were lit on a thousand hills, and flags fluttered in every village. There was an unusual lack of self-repression in the crowds. There was an illusion of happiness among the common folk, who, as a rule, take their pleasures sadly, or at least without exuberance of spirits.

This year has brought new bewilderments and a growing sense of fear that the horrors of war may be near at hand, and that poison gas may be creeping through the streets of crowded cities while incendiary bombs are smashing little houses bought on the hire system—and all the rest of it. Otherwise, why this colossal programme of rearmament? Otherwise, why these Home Office instructions for antigas defence? Why these speeches by Cabinet ministers to make the people's flesh creep? The newspapers keep the nerves of their readers constantly on edge by recording the threats of convulsion in Europe, the savagery of Civil War in Spain, and "incidents" which keep breaking out in the volcanic state of this world of seething passions and blind forces.

The crisis of the Crown was a shock to English tradition and its sense of security at the top. It has left uneasiness in many minds, despite the quietude of the transition from one King to another. Foreigners marvelled at the steadiness of our folk in this time of crisis, and that was true. It was a marvellous phenomenon—that appearance of a nation giving its verdict, accepting the change with absolute unanimity. But there was bewilderment, privately expressed, a deep sense of disappointment and dejection, in spite of loyalty to the Throne and to the new King, in all traditional minds which are most numerous in England. It was the breaking of a spell—the spell which Edward had upon the popular mind. There was a sense of something lost and something shaken.

The nation is confused, divided in ideas, uncertain of its future. The idealists have lost faith in their own hopes and dreams. They believed in the League of Nations as an institution upholding justice, protecting law, preparing the way for the elimination of armed conflict by ways of reason and conciliation. The League of Nations is sick unto death. The tragedy and crime of Abyssinia was an almost mortal blow to its prestige. Its impotence was revealed. Sanctions failed. Law was not upheld. There was no justice. So that hope has gone—for a while.

The Spanish Civil War has not been out of English thoughts since it first began. Like a blinding light thrown onto an arena in which men are fighting like beasts to the death, the daily news from Spain reveals how little man has advanced from primitive savagery, how merciless, though he fights in the name of Christ; how diabolical, though he fights in the name of humanity.

The Spanish Civil War has not been an alien affair which leaves untouched the English mind watching it from afar. It has had grave and dangerous effects upon our own mentality, and later on it may have grave and dangerous effects upon our actions. The aid given to General Franco by the dictatorships of Germany and Italy has exasperated and inflamed the anger of the Left minds in England, who see in this another cause of hatred against Fascism and another challenge to democracy and liberty, in which they profess to believe, and in which some of them do believe. The aid given to Caballero, and his Communists, Anarchists, Syndicalists, and Socialists, by volunteers and arms from France, Russia, Czecho-Slovakia, Houndsditch and Hoxton, seems to minds on the Right, and to many Catholics and Christians, a clear revelation of antichrist, working to overthrow religion, order and civilisation by the massacre of priests and nuns, the burning of churches, and assassination of innocent folk by murder gangs. They see the hand of Russia reaching out to stir up the flames of revolt against all Christian and civilised ideals. They see the advance of Communism, not only in this Spanish conflict, but in France and all countries who have given aid to the Spanish "comrades" under the banner of Bolshevism.

The British Labour party has been greatly agitated by the Spanish struggle and has accepted the government's policy of nonintervention with only grudging consent. Newspapers formerly in the Liberal tradition have taken open sides with the Spanish Communists and, day after day, have accused the government of cowardice in not stopping German and Italian reinforcements of Franco's army. They would have supported direct intervention on the side of the Spanish Loyalists, even at the risk of a general European war. They are propagandists of religious fanaticism based upon hatred of the Fascist creed and upon faith in something they call democracy, though

Communism, as well they know, is a denial of liberty and democratic rule.

The Left-minded people in England are more fanatical than the Right. The Labour party has become definitely militarist in its allegiance to that mystical phrase "Collective Security," which at the present time has no meaning or substance, and if Labour ever came into power it would be far more likely to plunge this country into war on behalf of this ideal than the Conservatives, who are more realistic in their foreign policy, though not realistic enough to see that Germany and Great Britain should arrange the peace of Europe, with France and Italy in a Western pact, or with France without Italy if Mr Mussolini is out for trouble.

2 *The Middle of the Road*

This ranging up of rival extremists is a departure from the historical attitude of England in her foreign policy and a complete break with the traditional temper and character of the English people, who are essentially and instinctively neither Right nor Left but in the Liberal centre. They still stay there, I am firmly convinced. Get away from London, get beyond the groups of intellectuals, theorists and fanatics, and one finds everywhere in England the old mistrust of fanaticism, the old shrewdness of judgment between the clamour of rival factions, the old belief in temporising, and compromise, and give-and-take which has been the genius of the English people for a long period. They don't want to go to war for a theoretical ideal of which they are sceptical. They don't want to go to war for Russian Communists or Czecho-Slovaks. They don't want to be dragged to the shambles for a phrase called "Collective Security" or for that old mantrap, the Balance of Power.

"Self-interest" is the gibe flung at this attitude of mind by flaming idealists, who would have us fight singlehanded on any front for their ideas of abstract justice. Self-interest certainly, but it involves national preservation—and the preservation of civilisation, the beauty of life, liberty, to say nothing of babies in their cradles and the blood of our young manhood. Lose or win, another world war would for England be the end of everything, as it would be for France and Germany. We lost the fine flower of our race in the last war—a million of our best. Those who would have been our leaders now went down into the mud of Flanders and the Somme. We have not yet replaced them. Are we to complete our ruin by bloody adventures on behalf of Russia or Czecho-Slovakia? The answer, I believe, in the minds of the English people outside the range of the Left Book Club is very definitely: No! I am bound to say that, though, I believe in Collective Security as the ultimate ideal if it is collective and secure—but not without Germany, Japan, Italy and the United States.

And yet they are conscious, these middle-minded people, of bewilderment and lack of any clear conviction. They were the people—eleven million of them—who voted in the Peace Ballot presented to them by Lord Cecil and others, and gave their approval to support the League of Nations Covenant, if necessary, as far as imposing sanctions upon an aggressor nation. They believed, as I did, in Collective Security and would do so still if it had had the united support of all the great Powers. But they now have seen that there was no such unity of action against an aggressor nation, as Italy was judged to be. France "ratted." Germany was out of it. The United States was out of it. Further action in regard to sanctions would have meant a straight fight between this country and Italy. How could that be called Collective Security? They have lost their faith in the League, and as yet they have found no other shrine at which to worship. They hope that this rearmament of Great Britain will give pause to bandit nations, but they hate the bill of costs and wonder what use will be made of all these stocks of shells and ammunition now being piled up. To the average man in the teashop or the third-class carriage, with whom I talk now and again, rearmament is a temporary safeguard which, no doubt, is necessary, but which is not exactly reassuring in the hands of the present, or any other, government.

"They may want to use those toys," says the man who remembered the last war.

"Nobody wanted the last war, but it happened. Some fool at the Foreign Office may walk into a trap. Then we shall be for it again, I suppose. It's all raving lunacy. If you call this civilisation, then civilisation ought to be blotted out! If I smell poison gas in High Street, Kensington, or the Brompton Road, I shall walk out and breathe deeply of it, because the game will be up, as far as civilisation is concerned."

I have heard those words said. Many people are thinking the same thing. There is a dark pessimism in many English minds.

I went one night to a meeting at Londonderry House. It was on behalf of the Red Cross libraries for hospitals, and a number of dames and dowagers had assembled to hear a debate between an array of famous writers, under the chairmanship of Lord Esher. The subject was: "I find this world a good place to live in—or I don't."

We sat uncomfortably on gilt-backed chairs in the great salon of this noble house. The famous writers had more comfortable seats facing their audience. They were Humbert Wolfe, Day Lewis, Margaret Kennedy, Rose Macaulay, Margaret Irwin and T. S. Eliot. I listened to their speeches. They were witty and amusing with verbal fireworks. Humbert Wolfe, poet and orator, was in good form and raised a laugh at every sentence and played with ideas like a juggler with glittering balls, keeping them up with perfect ease. Miss Macaulay was called upon suddenly to take the place of the Rev. Dick Sheppard, down with asthma, and said some very good things. So did they all. But there was an underlying gloom in these speeches. They evaded the question of the debate by the most ingenious flippancies. They dared not look at the world around them. They could not find a good thing to say about it. They were jesters, with death knocking at the door. They laughed like Boccaccio's characters with the plague around them. Miss Margaret Irwin tried to cheer us up by saying that however bad the world might be at present, it was no worse than it had always been. Was not life always horrible? Why, then, should we complain about our present state? The only way to be happy, said Lord Esher, is to wear blinkers and not see what is going on each side of us. There was no word of hope, of beauty, of laughter, or of happiness.

Mr Day Lewis, speaking as a member of the Left Book Club, dropped the mask for a moment. "People like ourselves," he said, "who are writers and poets, look out of a window upon a crazy world. Sometimes we think we must be mad ourselves. Perhaps we are, but outside our window the world is even madder. To secure peace people are arming to the teeth and making bombs to blow other people to bits. In a world of plenty and overproduction people are starving. It's a lunatic world!"

He regarded it with despair, but in his young soul there was a dream. Everything might be changed by Communism. Willingly would he surrender free speech and free thought that those now hungry should be fed. It did not occur to him that there is a hunger of the mind as well as of the body; and that denial of freedom does not produce more bread, even in Russia, where they are also arming to the teeth and seem as mad as the rest of us, judged by recent trials.

One cause of this distress in our English minds is, I think, the consciousness that we are on an island—not geographically but intellectually—surrounded by a sea of passion which threatens to swamp us or, at least, makes an unpleasant noise in our ears. We are a civilised people and the world is becoming uncivilised. Most of us still believe in freedom of speech and thought within the framework of our social order. We still believe in tolerance of minorities. We hate cruelty and brutality, though that gentleness is not old in our tradition. In hundreds of thousands of homes in England there is the conversation of free minds, a decent level of culture, some homage to beauty, a love of gardens, flowers, birds, and the pleasant ways of life. As a people we do not flame out into political passion, and detest fanaticism of any kind. Instinctively we are law abiding, free from any violence of revolt. No dark and deadly conspiracies lurk in the underworld. Even the inhabitants of the distressed areas are marvellously patient and untouched by revolutionary bitterness, though they have been given too little aid beyond the dole. Apart from those black areas of unemployment—not quite so bad now, and with a promise of rescue—our people have a fair standard of living with a margin for amusement and self-education, if they are out for that, as many are. The standard of intelligence is rising, despite the danger of mass-produced idiocies.

I am always impressed by the intelligence of the average mind. Those young men and women who go walking on week ends between one youth hostel and another read well, think well, and talk well. At least, they talk with an appeal to reason and with good nature for those who hold opposite ideas. They don't knife each other because they disagree. They don't have private bomb factories for blowing up railway lines or killing their politicians. In the rooms of undergraduates there is good talk between the inevitable absurdities of the younger mind and, anyhow, a certain code of courtesy and an unfailing sense of humour. Talk to a city clerk over a marble-topped table in a Lyons café, and you will find him polite, shrewd in judgment, awake to the world around him, interested in some harmless hobby, tolerant, kindly, and unembittered, however small his salary.

We may claim to be civilised. In spite of all our weak points, our stupidities, and our growing menace of mass-produced minds, we are still, I believe, a credit to democracy, though not so good in intelligence or physique as the Scandinavian nations. But this democracy of ours is, we think, menaced by the dictatorships and the ideologies, and the rise of blind force, violence, political hatreds and murderous passions. We wish to live in peace but see ourselves dragged into conflict. We believe in tolerance but find intolerance enthroned. We want to improve the security of life by appeal to reason, by a friendly method of conciliation, but find that reason does not prevail at the council tables. We—being civilised—wish to escape from discipline, regimentation and the spirit of militarism but find that all other countries are arming, drilling, and parading with gas masks. Being civilised, we have perhaps become a little slack and a little soft, preferring a patch of garden to a barrack square, and a lawn mower to a machine gun, and a book to a bomb, and a symphony concert over the wireless to the sound of bugles and the beat of drums. Thoughtful minds in England—the book lovers and the beauty lovers and the ramblers through Surrey woods—have a sense of uneasiness, a distress in their souls, because they are afraid that intelligence is in retreat before primitive instinct, and that their liberty, their ways, their little bit of civilisation, may be menaced by the coming of the Goths out of the primeval forests. They hear from afar the howling of wolves. Perhaps it will be necessary to obey the orders of a sergeant major and step up briskly to rasping commands in a barrack square. Horrid thought! What an interruption to civilised tranquillity!

3 *Lack of Leadership*

The English people dislike discipline. I have always hated it myself like poison. But a certain amount of it might be good for us. We have carried our individualism too far in resisting the community spirit and organised teamwork. There is much to be said for the German Labour Camps, in which every young man and woman must serve for a time, whatever their class or opportunity of work. There is nothing to be said—let us admit it—for the groups of young men propping themselves against the walls of Labour Exchanges or coming out like young wolves from their lairs at night to get free food on the Embankment or under the Admiralty Arch. They should be rounded up and put into Labour Camps, willy nilly, for at least a year's service, instead of being allowed to drift into vice and demoralisation.

The blackest mark on our social record in the postwar years is the lack of any organised service for the unemployed, any kind of recruitment for service of some kind—preferably on that wasted land of ours which should grow more food for our people—a thought which occurs only to our great brains when they get funky of a new war. Much heartbreak would have been avoided by some scheme of compulsory labour for the generation of young manhood; much comradeship, and cheerfulness, and laughter, and improved physique could have been gained if only the Labour government, or the so-called national government, had had the courage to enrol the unemployed in England in service battalions for work on the land when other work was short, with good leadership, mild discipline, physical exercises, and something of the spirit of those who once went singing "Pack up your troubles in your old kit bag", without

THE NEW COMMONWEALTH

the same red fires at Journey's End. We let them drift, and hang about, and slouch around, getting bored—boredom, so many have told me, is their greatest curse—getting dejected, getting unemployable. If only we had had a leader of inspiration and courage to take this job in hand in the right spirit, with a call to comradeship, we should have brought rescue to derelict communities.

Where are our leaders with such vision and such courage? It is pitiful and alarming that we lack any inspiration of leadership or any coming forward of young men with character and a touch of genius. A million went west in the war. We have not made up the loss. There is something lacking in the spirit of our young manhood today. Those crowds who watch football matches, and bet on them, are not playing games.

In the universities there is contempt for the "hearties" who play rude games by those who prefer the cinema or the Left Book Club. Even the intellectuals allow themselves to be weakened by the false mirage of Communism instead of getting to work on ideas of practical and immediate possibility.

Looking down on the House of Commons from the Strangers' Gallery, one's heart sinks at the mediocrity of that assembly. There is nothing dynamic there. The two Front Benches are respectable and dull.

The Labour party, with a few exceptions, is without quality. The Conservative party fails to produce any sign of a coming leader with a touch of the old fire of those who once led it. It is a tame assembly of sheeplike members who herd into the right lobbies when the bell rings. The only men of distinction and character—two or three—are those whose days are nearly done.

Perhaps that is too harsh. I feel it is, now that I have written the words. There must be on the back benches, here and there, young men of promise. But they don't get a chance. The Front

Benches are utterly selfish in the length of their speeches and their allegiance to a machine which is crushing out the spirit of the parliamentary arena, ironing out the individual point of view, denying the limelight to the young crowd. The French group system, not without objection—heaven knows—is, to my mind, preferable to a parliamentary system conducted by the pomposities of the Front Bench, controlled by the Cabinet, and disciplined by the Whips.

Something will have to be done about it, or the parliamentary system, which, after all, is the safeguard of democracy in the English sense of that much-abused word, will fall into decay and contempt.

The past twelve months have been an ordeal in England, testing, and perhaps shaking, the nerve of that section of society —that small section—which is sensitive to the international situation and to the perils and portents of our own state. That enormous rearmament programme sits heavily on the imagination of those who count the cost and look ahead to what may happen when it is completed. It is already disrupting the national industry by recruiting every class of labour for munitions and commandeering all available material—steel, timber, every kind of metal—for purposes which have no productive value beyond the machinery of slaughter and no selling power in the world's markets. Prices of these commodities are rocketing to fantastic heights. The government buyers are in the hands of rings, monopolists and profiteers who are becoming millionaires out of this great gamble in which the moneyed public is up to its neck. I hate to refer again to the Royal Commission Report on the Arms Industry, but if that had been adopted, these abuses would have been prevented and there would have been the chance of control, efficiency and economy, instead of the present lack of authority and complete surrender to the profit-making interests.

All that belongs to the dark side of our English scene today, and I have not put in the blacks too heavily, I think. But there is another side more pleasant to contemplate. The mass of the English people remain untouched by the despondency of the intellectuals, the fanatical theories of political extremists, the flesh-creeping forecasts of the prophets of doom, and all morbid, dreadful and horrid dreams. They have their jobs to do and not much time or use for that kind of thought. They have their little gardens—their little private paradises. They are getting good wages, if they have work, as more have than at any other time in English history. Compared with twenty-five years ago, their social state outside the distressed areas has been raised as though by a magic wand. They have got rid of the old squalor, the old penury, the old grinding drudgery, of sweated labour. They have more ease, more leisure, more amusement, more interests reaching out to them by the B.B.C. and by the adventure of a little car which gives them a way of escape from narrow lives and mean streets.

England is not to be judged only by the monstrous ant heap called London or by the tabloid press which panders to the lowest common denominator of mob psychology. There is still the English countryside, where life goes on traditionally in old farmsteads and small villages. There are the cathedral cities where time stands still, and where there is tranquillity of mind. In the old market towns the young farmers who come in with their sheep and cattle belong to Hardy's England, and their minds follow the same furrows. Their blood is the same. Their character has not been changed much by modern fretfulness and "nerves." The young craftsmen and labourers who ride away from their work on push bikes or motor bikes are, I find, exactly like the lads who joined up in 1914, when some of them thought it was going to be "good fun", not knowing the grisly humour they would find.

The shopkeeping mass in England, in every little town and village, as far as I know them, are cheerful and very sweet mannered. Whatever the pessimists and the critics of English life may say, I am certain that our folk have a sanity, a steadiness, an incapability of passion and hatred, a good-natured tolerance, a kindly courtesy, a sense of humour, and a moral tradition which keeps us free from the political turmoil and the ferocious vendettas which make such hell in many European countries. All foreigners think so when they come to visit us. I am sure they are right. We don't know our own luck in being free to think, to speak, to live without fear of spies, inquisitors and murder gangs. We don't know our own luck in having a national mind which keeps very steadily to the middle of the road.

We face a new reign under a young King, to whom the Crown came unexpectedly and in a tragic way. We face an uncertain future, not without danger, and certain to bring new ordeals to test the courage and the wisdom of the younger generation whose world it will be. Let me give them one word of hope, in which I believe. I dare to say that the expected war is not going to happen. Let us kill that bogey in our minds. It will not happen if we do not wish it to happen. Let us burn those gas masks which are very spoiling to the human face and all ideals of beauty.

Epilogue

The Coronation

NEVER BEFORE, I believe, was there such tremendous display and showmanship for any king's crowning as that prepared for the coronation of George VI. It was inspired by the determination of our government and people and Press to make this an opportunity of showing to the world, and to themselves, that in spite of a temporary crisis which shook the Crown, and the anxieties of foreign affairs which had led to fear and an enormous programme of rearmament, frightful in cost, we were all right, if all the world were wrong, and that the Crown was all right, and that the Empire was steady and strong and powerful, and that England was still England.

London became like a city preparing for a siege. Barricades went up. Armies of workmen invaded the West End. Forests of timber and steel were stacked along the line of the royal route. Presently stands were built in many streets. Elderly gentlemen lost their way to their own clubs hidden behind these planks and girders. They strayed through forbidden portals and said "God bless my soul!" when they found themselves in clubs on the wrong side of their political horizon. When the flags and the trophies, and the garlands, and the heraldic devices, and the coloured hangings covered up the wooden scaffolding, it all looked strangely medieval, like London in the times of the Tudors, when Elizabeth rode on her way after the Armada. Other minds, less romantic, thought it looked like one vast circus ready for the greatest show on earth, patronised by the nobility and gentry.

Drapers' shops and chain stores were having a great time, selling thousands of miles of bunting and millions of gilt lions and unicorns. Every village from John o' Groats to Land's End fluttered with Union Jacks. Every village prepared its own Coronation celebrations. Bonfires were ready for the touch of a match on thousands of little hills and high peaks. The sixth George, following the eighth Edward, was going to have a full proof that his people accepted him with an allegiance and loyalty untouched by any shadow of what had happened in December.

It was unfortunate and ill-timed that the busmen should go on strike just before the Coronation. They would have had more public sympathy if they had postponed their grievances until after this event. It created horrible inconvenience when vast crowds were surging into London to see the decorations; and it put a strain on the patience of city clerks and shop assistants, but not beyond their wonderful reserves of spirit and good nature. They set out to walk—those battalions of shopgirls, with high heels and high courage. They struggled laughingly into underground carriages already packed to suffocation. Another misfortune was that our climate behaved badly—at its worst!—just before the day of days. It was a bad advertisement to all those kinsfolk from the Dominions and all the foreign visitors who came to England by every boat. England in May! They had looked forward to its fragrance and beauty. They found on the day before the Coronation November weather, wet, dark, cold, horrible. We all had pity in our hearts for those crowds who were preparing—God help them!—to spend the night in the parks and streets. They were already taking their places. The porter at my club spoke to me about them as he held a dripping umbrella over his wet oilskins.

"They're already beginning to line the route. Marvellous! That's what I say. What a heart! I wish I had a touch of it myself."

He had been one of the heroes of the Great War.

To me it seemed like madness. I could imagine nothing more desperate than standing out all night, getting soaked, chilled to the marrowbones, cramped and exhausted, while waiting all those hours to see the King, and all the King's horses, and all the King's men, through wet mist. Truly these "rain-soddened islanders", as a French writer called them, refused to be beaten by their own skies. By the grace of God it cleared, and the night and morning were dry for those millions who gathered along the Royal route.

At five o'clock on the morning of Coronation day, when I looked out of my windows, I saw crowds of them hurrying on their way like ghosts in the grey dawn. At six o'clock I sat in a taxicab upon one window of which was pasted a ticket with the mystical numbers Q2 which allowed it to proceed by a certain route to the north door of Westminster Abbey, past massed police who waved it on. Before me and behind me was an endless procession of motorcars. I felt my pockets. In one of them was a packet of sandwiches; in another a flask of potent liquid; in another a pair of field glasses. In my gloved hand I clutched a large card which gave me the privilege of entering the Abbey up to the hour of 7 A. M. I looked forward to the ordeal of a long wait with a fore-knowledge of its fatigue. But I knew that, whatever the fatigue, I should see in due time an unforgettable series of living pictures, wonderful in colour.

There were many people before me in the Abbey. Many of them were already in their seats in block numbered Q2, where

I was to find a place. We were high up and looked down from this great height to the dais with five steps where the King's throne was set three steps higher than the Queen's. People about me were grumbling because they could not see the altar and the place where the King would be anointed. An artist—my friend Matania—was in despair until he found by some magic of his own a better viewpoint. Through my glasses I could see the faces and even the expressions of some of the actors already down there. It wasn't too bad. At the rehearsal I had seen everything very closely and clearly. I had been to a previous Coronation. The ritual would be the same, though one could not see all of it. It was good to be here for a while, though before the end some of us drooped like withered weeds.

What did it mean, that pageant and ritual we had come to see? Had it any meaning more than a pantomime in a modern world? Was it more than a masquerade of olden times? Yes, more than that. All English history was in it—something of the spirit and faith of a people who from this rain-soaked island went out in ships across the seas and built new nations, carrying with them their speech, their ideas of liberty, their traditional character. That day from those new nations of the Commonwealth thousands of guests had come to do homage to the King who was theirs as well as ours. The Past called to the Present with a message—if one could hear it—for the unknown Future.

In the old Abbey where I sat in my place there was a murmurous quietude. Through the open doors, and a window in the lavatory near by, I could hear vague sounds from the multitude outside, massed in the streets.

Inside it was very dim at first, with lamps glimmering like stars between the grey columns. Presently the high clerestory windows brightened. Shafts of cold light struck aslant the great nave and touched some of the pillars. I could see part of the scene set for this royal drama.

All along the highway of the nave was spread a blue carpet reaching to the stage where the altar stood, though I could not see as far as that. On the stage itself the carpet was of a fawn colour turned to old gold by a flood of light from arc lamps. Here, facing the altar, was a worm-eaten wooden chair—the chair of Saxon Edward, king and saint—with its seat above the Stone of Scone whose story goes back to the mists. Further towards the nave, within my view, was the dais with the two thrones.

For the guests the whole Abbey had been turned into a vast auditorium with high tiers of boxes and galleries, draped in gold and blue, reaching almost to the pointed arches and blocking out some of the windows. Immediately opposite the dais was a winding stairway leading to the gallery for the royal family.

Places had been made for eight thousand people—the nobility and gentry of this realm, and all the political and social leaders. For two hours they kept coming into the twilight of this shrine, led to their places by glittering gentlemen called Gold Staves. Thousands of these people were in court dress and all manner of uniforms, British and foreign. They were living figures from some painted book of history whose pages come down to present days. Scarlet and gold. White and gold. Blue and gold. Black silk breeches and white stockings and shining stars. To their places went great soldiers and sailors who had served in a war not very old in memory. I had seen some of them before in dirty trenches. They wore orders of valour and service. All the people who pull the strings of our puppet play were within these grey old walls.

Down below I saw the glint of gold-worked tabards worn by Garter kings, heralds and pursuivants. Busy about the altar moved bishops and clergy in gorgeous copes. Hundreds of choristers in white surplices and black or crimson cassocks passed up to the choir. It was a scene out of a play by Shakespeare.

Presently, after a long while, the peers and peeresses of the realm arrived. Some of them had come to Westminster by barge, others by a threepenny train on the underground, others by car and road through the massed crowds. But they looked as if they had just come from the Middle Ages. The peers wore their long robes of purple red with capes of ermine and held their coronets under their arms as knights used to carry their helms. Some of them were very old and stumbled in their robes. Some of them were very young, and looked jaunty and debonair. The long velvet robes of the peeresses touched the old stones of the floorway, and one saw among them, here and there, pretty young faces and the grace of English beauty. Some of these people bear old names famous in English, Scottish and Irish history. Some of them still live in old castles and houses on lands held by their forefathers. But the roll call of the peerage is now crowded with new names and new men who have gained their titles by modern service and modern ways of power. They looked as noble and as feudal as those of the bluest blood.

Through the open doorways came the music of military bands. Inside the Abbey the organ played gloriously and its notes vibrated through the forest of stone. I heard the stamp of horses' hoofs and a rushing noise like a silver cascade as escorts of cavalry clattered outside. The boxes and galleries were now filled. This old church was crowded with modern life from which came a murmur of living voices, though no footfall could be heard on the carpeted stones.

But as I waited for the coming of the King and Queen I was aware of old ghosts about me. I heard old voices from the past, as far back as the Saxon craftsmen whose stonework still stands in some of these walls. Here on that worm-eaten chair many kings and queens had been crowned. Among them were lion men and tiger men, very fierce and cruel. Norman William had strode to this place in his chain mail. Richard, with a great sword at his side, had come here for his crown, though he spake no English. The early Edwards had helped to build this Abbey as we now see it. They had held their kingdom by sword and battle-axe. Henry of Agincourt, a friend of low fellows in his youth, stared down this nave with his falcon eyes. All the great figures of our story had come here for a little while, like shadows passing; saints and heroes and villains; fair women with tears in their hearts for the world's cruelty in times of passion, murder, plague, war, and the unending struggle of life by our forbears. By some spirit in them for a thousand years they were greatly daring in adventure. It is still unfinished, that adventure. That day another one began with the crowning of another king.

There was a living ghost in the Abbey. It was impossible not to think of him now and then, as all of us did, I am sure. It was the invisible presence of Edward VIII, who was proclaimed king not long ago but did not come to his crowning. He was now in exile, having chosen another way of life.

The whole world had sent their princes or ambassadors to this Coronation service of George VI, for whom we waited so long. Now and then I had a glimpse of oriental princes in silken headdresses. The Sword of Islam saluted a Christian king. The Blood Royal of Europe walked this way, though many dynasties had fallen after a world war. Here were the princes of four hundred million of Indian peoples in teeming cities by age-old rivers. Here were the dark chiefs of sun-baked tribes in swamps and jungles where that day their drums were beating because of a crown raised as a symbol above many races and creeds and human souls. Here came the rulers of the new Dominions, free and equal partners in our British League of Nations.

From the tumult outside, only very faint to our ears, came two little girls like princesses from the Court of Queen Anne. Princess Elizabeth bore herself gallantly, with her head up and a smile about her lips. Upon her head one day may be placed the heavy old crown. There may be another Elizabethan era, perhaps, if destiny decrees, with another great flow of genius and vitality and splendour of spirit. Who knows? By her sister's side was Princess Margaret, a rosebud from the springtime of Chaucer's England. They sat in chairs opposite my box and shifted about and twiddled their little fingers, waiting for their father, who was to have great things done to him. Other princesses arrived and went to their places up the winding stairway to their gallery with their long, long trains upheld by ladies in waiting—a pretty picture every time.

I saw Queen Mary pass by and remembered her suddenly as I had seen her at her own crowning when her eyes seemed to burn with the light of her own jewels. Now, an old lady, rather tired, perhaps, but glad that things had gone well after all—it had been an anxious time—she smiled upon her friends.

The King and Queen came at last in their golden coach to the West Door of the Abbey, received by the great lords of state bearing the regalia. The King wore his Cap of State and royal mantle of imperial purple, with its immense train held by young and noble pages. Some of us thought he looked pale and nervous and under a great strain, as well he may have been, but he bore himself well, with dignity and meekness. The Queen was good to see. She has always a softness and glamour in her eyes. This ordeal to which she came had never been in her girlhood dreams, though in her veins is the blood of Scottish kings as far back as Robert the Bruce. Her train was carried by six young beauties who seemed to have stepped out of Tudor England.

The Abbey now had its full living picture, always changing in its groups, wonderfully rich in colour. The nave was lined by the King's gentlemen-at-arms and by those old men in scarlet and gold—the yeomen of the guard—who take us back to stout Harry and all his ghost queens. Slowly the royal group went up to the high stage to the sound of glorious music.

The King's servants—his great lords—were busy about him. Presently we heard the clear words of the archbishop in his fine, deep, sonorous voice.

They were very old words. They enshrine the spirit with which the early Kings of this realm were accepted by their peoples and dedicated to their service and liberties. It was the ancient liberty of the English folk to choose their own king, though he might not be the eldest son of his father, but the younger brother of an elder brother not so acceptable.

So now the archbishop went to the four sides of the stage and asked a question in a clear, strong voice.

"Sirs, I here present unto you King George, your undoubted King. Wherefore, all of you who are come this day to do your homage: Are you willing to do the same?"

They were willing, it seemed. No man said nay. They accepted the younger brother of the elder brother who had renounced his throne, and there were loud shouts of "God Save King George!"

The King took his oath, promising to govern his peoples according to their laws and customs. After many prayers, sung and said, he was disrobed and stood in a simple tunic low at the neck. (I remembered that day when I had seen him bathing and the boys at his camp splashed water at him.) Now he sat on St. Edward's chair. Four Knights of the Garter held over him a canopy of cloth of gold which gleamed like metal. Mystical rites were done to him, because in the old days a king was made a kind of priest. He was anointed on the head and hands and breast, and dedicated to God and his peoples. They touched his heels with spurs, because he belongs to the Order of Chivalry, like any knight who made his vigil at Arthur's Court, vowing to defend the right and succour the weak, and afterwards, alas, did, very often, the exact opposite, as history tells. He was handed the Sword of State "to do justice, and stop the growth of iniquity, and reform what is amiss, and confirm what is in good order." When that was handed back he received the ring, the orb, and the sceptre; and this young man, who drives a motorcar, sat for a while, in a supertunic stiff with gold, like Alfred the Great in a pictured history book.

Now came the moment of crowning. The archbishop took the crown from the altar and, after some hesitation as to which was back or front, pressed it firmly down on the King's brows. The sixth George was crowned king of many peoples.

Silver trumpets sounded with a crash of melody. All the peers and Kings-of-Arms put on their coronets. There were loud cries of "God Save the King!" Away on Tower Hill guns fired with heavy dull shocks of sound.

"Be strong and play the man," sang the choristers, while the old archbishop blessed the King, praying that he might have fruitful lands and a quiet Empire.

Heavily robed, bearing the weight of the crown, holding his symbols of power, that young slim man was supported by his lords and placed on the throne of his fathers, as I could see. The jewels in his crown flashed out little sparks of blue, red and green light.

I watched the act of homage by the princes and peers, each one representing his own Order. It was the Duke of Gloucester who knelt before him first, and said old words, and kissed his cheek as others did. As he knelt I thought for a moment of the last Coronation when a young Prince of Wales, looking as though he had stepped out of a fairy tale, knelt before his father. The sun had touched his hair—very fair then—turning it to gold. But for the hand of destiny, and something in his own mind and will, he would have been receiving this homage, given now in full loyalty to his brother.

The Queen's Coronation was short and beautiful to see. So after a long while, as it seemed to us who had waited and watched, it all ended with the royal progress to the West Door when the King wore a different crown—the Imperial Crown which has among its precious jewels the "fair ruby" given to the Black Prince and worn by King Harry in his helm at Agincourt upon St. Crispin's Day.

The pageant faded. We awakened from a dream. All of us were faint with hunger and many with fatigue. By a word of power I and a few others who had to tell this tale to the world—it had already been well told by the B.B.C.—were allowed to leave the Abbey. Others had to stay for hours more, owing to a lamentable breakdown in police organisation. Most of the peers were kept prisoners in the Abbey until late in the evening, though I saw one of them as early as six o'clock being photographed in his robe and coronet by his admiring family above the area railings of a London square.

In the streets there was the tumult of a vast multitude of people who were eager to express their loyalty by tremendous demonstrations, and who were greedy for more pageantry, more romance, more royal drama, of which, it seems, they cannot have enough.

So the King and Queen drove on their way to the Future—that mystery—assured by these storms of cheers, and afterwards by a thousand messages, that they have the love and devotion of their peoples and the good will of the world.

The crisis of the Crown left no trace of its episode. No shadow falls over the Throne. The old traditional loyalty of our amazing folk stands unweakened. They assured themselves by the Coronation that all goes well. They let the world know, and the world sat up and took notice.

Now the time of pageantry is over. It is time to make peace with those who are willing to be our friends. We need quietude in our souls, if that be possible in this restless rush of life, always speeded up by a turn of the screw.

THE END